Finlay Dun

Landlords and Tenants in Ireland

Finlay Dun

Landlords and Tenants in Ireland

ISBN/EAN: 9783743344389

Manufactured in Europe, USA, Canada, Australia, Japa

Cover: Foto ©ninafisch / pixelio.de

Manufactured and distributed by brebook publishing software (www.brebook.com)

Finlay Dun

Landlords and Tenants in Ireland

LANDLORDS AND TENANTS

IN IRELAND

BY

FINLAY DUN

AUTHOR OF 'FARMING AND FOOD IN AMERICA'
'VETERINARY MEDICINES, THEIR ACTIONS AND USES' ETC.

LONDON
LONGMANS, GREEN, AND CO.
1881

All rights reserved

PREFACE.

During the past winter, at the request of the proprietors of the 'Times,' I visited Ireland to inquire into the subjects of land tenure and estate management, and the condition of tenants and labourers. The results of my inquiry were published in the 'Times' in a series of letters, which, by the courtesy of the proprietors, I am now enabled to reproduce with such additions and alterations as have seemed necessary.

FINLAY DUN.

Estate Offices,
2 Portland Place, London, W.
April 5, 1881.

CONTENTS.

CHAPTER		PAGE
I.	INTRODUCTORY	1
II.	THE MARQUIS OF DOWNSHIRE'S BLESSINGTON ESTATES	13
III.	THE DUKE OF LEINSTER'S ESTATES	20
IV.	EARL FITZWILLIAM'S ESTATES	30
V.	THE MARQUIS OF WATERFORD'S ESTATES AT CURRAGHMORE.	43
VI.	THE DUKE OF DEVONSHIRE'S ESTATES	54
VII.	ESTATES BETWEEN CORK AND KILLARNEY	65
VIII.	LORD BANDON'S AND LORD KENMARE'S ESTATES	73
IX.	TRINITY COLLEGE AND THE KNIGHT OF KERRY'S ESTATES	82
X.	ESTATES IN DOWN AND ANTRIM	97
XI.	THE LONDON COMPANIES AND IRISH SOCIETY'S ESTATES	113
XII.	ESTATES IN DERRY, ENNISHOWEN, AND TYRONE	132
XIII.	THE SMALL OCCUPIERS AND OWNERS OF ULSTER	144
XIV.	DONEGAL MOUNTAIN ESTATES	158
XV.	ESTATES IN DONEGAL AND SLIGO	171
XVI.	SIR HENRY GORE-BOOTH'S SLIGO ESTATES	187
XVII.	LORD DILLON'S ESTATES.	201
XVIII.	LANDLORDS AND TENANTS IN MAYO	208
XIX.	TENURE AND TENANTS IN NORTH-WEST MAYO	222
XX.	ESTATES AND FARMING IN SOUTH MAYO	235
XXI.	LAND TENURE: GENERAL CONCLUSIONS	252

LANDLORDS AND TENANTS
IN
IRELAND.

CHAPTER I.

INTRODUCTORY.

THE landlords of Ireland are comparatively few in number, and many hold large estates. The tenants are numerous, their farms are small; one-half the holdings are under fifteen acres. Nearly half the area of the island is owned by 750 proprietors, each enjoying upwards of 5,000 acres. Many large estates unfortunately illustrate the evils of subdivided tenancies too small to furnish decent subsistence for their holders. In the poor county of Mayo, for example, nine owners hold upwards of 20,000 acres, or together half a million acres, being considerably more than one-third of the county. At the opposite extremity of the social scale, with few intermediate connecting links, are half a million small occupiers, half of whom pay on an average 6*l.* of annual rent. The land map of Ireland, officially prepared for the Doomsday Book, and reproduced at the beginning of this volume, presents the number of owners of upwards of one acre in each county, the names of the landlords of the largest domains, with the number of statute acres which they hold in each county. The peasant and yeoman owners possessing from ten to 500 acres—a very important class, on whom should depend much of the agricultural prosperity and social stability of the country—are few and scattered. Although the land sales under the Church Act of 1869 have added about 6,000 new owners, and those under the Bright's clauses of the Land Act of 1870 have contributed 710, the total roll of peasant and yeoman proprietors hold amongst them only one-eighth of the area of their country. In England this useful class of owners hold one-third of the land. The subjoined tables from the Doomsday Book, and from returns presented to the House of Commons, August 10, 1876, furnish the number of owners in Ireland, classified according to their different acreages, with the area held by each class :—

		Owners	Extent in statute acres
Less than 1 acre		36,144	9,065
1 and under 10 acres		6,892	28,968
10 ,, 50 ,,		7,746	195,525
50 ,, 100 ,,		3,479	250,147
100 ,, 500 ,,		7,989	1,955,536
500 ,, 1,000 ,,		2,716	1,915,528
1,000 ,, 2,000 ,,		1,803	2,514,743
2,000 ,, 5,000 ,,		1,198	3,675,267
5,000 ,, 10,000 ,,		452	3,154,628
10,000 ,, 20,000 ,,		185	2,478,493
20,000 ,, 50,000 ,,		90	2,558,850
50,000 ,, 100,000 ,,		14	1,023,677
100,000 and upwards		3	397,079
		68,711	20,157,511

Landlords, tenants, and labourers, it has hitherto been believed, have many interests in common. Recently, however, in various parts of Ireland their interests appear to have become seriously dislocated. They are disposed to array themselves in unfriendly antagonism. Capital and labour are unprofitably at variance. Several untoward seasons, bad crops, and low prices of some articles of produce have caused much widespread agricultural distress. As in Great Britain, many farmers have been entirely ruined. It is generally believed that 140,000 tenants, or one-fifth of the whole number, in Ireland are bankrupt. Many farms, in consequence, are worse cultivated or stocked than formerly; profits become still further reduced; the tenants' ability to pay rents and other dues is impaired. Credit, often too readily obtained in more prosperous times, is shortened. Repayments of old obligations are insisted upon. Without money, without credit, stranded, as it were, and almost disheartened, many farmers and their friends anxiously inquire into the causes of these difficulties and disasters.

Many and varied are the causes propounded. With half the population of Ireland deriving their livelihood from the soil, and more than half her income drawn from land, without the extensive diversified industrial resources of England or Scotland, the recent agricultural depression has told very seriously throughout Ireland. Landlords are blamed for absenteeism, for neglecting their duties, for allowing great portions of their estates to remain in unprofitable waste, for putting forth small effort to assist, guide, or elevate their tenants, for charging more than Griffith's valuation. Relatively to their number, it may, however, fairly be said that there are in Ireland as many good and improving landlords as there are good and improving tenants. Occupiers are blamed for apathy, idleness, and neglect of their opportunities. Many for years, with good security, have held useful land, which has not been drained, or has been tilled only in a very perfunctory manner. The State is blamed for supinely allowing large tracts of land in many parts of Ireland to remain in comparative waste, while a considerable proportion of the cultivated area is, moreover, very indifferently managed. Some of the legislative measures adopted for the relief of Irish agricultural distress have not worked as successfully as might have been anticipated. Not all the new landlords created under the Encumbered Estates Court have been improvements on those they superseded. The Land Act of 1870 has not fulfilled all the good expected from it. It has tended to paralyse landlords' improvements, and has not sufficiently encouraged or protected tenants' improvements. In harmony with Irish traditions it wisely recognises the possessory interest of the tenant. When paying less than 50*l.* of yearly rent, he is awarded compensation if he is wrongfully disturbed. To establish his claims he is, however, driven to appeal to a law court, to stand forth in antagonism to his landlord, and thus usually to destroy his chance of retaining his holding. Rather than thus run the risk of being removed, he submits to almost any advance of rent or to other arrangements detrimental to his interests. The Act is powerless even in Ulster to prevent excessive raising of rent, which, insisted on, either pauperises the tenant or practically evicts him. The fact that exorbitant advances of rent are sometimes made, and are possible, affords widespread material for agitation. Whilst granting compensation for the disturbance of tenants paying less than 50*l.* of annual rent, no protection is accorded to those above that

SHORTCOMINGS OF THE LAND ACT.

amount, who often bring to their vocation proportionately more capital and intelligence, who sometimes furnish the much-needed employment to the day-labourer and smaller tenant, and whose interests and improvements demand greater consideration and protection.

As in England, want of capital intelligently used is one chief cause of agricultural failure and distress. Nevertheless, neither landlords nor tenants take advantage of the liberally-provided facilities for borrowing money for building, draining, and other improvements. Tenants generally have been more indifferent than landlords in effecting such improvements; they have grudged the percentage, or feared an increase of rent. They are too generally disposed to adjure the State for aid, and to depend too little on their own imperfectly-used resources. Owners and occupiers alike fail to realise that no legislation can be expected invariably to ensure the satisfactory conduct of such businesses as landowning or farming, which demand for their successful issue individual ability, enterprise, special knowledge, and adequate capital.

Notwithstanding recent Acts facilitating the transfer of land and its acquisition by the cultivator, and affording, as does the Land Act of 1870, more security for capital expended, especially by smaller tenants, and in spite of extended opportunities for obtaining money for improvements on moderate terms, a proportion of landowners in Ireland do not yet fulfil aright their important trust, and, by ignorance, neglect, or rapacity, bring down loud and indiscriminate anathemas on Irish landlords. It is somewhat difficult to estimate the proportion of those who thus abuse their position and make poor use of their heritag

They certainly do not amount to $\frac{1}{25}$th of the 25,000 who now hold estates of ten acres and upwards. Being chiefly small holders, their maladministration probably does not extend over $\frac{1}{50}$th part of the whole area. This is, however, too large an extent to be mismanaged; it represents too large a measure of neglect or wrong; but, like some other evils, it is more readily recognised than remedied. Blundering waste and injustice to the tenantry have been most frequent and serious in Munster and Connaught; but, even with the protection of the Ulster custom, excessive and reiterated raising of rents has sometimes occasioned much dissatisfaction and has, naturally, pressed most heavily on smaller, poorer occupiers. Flagrant cases of unfair dealing have added to the widespread social and agrarian agitation.

On the many debatable land questions which at present distract Ireland some light may be thrown by a careful, unprejudiced survey of Irish estates and systems of land management. I therefore purpose to examine typical estates belonging to all sorts and conditions of men. I shall endeavour to describe several of the great properties held by noblemen and others whose titles date from past generations or centuries, entering into some details as to tenure, rents, agreements, improvements, and the mode of carrying them out and paying for them, making reference also to the condition both of the tenantry and the labourers.

On many Irish estates not only the cultivation of the soil but its more permanent equipments have been mainly effected by the tenant, sometimes holding under a long lease, more usually with a parole agreement running from year to year, with a six months' notice to quit, which by the

Act of 1877 was extended to twelve months. On many estates the labour and outlay, usually of small occupiers, has gradually reclaimed the bog and reduced the stony mountain-side to some sort of cultivation. The landlord generally has contributed to these improvements much less than his compeer in England or Scotland would have done. Houses, buildings, fences, and drains, seldom so substantially or thoroughly made as in Great Britain, but often fairly answering their purposes, in many instances have also been the work of the tenants. In this way, as already indicated, as a matter of equity has grown the occupiers' recognised possessory interest. Hence results the hardship of arbitrary eviction. Hence, moreover, arises one of the several difficulties in determining the vexed question, what is a fair rent?

In marked contrast to the general Irish practice, under which landlords delegate to middlemen or occupying tenants the substantial improvement of their property, are the estates which for generations have been systematically managed on what may be termed English principles, where permanent equipments have been chiefly effected or paid for by the landlord. On the best of these estates, pains have, moreover, been taken to roll into one conveniently-sized farm several of the small, often scattered, pendicles, on which even the most industrious thrifty tenant could scarcely earn a bare subsistence.

The lands of the great public companies, which recently have been threatened with wholesale extinction, deserve investigation.

Unfortunately, there is no difficulty in finding numerous examples of estates held by absentees, often, also, without any responsible resident agent, where the receiving and paying of rent is the only bond of connexion between landlord and tenant, where the owner's apathy and neglect are often reproduced and intensified in the occupier. By a return published in 1871 there were 1,443 absentee landlords, possessing 3,205,000 acres, or 16 per cent. of the area of Ireland; and 4,496 landowners who resided in Dublin, controlling 4,075,000 acres, or 20 per cent. of the total area. The average of the estates of these absentees was 2,220 acres.

More than half the area, especially of some of the western counties, is held by men who do not spend one week a year amongst their tenantry, who know nothing of their condition and wants, who contribute little or nothing to public or private charities. From one poor western county, where the tenants do not average 10*l.* of annual rent, nearly 100,000*l.* is every year carried out of the county by six of the principal absentee owners. This has continued even before recent troubles afforded some pretext for absenteeism. No wonder that at frequently recurring intervals the demand is made that absentees should be taxed!

Of a type almost more unsatisfactory are estates, fortunately seldom of large size, purchased often in the Encumbered Estates Courts, held frequently by non-residents, and illustrating all the evils of extravagant rents, insecurity of tenure, and ruthless appropriation of tenants' improvements. These are the cases that chiefly evoke the demand for State authority to fix fair rents, ensure some fixity of tenure, and afford security for payment of unexhausted improvements.

Facilities for the acquisition of land during the last

twenty-five years have, however, also introduced in many districts a most valuable race of landlords, who by precept and example have done much to improve the country. As strangers, they have not always been popular among the people; as improvers they have been regarded as disturbers, and, perhaps, as exterminators; they have, nevertheless, in many quarters demonstrated how much can be done by judicious outlay, not only in developing the resources of the land, but in finding the much-wanted regular employment for the labouring population, and in advancing their social condition.

By the Church Disestablishment Act of 1869, and the Irish Land Act of 1870, upwards of 6,000 occupiers have been converted into owners; and it will be useful, not only in an agricultural, but also in a social, aspect, to ascertain how these new proprietors have battled with recent bad times. Most have continued regularly to meet their instalments towards the principal and interest of their loans. Many have, besides, obtained capital for improvements, and, with energy and ability, are making good use of their possessions. It becomes an important practical question, alike of social and agricultural import, whether extended facilities should not be given for the multiplication of these yeoman farmers.

Still another class of noteworthy holdings are met with, the properties of middlemen, sometimes held on leases for several lives, or for long periods, on which obviously there is limited inducement to expend much, where subletting and subdivision have sometimes been carried to a ruinous degree, where the cultivating tenant is sometimes separated from the owner of the fee-simple by three or four middlemen, where rents, consequently, are apt to be excessive, but where, curiously, the occupier clings to the spot of his birth or early location, almost with the same affectionate tenacity as he does under more auspicious circumstances.

The occupation, or ownership, of portions of land under five acres is greatly more common in Ireland than in any part of Great Britain. Notwithstanding evictions and consolidations, emigration, and the diversion of the surplus agricultural population to the limited amount of other available work, one-fifth of the holdings in Ireland, or 117,580, are still under five acres. These small folks mostly live in a state of chronic poverty, liable in a single bad season to drift helplessly into positive destitution, their lot lightened only by the fine climate, by their wonderful hardiness, and their natural good spirits. They are generally fonder of politics than of farming. The leaseholders and owners among them are seldom better off than the rack-renters, who hold sometimes precariously from year to year, and are usually experts in propounding very advanced views on land tenure.

Although there are at present loud complaints of insecurity of tenure, occupiers in Ireland have more fixity of tenure than is enjoyed by their fellows in England or Scotland. For generations, without lease, with a kind of patriarchal, feudal, traditional right, very generally respected, they remain for generations in undisturbed possession of their holdings. Indeed, excepting for accumulated arrears of rent, evictions are very uncommon. The Ulster custom, legalised by the Land Act of 1870, has given Irish tenants throughout most parts of the northern province a permanent interest in their holdings. But even in other parts of Ireland analogous usages have gradually been gaining ground.

In their anxiety to obtain the much coveted 'bit of land,' with few other occupations to turn to, several years' rent is constantly paid to the outgoing tenant by way of premium, or good-will for the possessory interest, and in addition to any charges for unexhausted improvements. This payment for tenant right is usually recognised and acquiesced in by the landlord, who generally secures therefrom the discharge of any arrears of rent.

Of late years rents have been widely characterised as 'exorbitant.' As in Great Britain they are irregular; even on the same estate they are not always accurately graduated according to value; they are usually highest on small estates, and those which have repeatedly changed owners; in some districts they remain as they were thirty years ago; they are moderate on many of the larger estates; the small holdings are generally dearest. As elsewhere the worst land, proportionately to its producing capabilities, is most highly rented. Even by many intelligent tenants the economy of good buildings, roads, and markets, is not sufficiently appreciated, and allowed for in the rent. Throughout Ireland, during the last twenty years, rents have not risen in the same proportion they have done in Great Britain. The Income Tax assessments indicate that between 1857 and 1875 the gross annual value of the land of England increased 21 per cent.; the increase in Scotland during the same period was 26 per cent. The returns from Ireland are not available for comparison previous to 1862; but between that period and 1875 the increase on the valuation of Irish land was only 6 per cent., or about one-third that of the sister country.

In the following letters a description will be given of

land tenure and estate management, and of the various classes of owners and occupiers throughout different parts of Ireland. Such reports may prove useful in the present disturbed state of the country; may indicate where grievances and hardships really exist ; may mark the remedies which intelligent and energetic landlords, tenants, and even peasants are now employing for their own and their neighbours' welfare ; and, further, may foreshadow the direction and scope of future land legislation.

CHAPTER II.

THE MARQUIS OF DOWNSHIRE'S BLESSINGTON ESTATES.

The Marquis of Downshire has an estate of over 17,000 acres in counties Wicklow and Kildare, eighteen miles south of Dublin, around the neat little village of Blessington. He owns, besides, estates in county Down, Antrim, and King's County, and also in Yorkshire and Berkshire. Fortunately for the tenantry and the country several former marquises have been men of kindly, liberal spirit, determined to improve their inheritance and elevate the people upon it. The fourth marquis, who died in 1868, is still spoken of with good will, is affectionately styled 'the big marquis,' and was great in heart and good works as well as in body. Many are the stories current of his benevolence, of his riding round his estate with a pile of garments for women and children attached to his saddle, and goodly supplies of notes in his pocket, cheering the hearts of the desolate and distressed with kindly greetings and good gifts. Nobility and landlordism were made popular not only at Blessington but in many other parts of Ireland by these good deeds of the big Marquis of Downshire. With more men of his sort, poverty, discontent, and disaster would have been less common than they now are in Ireland. Farmhouses and cottages were put in order, land was drained and reclaimed; in 1846-4 and in other bad years useful work was found for the unemployed; a capital supply of water was brought into the village; planting, for shelter and effect, generally much neglected, was carried out.

The fruits of liberal management are very notable among the people themselves and in their holdings. The Protestant and Roman Catholic population agree most amicably; children of all denominations attend the same National Schools, in which pains are taken to have teachers of each creed. The people are industrious and thrifty, fairly tidy and cleanly, and above want. In the Blessington division of the Naas Union, out of a considerable population, only four old people are in the workhouse, and none receive out-door relief, which it must, however, be noted is granted very sparingly in Ireland. Instead of allowing the small tenants last spring to apply under Major Nolan's Act at their union for seed potatoes and oats, the Downshire trustees procured champion potatoes and black Tartarian oats, and distributed them where needful. Both potatoes and oats have produced admirable crops, amply testifying to the importance of more frequent change of seed.

The farms on the Blessington estate vary in extent from plots under an acre to farms of 400 acres. Some small accommodation fields rent at 50*s.* an imperial acre; outlying hill-land, some of it 700 feet above sea-level, is only worth 6*d.* an acre. As occasion offered, small holdings have been thrown together, tenants being paid for improvements made; nearness to Dublin has steadily absorbed surplus population. The holdings are now considerably larger than on most adjoining properties, either in Wicklow or Kildare. There are few leases or written agreements. Every confidence has been placed in the fair dealing of landlord and agent. Several families have been in undisturbed possession for upwards of 200 years. Ejectments are unknown, except where the tenant had become notoriously dissipated or vicious, or where payment of rent was persistently refused for two or three years. Subdivision and subletting are not allowed.

Here, as elsewhere in Ireland, Sir Richard Griffith's valuation, made forty years ago, is not regarded as inviolable. As in most such valuations, the poorer lands are often too high; many of the surveys being undertaken in August—when, in high-lying districts, grass, and, indeed, all crops looked their best—brought out too favourable figures. Some of the better lands are, however, as much underestimated. The price of most descriptions of agricultural produce having increased 20 to 50 per cent. since Griffith's valuation was made, renders it inadmissible as a fair criterion of rent. Moreover, when the valuation was concluded, being for rating and not for rental purposes, a deduction was made all round of fully 20 per cent. Notwithstanding outlay on the part of the landlord, and better cultivation by tenants, the present rental is not 20 per cent. higher than that of fifty years ago. The average rent for land adjoining Blessington, which grows four to five quarters of oats, and twenty tons of swedes, or of grass which will dairy or grow good young stock, is about 25s. a statute acre. The rental is generally 14 per cent. over Griffith's valuation. Its moderation is, however, attested by the keen competition for any vacant farm. Until the last two years, rents were always most punctually paid; even now the arrears do not exceed 10 per cent.; 10 per cent. was generally remitted from the year's rent of

1879; six months' grace is always given before the rent due is collected.

Rates are made on the Poor Law valuation, which is Sir Richard Griffith's valuation revised annually, with addition of new buildings and other improvements. The poor rate is 1s. 1d. in the pound; it has considerably increased during the last twenty years; one-half is paid by the landlord. The county cess, which goes for roads, bridges, &c., is 1s. 8d. per pound, has also somewhat increased, and is paid by the tenants. The tithe rent-charge, applotted by local valuers, is paid by the landlord.

Even in the best of times farmers generally have not made money unless by dealing or other business, but they have lived comfortably, brought up and placed out their families. Gradually the tillage area has diminished. The climate being so uncertain and the altitude great, oats are the only cereal cultivated. Labour is moderate in price, but not particularly good or reliable; most of the workpeople require a good deal of looking after; wages vary from 7s. to 9s. a week, often with a cottage and garden rent free. Ploughmen and herds have 10s. to 14s.; harvest wages are 3s., sometimes 4s., a day. There are no home industries, no weaving as in old times; the women do a little knitting, but chiefly for their own families. Needle-making, introduced into Blessington some fifty years ago, soon languished. A steam tramway projected to run from Dublin will benefit the neighbourhood, but a narrow-gauge railway would probably be more generally serviceable and, in the long run, prove more economical.

On a large adjacent estate of the Marquis of Waterford are some extensive quarries, producing the beautiful Wicklow granite, now carried over twenty miles by road to Dublin, at a cost of 10s. to 12s. per ton. The facility and cheapness of carriage which will be afforded by the projected steam tramway should greatly increase this industry, from which, even under present circumstances, a large number of hands get employment—quarrymen at 12s. to 15s. a week, and stone-cutters at 20s. to 30s.

Landlord and tenant in Ireland being at present often in antagonism, disputes as to rents being too common, tenants refusing settlement excepting on Griffith's or their own valuation, and using besides a new circulating medium with which to pay off unpopular landlords and agents, I availed myself with considerable curiosity of the invitation of Mr. William Owen, of Blessington, and his son, Mr. Arthur, to attend their rent audit on Miss Magan's Eagle Hill property, between the towns of Athy and Kildare, thirty-four miles from Dublin. The thirty tenants on this property entertain a friendly feeling towards their landlady and agent; there was not one demurrer as to rent; Sir Richard Griffith's well-known name was not once mentioned; a 20 per cent. deduction made in a few cases was, however, very gratefully received; the smaller tenants, who in spring had received seed potatoes and oats, to be paid for after harvest, were glad to have their obligation remitted; one widow who had lost her husband in July from 'the bronchitis on the chest,' pleaded for time, and was told not to vex herself, but make up something against the next settling six months hence; one conscientious gentleman reminded the agent that he was making no charge for a portion of newly-taken-in land, but was courteously informed that he had better get it into more profitable form before rent could fairly be charged upon it. Inquiry was repeatedly made whether any draining was requisite, and assurance given that any such essential improvement would be undertaken, not only for its own sake, but in order that no labourer willing to work should be out of employment during the dull winter months. Met in this spirit, the tenants are contented and fairly prosperous. With more energy they might do still better.

The estate, of 1,500 Irish acres, has been in the Magan family for a century and a half. Mrs. Magan, who died this year, like many Irish ladies, was herself a great agriculturist, and farmed about half her estates in four or five counties. Her daughter, the present proprietress, has the same fondness for farming, and has splendid flocks and herds roaming over the wide, rich pastures around her residence at Killyon Manor, in the county Meath. On this, the Kildare estate, the average rent per acre is about one guinea. The farms generally have been held upon long leases, some for three lives. The oldest tenant, whose memory goes back for sixty years, tells me that he does not remember an eviction. Several who left voluntarily have had compensation; rates are advancing; subletting and conacre are forbidden; but, in the event of any tenant desiring to give up, any respectable man nominated by him would be accepted, or, as has been done by Mrs. Magan even before the Land Act provisions became law, compensation would be paid to the out-going tenant for improvements made by him. About half the tenanted land is under tillage; a sort of four-course rotation is generally pursued of oats, potatoes, and oats or barley sown with seeds, which are allowed to remain down for two and sometimes three years. No interference occurs as to cropping or sale of produce. Hay is worth 40*s.* to 50*s.*;

oat straw about half that figure; swedes, which are generally very good, sell at present at 10s. per ton. Herdsmen have about 12s., ordinary labourers 9s. per week; but if fed, as some are, by their employers, they get 1s. per day. The hours of labour extend from 7 A.M. to 7 P.M., when the men return to their cottages on the farm or to the village. As in England, the younger men are not so steady, interested, or competent as the older. Alike to labourers and tenants permission is given to cut peat on the hundred acres of bog which flank the estate, at the rate of 5s. per two perches, from which a good winter supply of peats is obtainable, worth 1s. 3d. to 1s. 6d. a standard, which is a pile 4 feet long, 4 feet deep, and 2 feet wide.

The drive from Blessington to Eagle Hill passes through an improved and well-farmed district, and over portions of the estates of Mr. John La Touche, of Harristown, and Major Borrowes, of Giltown. The latter gentleman has laid out his demesne land in admirable square fields, enclosed with capital stone walls and thorn fences, and on which are grazing superior shorthorns and a choice lot of Kerries. The tillage and stock management evidence much skill, care, and enlightenment, and secure, I am assured, handsome returns. Throughout the remainder of his large estate, Major Borrowes has also carried his enterprising improvements; has built houses, farm premises, and cottages; has done a considerable amount of draining and fencing; and has placed his tenants, like himself, in the fair way of farming profitably.

CHAPTER III.

THE DUKE OF LEINSTER'S ESTATES.

Many of the larger estates throughout Ireland have been well and liberally managed. The rents have been moderate; they have seldom been raised. Long credit, not always judicious, has frequently been given. Deductions have often been made in bad times, and help in many ways has been accorded to those in difficulty and distress. Tenants interrogated as to arrears speak quite cheerfully of owing three or four half-years' rents. Tenants' rights have been respected. Families of occupiers, although frequently holding from year to year, have often lived on the estate as long as the family of the owner. Evictions, except for hopeless arrears of rent or gross immorality, are unknown. Improvements effected have generally been initiated, encouraged, usually in part paid for, by the landlord. The chief blame which attaches to many landlords seems to have been allowing their tenantry to sit still in contented apathy, making small use of opportunities, satisfied with half crops, pursuing antiquated, exhausting practices, often living in squalor and poverty. Alike among tenants and labourers, there has been and still is a want of energy, enterprise, and education. On many estates all classes of occupiers would be benefited by wholesome stirring up, which Irish tenantry greatly dislike. An old-fashioned, happy-go-lucky, fox-hunting squire has generally a larger share of their sympathy and regard than the improving landlord anxious to develop his estate by building good, comfortable houses, by drainage, by thorough cultivation of the arable land and enriching the exhausted pastures. Irish tenants are born politicians, orators, and sportsmen; but they do not always exhibit strong predilection for the steady industry required for successful farming. They frequently require to be put upon the right track, and by precept and example shown how modern farming can be successfully prosecuted. Such lessons are sometimes furnished by more intelligent neighbours, sometimes by improving landlords.

The Duke of Leinster's estates illustrate the beneficial co-operation of liberal landlords and a good class of tenants carrying out successfully general improvements. The measurement and valuation of the estate are as follows :—

	Acres	Government Valuation
Kildare	67,227	£46,571
Meath	1,044	1,075
	68,271	£47,646

From the demesne and park of 1,000 acres at Carton, two miles from Maynooth, the northern portion of the property extends towards the Liffey and is now chiefly in grass. The remainder of the property around Athy is fully half arable. In the management of his estates, the Duke has shown praiseworthy anxiety to improve all classes of his tenantry. His policy has been to charge moderate rents, to give his tenants the security of written agreements, to effect at his own expense permanent improvements, or if these are carried out by the tenant they are made the subject of specific agreement, and paid for if the party who provided them happens to leave. The rents generally are about 10 per cent. over Griffith's valuation; they range from 15s. to 25s. per statute acre. Many of the farms I examined appear with intelligent management to afford even in these hard times good prospects of fair profits. The soil is a useful loam, generally on sandy, porous subsoil, grateful for liberal treatment, which is, however, sparingly given. Several adjacent farms, apparently nearly alike in natural fertility, from the treatment to which they have been subjected now differ 10s. to 15s. in acreable value. On the well-managed the tenants are thriving; on the others they are grumbling and losing money.

Despite complaints of poor returns, there are, however, numerous applications for any vacant farms; bonuses are cheerfully offered for the good-will; more than one or two are sublet at nearly double the rent which the Duke receives. A Dublin dairyman recently gave one of the tenants 600*l.* for 17 years' unexpired lease of 140 statute acres, rented at 200*l.*, and seriously run out by continuous cutting and sale of hay. With liberal doses of Dublin manure the farm is already showing evidences of improvement. Another very energetic tenant has delivered on his farm Dublin manure to the value of 200*l.* annually, ensuring profitable growth of potatoes and other crops. It is to be regretted that such practice is not more common. In Ireland it seems more difficult than in England to rouse or amend idle or neglectful occupiers. So long as the rent is paid, the landlord or agent is thought to have no cause of complaint. As old leases, some of them granted last century for several lives, have lapsed, additions have been made to the rental; but reductions granted during the famine years of 1847 and 1848 have not been revoked; and last year 25 per cent. was given to all yearly tenants under 50*l.* of annual rental, and 15 per cent. to those ranging from 50*l.* to 100*l.* Leaseholders received help, according to the circumstances of each case.

Of the 400 farming tenants, the larger proportion occupy from seventy-five to 400 imperial acres, which in this part of Leinster appears to be the most generally suitable size. Excepting for accommodation fields in the neighbourhood of towns and villages, the number of occupations under twenty acres has been steadily diminished. The Duke is averse to giving less than forty to fifty acres, which will employ, according to the amount of tillage, one or two horses, which may be worked mainly by the help of the tenant's family, and should engross his full attention. A smaller area seldom secures full or continuous work or a sufficient, decent livelihood. The tenants are generally contented and well-to-do, and volunteer the statement that the Duke is always accessible and ready personally to see them and hear and remedy any grievances. With the security which is always strongest on the larger estates, and especially since the Act of 1870, there are fewer applications for leases. Many tenants are perfectly satisfied to go on with yearly agreements; a few have leases for twenty years; under special circumstances improving tenants disposed to lay out money have leases for thirty-one years.

Farmhouses and premises adapted for 150 to 200 acres cost from 700*l.* to 1,000*l.* These have generally been built wholly or in part by the landlord; when put up by leaseholders they have sometimes been taken to at a valuation, and interest charged at 3 to 5 per cent.

Solicitous for the decent, comfortable housing and improvement of the peasantry, the present Duke has done much in repairing and building cottages. The old mud and thatched cabins have been removed. During the last three years fifty new cottages have been built, and thirteen more are in course of construction. Of stone or brick and mortar, slated or tiled, and fairly well finished, they cost 130*l.* each, or a trifle less if erected in pairs. Every farmer of sixty acres who requires a cottage has one put up at a convenient point on his farm. They are generally 24 feet by 16 feet; a small room and pantry are partitioned off from the kitchen, which is usually open to the roof. Over the two rooms is a loft, reached by a ladder and used for sleeping accommodation and storage. These decent arrangements are not always fully appreciated or taken advantage of. Many of the new cottages are not tidily kept; pigs and poultry share the right of entry with the children; potatoes and swedes are piled on the paved or tiled floors; defying regulations, more than one family crowd in and impair comfort and decency.

Great improvements have been effected during the life of the present and former Duke, and under the intelligent rule of Mr. Hamilton, the present agent, and his father. For cottages, farm buildings, and other improvements money has been borrowed from the Board of Works at 6½ per cent., and the tenants are generally charged 4 to 5 per cent. upon the outlay. The former Duke of Leinster usually spent 5,000*l.* to 6,000*l.* a year on improvements; the present Duke has expended in the last six years, or since his father's death, 75,000*l.* on improvements; including buildings and arterial drainage, the expenditure has reached 12,000*l.* a year, or fully 20 per cent. of the gross income from the estate. Half the poor-rate has always been paid by the landlord; under all new agreements half the county cess is also allowed; and, like other liberal resident proprietors, the Duke of Leinster supports local charities and contributes to schools and churches. Migration and emigration have been liberally aided. At Maynooth alone are forty pensioners, who, besides comfortable cottages, have 6s. per week and gifts of clothes and other good things.

When distress overtakes the thriftless, improvident peasantry, still too numerous in most parts of Ireland, these larger proprietors have afforded immediate succour in the way of food and, better still, of labour. Last winter about Carton draining, road-making, and other work was promptly found for hundreds of destitute unemployed. Similar occupation, usually at 9s. a week, was also given by other proprietors on adjacent estates. For several months Lord Cloncurry paid for such surplus labour 70l. to 80l. a week. He had bought out several wretched tenants, who were farming miserably and drifting deeper and deeper into difficulties; for several years he has been farming in an enterprising and improving manner, finding plenty of constant, regular work, expending on this item alone 4,000l. a year. Such improvements bring, however, into unpleasant contrast the thriftless, do-nothing management of the small holders, who, although hopelessly bankrupt, fail to realise that constant work at 1s. 6d. to 2s. per day is preferable to starving as the holder of a small, beggared farm. Lord Cloncurry's ricks of hay on the approach of winter were burnt, other threats of violence were made, and, instead of spending the winter in Ireland and vigorously prosecuting his useful improvements, he has removed his household and stud to Melton Mowbray. Unfortunately, this driving away of improving landlords and of capital has not been peculiar to the Maynooth district.

The Leinster lease, introduced eight years ago, has been the subject of considerable discussion. In the somewhat uncertain state of law and custom regarding land tenure, the Duke now lets no land excepting under the regular printed agreement. Two tenants determinedly refusing to sign have been got rid of, and another recalcitrant is to be evicted from a farm which is certainly in a condition of dilapidation and neglect which in Great Britain would alone justify his removal. Besides a somewhat similar form of yearly agreement, two forms of lease are in use on the estates—one applicable to tenancies under 50*l.* of annual value, the other applicable to tenancies above 50*l.* The usual demise and description of lands and tenements are made, reserving to the landlord minerals, timber, game, and fishing, ingress, egress, and regress. The indenture enjoins maintenance, and repair of buildings, fences, &c., and imposes additional yearly rents for all permanent grass broken up for tillage, and all arable land over-cropped or used contrary to an approved course of husbandry. It interdicts subletting, assigning, or conacre, without permission of the lessor. It forbids erection of unsuitable buildings. Provision is made for the determination of the tenancy in the event of the bankruptcy of the lessee, of his breach of covenant, or of his rent being twenty-one days in arrear. Half the poor-rate, and more recently half the county cess, is payable by the landlord, but no part of any Grand Jury cess specially imposed for malicious or wanton outrage upon person or property. The tenant covenants to take the farm under these conditions ; to cultivate the land in a good and husbandman-like manner ; to alternate green and corn crops ; not to grow in succession two crops which ripen their seed ; to repair and maintain buildings, fences, and other appurtenances ; to pay rent half-yearly ; to bequeath the lease to one person only ; but on quitting the holding he undertakes to make no claim for compensation under any of the clauses or provisions of the Landlord and Tenant (Ireland) Act, 1870, 'in respect of any money or money's worth paid or given by him on coming into said holding.' Permission to destroy rabbits by ferrets or nets was formerly accorded ; but by the Ground Game Act of 1880 the tenant now has concurrent rights with his landlord in hares and rabbits, which will doubtless prevent the recurrence of disagreements which have occasionally taken place between tenants and gamekeepers. For farms valued at 50*l.* and upwards the clause relating to compensation for any premium or payment for good-will given by the tenant on entry is omitted ; but instead is introduced a provision 'that the lessee, his executors, administrators, or assigns, or any of them, shall not make any claim for compensation in respect of improvements, except improvements made with the written consent of the lessor, his heirs or assigns, save and except that portion of buildings set out in the schedule hereto annexed, which has been erected by the lessee.' In brief, no compensation is allowed for disturbance or for improvements effected, unless with the consent of the landlord.

In England or Scotland such agreements would not be considered unreasonable or stringent. Like laws, contracts respecting land are made, not for the well-doer, but for the possible evil-doer. In Ireland, however, there has been considerable outcry against the Leinster lease. In conformity with the provisions of the Land Act of 1870 all tenants under 50*l.* of annual value are entitled on their way-going to payments for all suitable buildings and other improvements effected by them. No interference is attempted with these claims. The unpopular clause in the indenture applicable to smaller tenancies, although it does not forbid the outgoing tenant receiving a bonus from the incomer, discountenances his being mulcted and burdened on his entry by heavy charges, and covenants that such charges shall not be made in future, as they sometimes have been made in the past, a claim against the landlord. Holders of land valued at more than 50*l.* annually, presumed by the Land Act of 1870 to be able to make their own contracts, under the Leinster indenture are entitled to compensation for improvements only when effected with the permission of the landlord. Such a provision is reasonable. Those who have experience of land property know how money, especially if belonging to other people, is ignorantly, injudiciously, and wastefully expended. Not many tenants have the special knowledge or experience economically to plan and carry out drainage works, much less road-making or building. Irish tenants have often peculiar views as to the placing of their house; rightly or wrongly they prefer it on the site of the old one, no matter how near it may be to the cattle or pig yards. Their ideas of drainage of house and buildings and of water supply are most elementary. Alike in the interest of landlord and tenant it hence appears desirable that the landowner should retain some control as to the extent and conduct of farm improvements for which he may at any time have to pay. On the Leinster and on other well-managed estates permission is, however, readily accorded to carry out any desirable, carefully considered improvements suggested by the tenant, and an undertaking is given in the agreements to make remuneration for such outlay, at the determination of the tenancy. 'Unexhausted tillages and manures' are fully allowed for under the provisions of the Act of 1870, but it is enjoined that 'no allowance shall be made for artificial manures used during the last two years unless with the written consent of the lessor or his agent.' This might prove discouraging to an improving tenant. Where manure is so much desiderated and so sparingly used it is undesirable in any way to discountenance its application in any form. Any excessive claim for artificial manures might be guarded against by providing that no repayments shall be made for more than the average outlay of the previous five years as shown by approved bills. These should be bigger than they generally are, for on the Leinster property there are no restrictions as to the sale of produce; a great deal of hay is cut and carried off, swedes as well as potatoes are freely sold, and no sufficient restitution is made to the beggared soil. But, although condemned by critics who, perhaps, do not always carefully examine them, the Leinster contracts appear to work successfully, and are approved by the most thoughtful and experienced of the tenantry.

CHAPTER IV.

EARL FITZWILLIAM'S ESTATES.

EARL FITZWILLIAM has estates lying tolerably compactly in the counties Wicklow, Kildare, and Wexford, and extending to 91,655 acres. For many generations one or more members of the family have taken an active, personal interest in this property, have spent considerable portions of the year at Coollattin, and have devoted money, time, and trouble to education, charities, and the improvement of the widely scattered population, as well as to developing the resources of the thin, poor land which constitutes the bulk of the estate. Giving the land and other help, the present Earl induced the Dublin, Wicklow, and Wexford Railway to extend their line sixteen miles from Wooden Bridge through the property to Shillelagh. Great pains have been taken to house the cottage and smaller farming tenants properly, to find work for them, and to prevent their becoming too numerous for the available employment and means of subsistence. Earl Fitzwilliam considers that holders occupying five to ten acres, regarding themselves as farmers, are seldom so well off as regular labourers. Attention to their own little piece prevents their accepting regular employment. This land is not good enough or sufficiently handy to market for gardening or fruit-growing. Even with good culture, ten acres do not furnish sufficient produce, supplemented by the sale of the young cattle or pigs, to support a family in comfort. The cultivation of ten or even twenty acres costs, moreover, relatively more than the cultivation of forty or fifty acres. It is seldom that the tenant has any trade or other resources wherewith to supplement his earnings from the farm. Now that grass so largely supersedes tillage, fewer hands are wanted. The middlemen whose leases have dropped in during the last few years have had a surplus of poorly-paid labourers and small tenants, many of whom have been wisely removed. For seventeen years the Hon. Mr. Ponsonby, now Lord Bessborough, contributed heartily in carrying out these and other estate improvements, which were begun by Earl Fitzwilliam's grandfather and carried on by his father.

Exclusive of cottage tenants—including, however, town and accommodation lands let to shopkeepers and townspeople—the tenancies ranging from one to twenty statute acres, and rented at 20*l.* and under, number 1,070; those over 20*l.* and under 50*l.* are enumerated at 351; those ranging from 50*l.* to 100*l.* reach 107; between 100*l.* and 200*l.* there are 56; between 200*l.* and 300*l.* there are only 22; while 17 pay over 300*l.* of annual rent. The rents range from 2*s.* 6*d.* an acre for mountain land and bog to 45*s.* for useful grass land near towns or villages.

Earl Fitzwilliam and his agent, Captain Duncan M'Neil, most courteously placed at my disposal the estate books, from which I extract the following figures, showing how the people have for many years been watched over and helped in their troubles, and the capabilities of the estate steadily developed. The disbursements for aiding the poor and helpless have been very large. No such liberal assistance could have been so systematically and continuously expended by small proprietors. No mere annuitants could have been expected to make such large outlays.

	£	s.	d.
Emigration from March 25, 1833, to March 25, 1847, cost	4,568	10	6
Emigration during famine years, from March 25, 1847, to March 25, 1856	19,017	11	5
	23,586	1	11

Ships were specially chartered for those who chose to proceed to America; whole families were deported together, and painful partings were thus greatly mitigated; a good commissariat was ensured on board ship: and six weeks' work was arranged for near the point of debarkation. The contingent was then moved West, and another shipload took up their quarters and work.

Those who remained at home were also largely assisted.

	£	s.	d.
Donations, clothing, and food during famine years, from March 25, 1844, to March 25, 1856	7,956	9	4
Disbursements for seed oats, potatoes, rye, barley, &c.	3,554	3	2
Donations and pensions from March 25, 1856, to March 25, 1859	2,057	7	4
Ditto from March 25, 1859, to March 25, 1869	7,503	2	9
Ditto from March 25, 1869, to March 25, 1879	7,771	17	8

These donations and pensions continue year by year, and range annually from 700*l.* to 800*l.*, while subscriptions to hospitals, dispensaries, and other such charities absorb annually 300*l.* Last year, to assist the poorer tenants whom the bad season had left without seed potatoes and oats, 867*l.* 18*s.* 5*d.* was, in addition, expended on carefully-selected champions and seed grain, which were charged to the people at half their cost price. To improve the people, and render them, if possible, independent of charity, education has always received anxious consideration. Help has long been given to schools irrespective of creed. Buildings have been provided, enlarged, or improved, and teachers' salaries augmented.

	£	s.	d.
Education payments, chiefly in aid of poorer schools, from March 25, 1844, to March 25, 1859	8,861	15	4
Ditto from March 25, 1859, to March 25, 1869	5,198	2	0
Ditto from March 25, 1869, to March 25, 1879	4,763	17	2

Now that the National system is so generally adopted, the disbursements for education are not so heavy as formerly, and 500*l.* proves a sufficient grant for recent years. Lads are taken in without fee to the building establishment, at low wages, and are taught the various trades carried on there.

The blessings of a resident and kindly-disposed proprietary in such a poor country as Ireland, where farming is almost the only industry, may be gathered from the accounts extracted from the estate sheets at Coollattin for the year to Lady Day, 1880, and fairly representing an annual average of over 12,000*l.*

This great outlay, recurring year by year, represents untold comfort and contentment in many a household, and the repeated turning of ready money, which in many western districts is so wofully scarce that barter has to be resorted to. It tells of industrious habits, self-dependence, and prudence; for no idler, drunkard, or evil-disposed man is allowed to remain in Earl Fitzwilliam's employment. It is obviously only property in the hands of extensive and wealthy owners on which an outlay so large in proportion to income can be justified.

In still another direction Lord Fitzwilliam is doing great good. His extensive home farm, reclaimed from a bog at a cost which shows a charge of nearly 40,000*l.*, illustrates what may be effected by the proper feeding both of plants and animals. From this farm there are distributed annually to tenants and others several score of wellbred young shorthorn bulls, Border Leicester rams, and, latterly, Shropshires—a practice which tends greatly to the improvement of the farmer's rent-paying stock.

The houses, farm buildings, plantations, and fences throughout the estate are maintained in good order by the efficient staff of artisans and labourers, well organised and looked after. Forty years ago a great deal was done towards building or thoroughly repairing the houses and premises of most of the larger holders. On a large, well-managed estate each year brings, however, the need of improvements and repairs. The way in which they mount into large figures and cut heavily into the gross returns may be gathered from the subjoined figures :—

	£	s.	d.
Building and repairs from March 25, 1844, to March 25, 1859	77,001	0	4
Ditto from March 25, 1859, to March 25, 1869	65,991	18	3
Ditto from March 25, 1869, to March 25, 1879	84,772	4	3
Disbursements for drainage, reclamations, river cuts, fences, &c., from March 25, 1844, to March 25, 1859	42,676	12	11
Ditto from March 25, 1859, to March 25, 1869	16,719	2	9
Ditto from March 25, 1869, to March 25, 1879	16,064	8	11

Apart entirely from what has been done by the tenants themselves and of which they are enjoying the good fruits, here has been an outlay by the landlord, continued during thirty-six years, now aggregating 303,000*l.*, or six years' gross rental of the estate, benefiting tradesmen and labourers during the carrying out of the work, and permanently and substantially increasing the food-producing capabilities of the property.

Tenants who require help or materials for their buildings or other improvements are enjoined to send in to the estate office applications and particulars of their requirements by the first week in February. An inspection is made and their claim is considered. Of such applications, 117 were received in 1878; in 1879 the number fell to fifty-seven. This falling off is an index of the worse times. Tenants have not money to spare for undertaking even their own share of such improvements. The proposed addition, repairs, or even tidying-up is postponed until more prosperous times. Nearly all these improvements are made by holders under 50*l.* of annual value. In dealing with building work several modes of procedure are adopted. Receiving timber and slates, most tenants prefer to do the work themselves, and thus prevent the accession of rent which would accrue if 4 or 5 per cent. interest were charged on the outlay undertaken by the landlord. Where a change of tenancy occurs, repairs are sometimes done by the landlord, and interest becomes merged in readjusted rent. Tenants, however, have been encouraged to do as much of their improvements as possible, and thus keep down their rents. Any money allowed to the tenant, with particulars of materials furnished and work done, is booked, and a copy is also usually indorsed on the tenant's agreement.

Buildings and premises generally are not so extensive and substantial as on the best English estates; but with only one-fifth under tillage they do not require to be so commodious. On a holding of sixty to seventy statute acres, valued at 50*l.*, which may be taken as a fair average of these smaller farms, the house has cost about 150*l.*, and the stable for two horses, cattle sheds, and pigsties about as much more. There are no field hovels, which would be very useful, especially as the young cattle and horses are kept out in the fields during the great part of the winter. Many of the older premises have been put up by the tenants, and are thatched. Tenants, however, receive considerable assistance in maintaining their buildings, and without cost are furnished with such home-grown timber as they require.

To replace the old, worn-out cabins, 140 labourers' cottages have been built since 1858, at a cost of 8,500*l.* They have been put up in towns and villages or at convenient points over the farms. Some are let with the larger holdings, but none go with farms under 50*l.* of annual value. All are maintained by the landlord. They are generally built in pairs, at a cost of 140*l.*, with 10*l.* or 15*l.* extra for setting out gardens. They have on the ground floor a kitchen and parlour (this latter sometimes divided), each about 12 feet by 15 feet; they are lofted over one or both rooms. They are built of stone, occasionally of concrete, when they cost about 10*l.* each less. With a garden, usually of a quarter of an acre, occasionally of half an acre, they are let at the rate of 2*l.* to 3*l.* annually;

but the tenancies are monthly; the rents are collected quarterly. A memorandum of agreement is signed by all cottagers. Estate rules exist, which strictly prohibit the taking in of lodgers. Although much has already been done, Earl Fitzwilliam considers that very much more is required; but this is a matter demanding time as well as money.

In towns and villages houses and shops are let yearly or on lease, and usually along with them town lots affording grass for cows varying from one to twenty acres, and rented, as a rule, at from 20*s.* to 55*s.* a statute acre. On these town lots subletting and the erection of buildings without permission are interdicted.

The families of many tenants have been on the estate for upwards of a century. Several speak of their great-grandfathers occupying where they still live. Since 1870 many leases for thirty-one years have been granted in cases where new tenancies became necessary, but these, as a rule, were confined to the larger class of farms. Most of those under 50*l.* of annual rent are held from year to year. The leases and agreements make the usual reservations to the lessor, covenant for the proper maintenance and repair of premises, for insurance against fire; and, for proper cultivation of the land, one-fourth, and in some cases one-third of the tillage, it is specified, shall be manured in each year. There are no cropping clauses, and no reservations as to sale of produce, excepting during the last three years of any lease, when no straw, hay, or roots are to be disposed of. Without written consent no public-house, beershop, or other business establishment is to be erected or opened. Cottages are to be occupied only by farm servants. Subletting is forbidden. It is provided that no building or other improvements shall be paid for, unless made with the previous approval and consent of the lessor. Game and rabbits have hitherto been reserved, but tenants have had liberty to net and ferret rabbits. Arbitration in the usual manner is provided to decide any disputes between landlord and tenant. The tenancy is determined in the event of the holder becoming bankrupt, neglecting to fulfil his covenants, or falling into arrears of rent. The terms of these agreements, although regarded as stringent in Ireland, could not be objected to by intelligent British tenants. Freedom of cropping and of sale, and payments for suitable improvements undertaken with the landlord's approval, are freely granted.

Secure in the fair dealing of the landlord, improvements are made with every confidence that no undue advantage will be taken, and that due allowance will be made in the event of the tenant's death or removal. One gentleman states that his father, fifty years ago, laid out 4,000*l.* on house, buildings, and reclamation of bog. Another improving tenant, with a lease for life, twenty years ago, enlarged his house and put up capital farm premises at a cost of 3,000*l.* These farms being under lease their rent of necessity remains the same. On one outlying farm 1,800*l.* was allowed for buildings and agricultural improvements made during a life lease which extended over nearly seventy years. On small and large farms alike, now, as previous to the Land Act of 1870, allowances are made for tenants' improvements. On the death of an occupier the widow usually remains in undisturbed possession without revaluation. If a son or other relative follows, the property is inspected and reported on, and the rent, if low, is slightly raised, the increment being determined by comparison with the Government valuation, and with valuations of the estate made in 1837 and in 1851, while the relative amount of the landlord's and tenant's improvements also receives due consideration. The principles of tenant right are thus recognised. Holders over 50*l.* of annual value who may be excluded from participation in compensations granted under the Land Act of 1870 are believed to need, quite as much as the smaller men, the fostering care of the Act and the inducement to lay out money. They are encouraged to improve; advice and help are given in carrying out suitable economic improvements; unexhausted outlays are scheduled and paid for much in the same manner as under our Landlord and Tenant Act of 1876. For gates and internal fittings, for grass seeds, and manure unused, all tenants are allowed, deduction, of course, being made for rent due; in point of fact, no deductions are ever made for dilapidations.

Excluding cottages, houses, and small townland pieces, there are every year twenty to thirty changes of farm tenants. They result mainly from the death of old tenants and the removal of others. Ejectments, in the usual acceptation of the term, rarely occur on this property. The outgoing tenant, if infirm, is sometimes provided with a pension; the man desiring to emigrate takes his valuation and joins his friends in America; most change for farms more suited to their means or taste. One change usually leads to several; a succession of promotions ensues; the smaller folks getting a rise, and usually increasing their area. Such changes are encouraged for the purpose of improving the position of the industrious and prosperous tenant, and of suiting the reduced means of his less flourishing neighbour.

It is difficult to determine whether the small or great holdings are best cultivated or afford most economical returns. The results depend upon the man, his intelligence, industry, and energy, rather than upon the number of acres occupied. The advantages of the proportionately larger capital which the bigger farmers have in implements and machinery is often counterbalanced by the continuous personal labour of the smaller holder. As regards this part of Leinster, probably the most successful results are attained with farms of 100 to 150 acres. The amount of capital employed per acre ranges from 3*l.* to 4*l.* Some of the larger holders have commodious, comfortable houses, which have frequently been built and provided with good gardens and surroundings by the squires or middlemen, who, with long leases, often held several hundred acres, and had subtenants and cottagers. As these leases have determined, Earl Fitzwilliam has converted them into direct tenancies. Captain D. M'Neil informs me that about three-fourths of the tenantry of all descriptions are Roman Catholics. Of the larger holders, nearly three-fourths are, however, Protestants. But these are not, as might be supposed, recent introductions; they include most of the oldest families, several of whose ancestors came over with Cromwell. Fifty years ago the Roman Catholics were notably of lower social and educational standard than their Protestant neighbours, but such distinctions are not now discoverable.

Farms are entered upon indifferently at Lady Day and Michaelmas. The latter is the more costly entry, as more crops have then to be taken to. The half-yearly gales or audits are held on the second and third weeks of May and December, but reasonable time is invariably given for settlement. No uniform percentages have been given even during recent bad years. Fortunately, they have not been required. Special cases have been met by special allowances in money or in other ways. On such a large estate, allowances, even when very carefully made, speedily amount to large figures. From the estate books are extracted the following details of deductions:—

	£	s.	d.
Allowances on rents from March 25, 1844, to March 25, 1859	42,903	15	9
Ditto from March 25, 1859, to March 25, 1869	22,329	6	4
Ditto from March 25, 1869, to March 25, 1879	11,521	17	4

Recent rents have been well met, testifying to the prosperity and solvency of the tenants. Arrears in 1846 stood at 10,000*l.*; as a result of the famine years, they reached 26,924*l.* in 1853, when 15,000*l.* was written off. The arrears at present do not exceed 5,000*l.*, or one-tenth of the rental.

Turning to the other side of the account, the particulars of which are also furnished with obliging readiness, it appears that, notwithstanding good management and liberal outlay on improvements, the rental does not increase rapidly, and now stands at but little over Griffith's valuation, which is 47,689*l.* 0*s.* 6*d.*

The increment in rental, since 1880, is as follows:—

	£	s.	d.
Annual rental, 1800	24,051	18	8
,, 1846	38,983	8	10
,, 1859	42,344	17	10
,, 1869	45,165	7	10
,, 1880	49,674	16	1

From the rental of last year was deducted for taxes, rates, tithe rent-charge, &c., a sum of 6,221*l*. 17*s*. 11*d*.; the expenditure for management was 3,578*l*. 5*s*. 11*d*.

The facts and figures thus extracted from the estate books demonstrate that Earl Fitzwilliam derives small pecuniary advantage from his Irish estates. He does not appropriate 1 per cent. per annum from their gross value. I am permitted to state that 13,000*l*. was the total amount which passed to his private account in 1879. Nearly three-fourths of the gross rental is spent upon the property. The money returns are small, but the prosperity, peace, and progress, spread through a wide area have hitherto been large. It is, however, to be deplored that even this fostering care and vast outlay have failed to secure for this estate immunity from the demoralising influences and the troubles consequent on Land League agitation.

CHAPTER V.

THE MARQUIS OF WATERFORD'S ESTATES AT CURRAGHMORE.

FOLLOWING family traditions, the Marquis of Waterford for fourteen years has expended much thought, personal labour, and expense in developing his estate and improving his tenantry. During half the year he resides at Curraghmore, where the park and grounds extend to 3,500 acres, and wood and water, mountain and glen, nature and art contribute to produce one of the most beautiful places in Ireland. When at home on the weekly pay-night, the Marquis is at the office, ready to hear and, if possible, redress any grievances. He takes a personal interest in and supervision of all details throughout his estate. At least once in twelve months he visits every tenant. Any measures seriously minimising the personal interest of such a landlord in his property or contracting his ability to benefit his poorer neighbours must surely prove disastrous. In Ireland, much more than in England, capital and the intelligence rightly to use it are greatly wanted. There is everywhere abundance of manual labour, but discretion and experience to encourage, guide, and stimulate it and money profitably to employ it are required.

During the proprietorship of the present Marquis, and long before, no tenants have been disturbed; few accessions have been made to rents; tenants' improvements have often been paid for without increasing the rent. Frequently, in their anxiety to obtain land on good estates, extravagant rents are promised. The Marquis of Waterford assures me that he has frequently been offered double the fair rent. Not long ago one young fellow came to treat for a farm, and was disconcerted on being told that there was one condition which he proposed which was fatal to his application—he had offered 50 per cent. more rent than he could afford to pay. It is not all landlords who know the value of their property, and who wisely demur to accept excessive rents even from responsible tenants. But in Ireland, as in England, tenants are not all responsible as regards the possession of sufficient capital. It is difficult to get men who have the 3*l.* per acre which is regarded as a fair amount for setting up business in county Waterford. False representations are apt to be made as to the means of the prospective tenant. A bank deposit is frequently shown for several hundred pounds. A couple of friends, informed of their neighbour's scheme, become security for the required amount, on condition, however, that the accommodation is merely nominal. The would-be tenant forthwith opens an account, shows his bank-book or deposit receipt, and gets credit for resources over which he has practically no control. Once in possession of a farm, especially on a good estate, on which the rents are understood to be moderate, the tenant has credit. His possessory interest, which in the smaller holdings has the legal recognition of the Land Act of 1870, enables him to obtain advances from merchants and bankers, while his resources may also be strengthened by marrying a wife with money.

Although prevented from subdividing his holding, the tenant, aged, crippled in means, or desirous to remove, has always been at liberty to name his successor, who, if respectable and possessed of sufficient means, is accepted as tenant. The landlord's veto, I am assured by Captain George Gandy, the Marquis's agent, often proves a useful protection to the man in possession against the severity or rapacity of shopkeepers, bankers, and other creditors, who are certainly less likely than the landlord to deal considerately with the struggling creditor. The Marquis always recognises the tenant's possessory rights. Owing, however, to bad times, want of capital, reduced competition, and uncertainty and agitation regarding the vexed land question, the value of tenants' as well as of landlords' rights has of late years diminished. Besides the value of improvements they have made and of acts of husbandry, landholders giving up are allowed several years' rent. The arrears, which in such cases usually extend back for several gales, and the balance of ready money paid to the waygoer, generally represent six or seven years' rent. Conjoined with fair rents, such a custom affords the best practical security to the tenant, and is tolerably effectual in preventing his capricious eviction. A landlord must obviously have some very substantial reason for removing a tenant if he is thus willing to sacrifice about 25 per cent. of the value of the fee-simple of his property. The tenant receiving such a premium should have capital to make a satisfactory start elsewhere. Widows are not disturbed, but allowed to make the best of their holding for their children. They are usually very thrifty and industrious. Remaining at home and attending closely to business, they are, as a rule, notably prosperous.

In forcible illustration of the security of the tenant on this and many other estates in the South of Ireland is the value of the possessory interest and the manner in which it is appreciated and disposed of. The exhausted resources of an elderly tenant are readily recruited if he has a marriageable son or daughter. With the easily obtained consent of the landlord he makes over the farm to the son or son-in-law, reserving for himself and 'the old woman' a room in the house, or a cottage and garden, with aliment or a specified annuity of flour, milk, and potatoes. Endowed with a farm and home, the unmarried tenant becomes an object of interest to saving parents, who have diligently accumulated dowers, sometimes of several hundred pounds, for the younger members of their families. There is not much sentiment expended over these matches. They are generally arranged by the parents. The most interested parties may have scarcely seen each other, occasionally their ages are somewhat ill-assorted; but the unions are reported to be quite as happy as those which have originated in love, instead of mutual interest. For the farm, the most profitable issue of such arrangements is where an only daughter remains on a holding, to which the bridegroom then brings the dower, with the help of which a fresh and energetic start may be made. In these engagements fair shrewdness and sense are generally exhibited, and on the Waterford estates only once in fourteen years has any objection been made to the son-in-law introduced or the arrangements proposed. Among all the better class of tenantry marriage settlements are common.

Unfortunately for the prosperity of the young couple, the dower is not always available for the cultivation of the farm. But it is not kept idle. It portions another daughter or younger son, who thus also acquires the *summum bonum* of Irish ambition—a bit of land. What matters that the house may be a hovel, the farm without equipment and beggared? It is, nevertheless, a home. The hundred pounds or two saved by the self-denial of a lifetime, within a few months passes through half-a-dozen hands, purchases the tenant right of half-a-dozen holdings, and launches on their wedded career half-a-dozen couples.

The Marquis's estates in county Waterford extend to 35,128 statute acres. The Poor Law valuation is 23,128*l*. The actual rental, exclusive of town lots, is 24,615*l*. Exclusive of town and cottage tenants, there are 474 landholders, ninety-four of whom pay less than 10*l*. annually. The majority of the rents range from 60*l*. to 70*l*. The land varies much in character and quality; some of the hill, or, as they are called, mountain tracts, partially clothed with furze and heather, are often conveniently apportioned to the lower farms at 2*s.* 6*d.* to 5*s.* per acre. The deep, good land on the Dungarvan portion of the property reaches as high as 50*s.* an acre. There is abundance of water from springs and rivulets, many of which might be utilised for irrigation. The Garravoone estate, bought by the Marquis of Waterford a few years ago at twenty years' purchase, has since been much improved; timber and slates have been freely furnished to all tenants who would rebuild or repair their dilapidated premises. Instead of raising rents, six and sometimes twelve months' arrears were wiped out. On this, as on all parts of the estate, the principle of 'self-help is anxiously inculcated. To any improvements required or asked for the tenant is expected to contribute, usually in the proportion of one-half. A great deal of good work is thus cheaply and effectually done, towards which the landlord's expenditure averages about 600*l.* per annum. This, however, does not include the value of the home-grown timber often used for building. Farmhouses suitable for 150 acres usually cost 200*l.*; cow-shedding and other buildings absorb about 300*l.* Outside walls and roofs are stout and good, but the interior fittings are fewer, plainer, and less expensive than on most English estates.

Dividing the fields more symmetrically than formerly, many miles of clay and turf banks have recently been formed, $4\frac{1}{2}$ feet to 5 feet high, 4 feet wide at the bottom, and 2 feet at the top, costing 1*s.* 2*d.* per perch of seven yards, while on the top is planted furze, which, when cut, proves useful for fodder, and when growing luxuriantly, as it readily does, affords admirable shelter. Along farm boundaries and roadsides bigger clay fences are faced with large stones, which are abundant and readily got. These more solid structures cost about 4*d.* per yard. Throughout the estate are numerous 9 feet iron gates, with eight bars, $4\frac{1}{2}$ feet high, weighing $3\frac{1}{2}$ cwt., furnished by the estate blacksmiths at 35*s.* each, and supplied to any tenant who will build substantial stone piers from which to hang them.

The following table exhibits the size of farms in two different parishes, their Government valuation, and their actual rental :—

Clindonnell.

	Irish	Rent per acre	Poor Law Valuation	Actual Rent
	a. r. p.	s. d.	£ s. d.	£ s. d.
Chas. Carrothers, Mountain Farm	205 0 0	—	38 0 0 }	51 16 0
Ditto, Quarter Farm	39 1 33	—	12 0 0 }	
Michael Whelan	34 2 6	20 0	35 10 0	35 0 0
James Hembery	40 3 17	17 6	30 0 0	32 0 0
Michael Hembery	39 3 23	18 6	30 0 0	38 0 0
Reps. of Maurice Power	62 1 35	14 0	37 0 0	40 0 0
Maurice Whelan	67 2 8	14 0	40 0 0	44 0 0
John E. Power	43 0 14	22 0	40 0 0	48 0 0
Richard Kennedy	87 1 0	24 0	93 0 0	110 0 0
Bally-Neale and Bridgetown.				
John Ryn	110 0 17	36 0	164 15 0	200 0 0
Wm. Shannan	85 3 14	34 0	130 0 0	146 0 0
Reps. of Wm. Moore	22 2 0	32 6	27 10 0 }	101 4 0
„ „	52 2 2	25 0	65 4 0 }	
John Walsh	70 1 7	20 0	76 0 0 }	140 0 0
Reps. of Pat. Walsh	70 1 7	20 0	70 0 0 }	
Patrick Phyn	13 0 6	25 0	18 0 0	18 0 0

Three Irish acres make five Imperial acres.

Poor rates in various baronies range from 1s. to 4s. County cess, increased by the building of bridges and the deficits f the railway, for which the county became security, are from 2s. to 3s.

Dairying and dry stock, usually in about equal proportions, occupy the Waterford farmer. Only a limited area, seldom exceeding one-fifth part, is in tillage, producing the straw, fodder, and a few roots requisite during the short winter. Comparatively few sheep are kept, partly owing to the heavy losses sustained two years ago from liver-rot, the result of flukes, and the shrewd suspicion that the pastures may not yet be clear of the parasites.

Lord Waterford is busily occupied with the better housing of his cottage tenants. In the towns and villages many cottages are in the hands of middlemen, who squeeze the tenants unmercifully, and often exact 200 to 400 per cent. over and above the rents that they pay to their superior. Pending the leases and other current agreements, it is difficult to buy out or make satisfactory arrangements with these middlemen. In the straggling, poor town of Kilmacthomas, as well as in many villages, are houses without back entrances, without gardens or allotments, and often in a state of dilapidation. The want of half-an-acre of garden ground with each cottage is a serious evil in Ireland where agricultural labour is irregular and precarious, where other occupations are rare, where many of the farmers are not much removed above the labouring class, and seldom provide regular, constant employment. Wages are 9s. to 10s. per week; ploughmen and herds, boarded in the farmhouse, have 9*l.* to 10*l.* a year; servant girls receive 7*l.* to 10*l.* Tea and bread and butter are sometimes now bargained for, especially by the girls. The tea, bread, small portion of bacon, and other etceteras consumed by master and servants, inexpensive and reasonable although they appear, I am told by careful housekeepers add 20s. per week to the expenditure on a farm of 100 acres, as compared with the moderate commissariat expenses of thirty years ago, when potatoes, stirabout, and butter-milk constituted the dietary both in parlour and kitchen.

Lord Waterford's gardens, his stables—where upwards of fifty horses are kept—his home farm, his woods and improvements, afford much regular employment. Besides salaries to heads of departments and foremen, 100*l.* is paid every week in wages at Curraghmore. Every year about sixty acres of mountain or waste are planted, usually with larch, spruce, and other firs, usefully finding labour, greatly improving the appearance of the country, and promising in twenty years handsome returns. If all tenants are to be endowed with absolute fixity of tenure, will not serious difficulties be placed in the way of planting, whether for shelter or amenity? On the home farm are thirty superior shorthorn cows, from the best of which the bull-calves are sold, when dropped, at 40*s*. to 60*s*., and are making their mark among many of the farmers' dairy herds.

Adjacent to Lord Waterford's, the College of Physicians, Dublin, have 3,418 statute acres, divided among twenty principal tenants and a number of smaller struggling occupiers. The buildings are generally poor and dilapidated, the land starved and neglected—an apt illustration of the evils of absenteeism. This is the sort of estate one would gladly see passing into more energetic hands. The majority of the tenants do not, however, show much smartness; their want of success as occupiers does not justify any great expectations of activity or enterprise being developed, even if they became owners. It is doubtful whether many of them could find ready money to pay even one-fifth of the purchase-money. A notable exception is Peter Wall, of Ballygiven, who appears to concentrate in his own person the *nous* and enterprise of the estate. Naturally dissatisfied with the returns of his poor holding, he purchases all the manure he can collect from the town of Carrick, three miles distant, keeps several horses drawing it to the farm, and has the satisfaction of producing alike on his tillage and top-dressed grass about four times the return which his neighbours secure. This telling illustration of liberal treatment is not yet sufficiently imitated.

Sir Henry P. T. Barron, county Waterford, has a good

estate of 6,218 acres ; the Government valuation is 3,625*l.* ; the actual rental 4,000*l.* ; the rents generally are 30 per cent. over Griffith's valuation ; the farms average fifty acres, but several reach 150 acres. The larger holders are generally doing best ; many of the smaller are in difficulties owing to long credits with shopkeepers, gombeen men, or banks. Not one-fourth of the tenants have leases ; many are without written agreements, and few now care to have them. Tenants are allowed to dispose of their interest. The agent informs me that 340*l.* was recently paid for the goodwill of a farm of forty acres—a premium reaching seven years' rental. Changes of occupiers seldom, however, occur ; although here, as elsewhere, it would sometimes be advantageous alike for owner and occupier that an apathetic, idle, and neglectful tenant, of whom there are not a few, should be moved on.

Mr. Joseph O'Neal Power has an estate of 8,312 acres in counties Waterford and Kilkenny, four miles from the city of Waterford, with a rent-roll of 7,000*l.* The farms average seventy-five acres. Holders occupying less than twenty acres have, of late years, struggled along with considerable difficulty. The tenantry generally, however, are contented and fairly well-to-do. The arrears of rent are trifling, and more pride than formerly is taken in keeping houses and premises tidy. Towards building, draining, and other repairs the landlord contributes, finds labour for the unemployed in times of distress, and is often called upon to replace losses from disease of stock or failure of crop. Payments for tenant right are recognised ; rents vary from 10 per cent. to 20 per cent. above Griffith's valuation, and do not appear to be excessive. Of course, no man regards his own holding cheap, but occasionally hazards the opinion that his neighbours 'should be tidily well off.' As is frequently the case elsewhere, it is not the low-rented man who is best off. Success depends on the capability of the tenant quite as much as on the goodness or cheapness of his farm. Four acres suffice to furnish a cow with summer and winter food. Rent and taxes seldom exceed 30*s.* per acre. While dairymen give, as they willingly do, throughout this district, 9*l.* to 10*l.* per head for ten months' use of a fair dairy of cows, the farmer should, under such conditions, with judgment and industry, make a fair livelihood. Many tenants with whom I conversed admit that, although they are paying 20 per cent. over Griffith's valuation, they are doing very fairly. One man, who pays not quite 100*l.* a year rent, dairies twenty cows, the receipts from which cover all expenditure, sales of young stock and of pigs going towards profit. A smart, pushing, young fellow, ten years in business, although entering his farm with a very limited capital, and complaining of its being over-rented, has, nevertheless, managed to save 600*l.*, with which he has good-naturedly set up his brother in a promising farm belonging to Lord Waterford. Another clever manager with 200 acres, part of it hill pasture, pays 90*l.* annual rent, or 16*l.* over Griffith's valuation, dairies thirty-three cows, and boards his young stock among his less prosperous neighbours. Such successes demonstrate that in this part of Ireland, even under an admittedly imperfect land system, industry and energy ensure prosperity.

CHAPTER VI.

THE DUKE OF DEVONSHIRE'S ESTATES.

Although the Duke of Devonshire by some may be styled a Sassenach and an alien, he and his predecessors have shown much interest in their Irish estates, and have done a great deal to improve them. Beyond narrow, personal concerns, beyond the mere development of his own demesne, his influence and purse have been widely used to benefit the country. In land shares and subsidies he has contributed upwards of 200,000*l.* in the making of railways in Waterford and Cork. Apart from the labour given, who can estimate the benefit which these enterprises exert, not only in providing markets, but in extending education and civilisation? Such big enterprises require big men. Accumulated capital is one of Ireland's greatest wants. In the West ready money is almost as scarce as in the Western States of America; in some localities barter is resorted to. An immense boon, therefore, is the landlord who, like the Duke of Devonshire, has the heart and means largely to benefit his neighbours.

The Duke has two estates in county Cork, and one in Waterford. That of Lismore around his beautiful castle is 16,892 acres. Griffith's valuation is 9,573*l.*; the actual rental is 19 per cent. over this valuation. This division of the property, including large farms near the towns of Lismore and Tallow, where the land is of superior quality, diverges more than elsewhere from Griffith's valuation, which almost invariably places a low estimate on the prime land. The number of tenants is 285, including 120 under 10*l.* of Poor Law valuation. During the last ten years there have been nine ejectments of farming tenants for non-payment of rent. Over three years' arrears on an average had accumulated against these defaulters. The Kinatalloon estate, lying between Tallow and Fermoy, embraces 13,312 acres divided among 166 tenants, only twenty-seven of whom are under 10*l.* of Poor Law valuation; Griffith's valuation is 8,113*l.*; the actual rental exceeds this by 6 per cent. The Bandon property, twenty miles west of Cork, includes 17,779 acres; excluding town and accommodation occupiers, it musters 215 tenants, only ten of whom are under 10*l.* annual rental. Griffith's valuation is 10,162*l.*; the actual rent 10 per cent. over. The same management extends over the three portions of the estate, which for forty years has been under the kindly, fostering care of Mr. F. E. Currey, J.P., who informs me that most of the present rents have been fixed within the last forty years, but some have existed for a longer period without change. Many tenants have remained at their present rents for over thirty years, and in no case is rent altered within a term of twenty-one years.

No respectable tenant paying his way is ever disturbed; no reiterated vexatious additions are made to rental. The way-going tenant is usually allowed to nominate a creditable, reliable successor, and on an average receives for his good will about five years' rent. Frequently a portion of the arrears is forgiven in order to leave the tenant something to make a fresh start either at home or in America. Mr. Currey, who has had great opportunities of observation, believes that for the counties Waterford and Cork Griffith's valuation is an uncertain and irregular test of rent, and is usually under the fair letting value. The instructions given during the prosecution of the survey varied considerably; the prices of agricultural produce were at one time left out of consideration; and in some districts four different valuers followed each other, so that relative or absolute uniformity of result was scarcely to be expected. Since the work was done about thirty years ago most agricultural produce has, moreover, advanced 25 to 50 per cent. Still another condition renders Griffith's valuation an unreliable criterion of rent. From the original valuations made of parts of these estates, and of which Mr. Currey had copies furnished him, nearly 30 per cent. was subsequently deducted previous to the awards being published.

Twenty years ago most of the smaller tenants held on parole; but it has been found desirable to guard against abuses, and especially against subdivision, subletting, the removal by the way-going tenant of his last crop, and irregularities of cropping. Printed agreements for yearly tenants and leases for thirty-one years are now given; but in the present unsettled state of the land question ordinary tenants on a well-managed estate contentedly entrust their interests to their landlords and the State. Pleasing although this trustfulness may be, there is more hope of tenants who exhibit some self-assertion, independence, and determination to have their contracts definitely fixed on a business-like basis. The chief features of the agreements and leases may thus be epitomised. After the usual reservations as to timber, minerals, and the arrangements as to rents, the tenant covenants to maintain, repair, and keep his premises insured against fire, to avoid assigning, subletting, and conacre, except in the case of potatoes, or other green crops properly manured—an accommodation frequently given to farm servants. Liberty is granted to dispose of the lease to one member of the family or, with the approval of the landlord, to a stranger. No house or cottage shall be erected without consent; subdivision of the house is forbidden, and no family is permitted to reside in the dwelling-houses or cottages excepting that of the tenant or his servants. The land under crop shall not exceed one-fourth, sometimes one-third, of the total acreage; no two consecutive corn crops shall be grown; straw and manure are to be consumed on the farm; no way-going crops are allowed, but payment is made for two-thirds of the value of any corn crop immediately succeeding a green crop, for manured green crops, for the unexhausted benefit of any manure supplied within twelve months to land on which no subsequent corn crop has been grown, for actual cost of seed and labour expended on other growing crops. These valuations are appraised by arbitration in the usual way. The Landlord and Tenant (Ireland) Act of 1870 notwithstanding, no remuneration will be made for buildings put up by the tenant unless with consent of the landlord, or unless they have been paid for by the tenant at the period of his entry. Exemption is further claimed from any Ulster customs. The agreement for smaller and annual holders covenants that 'the premises shall not be held to be subject to any usage corresponding to the Ulster tenant custom,' and that no claim shall be entertained for compensation for money given as premium on coming into possession, excepting when specified in the agreements. Without previous notice the landlord covenants for re-possession in the event of the rent being unpaid after twenty-one days, in the case of the tenant's bankruptcy, or of his breach or non-fulfilment of conditions.

All permanent buildings are done at the joint expense of the landlord and tenant, each generally paying about an equal moiety. Under this plan the tenant takes a personal interest in the work, and sees that artisans and labourers are kept up to the mark. On draining 5 per cent. was formerly charged; but now the work is usually done at the joint expense of landlord and tenant, and no additional rent is charged. The drains are made under supervision of the agent, are usually $3\frac{1}{2}$ feet deep, are cleared out 10 inches at bottom, flat stones are placed $\triangle$ shaped; where 16-inch or 18-inch flags are available the practice is to reverse them ($\triangledown$). Above this for 14 inches the drain is filled with smaller stones. Following the principle of sharing in the expense of all work, the landlord pays for cutting the drain, which costs 1*d.* per yard; the tenant draws the stones and fills the drains.

On the Waterford part of the property during the last twenty years 26,800*l.* has been expended on farm improvements; on the Bandon portion, 6,300*l.* The general works account ranges annually from 5,000*l.* to 6,000*l.* The garden accounts reach 400*l.*; woods and plantations usually about 700*l.* Labourers' wages take 25*l.* per week, and artisans' nearly as much. Not all the Americanised Irish are politicians and stump orators. One of the smartest and best tradesmen on the property, after several years' training in the United States, finding business dull, returned home, uses to good account his acquired adaptiveness and resource, and turns his hand to almost any sort of building work.

Charges for works and labour bills are not, however, the only deductions from the rental of a liberally managed estate. In Ireland much more than in England, and from rentals which are strictly moderate, allowances are freely made in times of too frequently recurring distress. On the Devonshire estates such allowances in 1846 reached 5,255*l.*; 1849, 5,826*l.*; 1850, 6,064*l.*; 1851, 6,610*l.*; 1852, 6,791*l.*; 1853, 3,472*l.*; 1862, 5,560*l.*; 1863, 5,569*l.*; 1879, 5,394*l.* In intermediate years fortunately less help was needed, and a few hundred pounds sufficed to tide over the difficulties which were brought under Mr. Currey's notice. To the smaller tenants allowances are frequently given towards making up losses among live stock. Two years ago one large tenant received 250*l.* on account of the destruction of his flock from liver-rot produced by flukes. Last year 112 tons of seed potatoes were distributed, at an average of about 1*l.* per ton below cost price. Subscriptions for charities, schools, and now for churches aggregate a large amount, in 1879 reaching 2,803*l.*

This long-continued systematic consideration and care for the interests of the property and the people exhibit their good fruits in the order and well-being observed in driving through the estate. The farmhouses, generally of stone and slated, are usually substantial and in good preservation, are often lime-grouted to keep out the driving south-westers, and many are tidily whitewashed. The other buildings are also in good order; 600*l.* to 1,000*l.* is the usual outlay represented in the buildings of a farm of 200 imperial acres, and half of this has generally been contributed by the tenants. Gardens and orchards are not sufficiently attended to; several good orchards are injured for want of cutting out old and dead wood, and by the accumulation of water-absorbing moss. On the farms and in the villages numbers of one-storeyed cottages have been erected, which are let with good gardens for 20*s.* to 50*s.* a year. Servants on the farms usually have their houses rent free. Instead of small, inconvenient, irregularly shaped fields, too numerous in the south of Ireland, on all large farms the fields have been laid out symmetrically, usually in six to twelve acres. The fences are clay and turf banks, occasionally stone faced and topped for shelter with furze. Thorn hedges are sometimes planted, but are apt to be browsed and destroyed by the numerous goats. Occasionally the superabundant stones, laboriously got out of the land, are utilised for walls.

The Devonshire estate comprises a considerable stretch of the fertile valley of the Bride, which runs into the Blackwater. In the vale of the Bride are located some prosperous tenants occupying 200 to 300 acres of good loam on sandstone, and, better still, occasionally on an outcropping limestone. They pay 16*s.* to 30*s.* per acre. Dairying is the chief business; good managers keep about thirty-five head of cattle, young and old, for each 100 acres.

Some men with taste for horses—and there are few in Ireland who have not—keep one or two good brood mares, and turn out a useful three-year-old hunting colt at 50*l.* to 60*l.* One gentleman, more fortunate than his neighbours, from a brood mare of superior stamp for a dozen years paid the rent of his 100-acre farm. As a good type of his class, Mr.

POVERTY STRICKEN SMALL HOLDERS.   61

Peter O'Neil, who holds the Garran Ribben, or 'ribbon garden,' measuring 347 acres, pays annually 225*l.*, dairies thirty-four cows, makes butter—which this year has averaged 1*s.* per pound—rears most of his calves, feeds out his bullocks when about three years old, breeds a few young horses, managing to sell three or four annually at 40*l.* to 50*l.* apiece. He has about fifty acres in tillage, and makes good use of the beautiful stream which flows through his farm, irrigating about forty acres, and securing in consequence good grass by the 1st of April, or about a month earlier than it springs on the ordinary meadows. Such irrigation might be readily and profitably extended on many farms. One of the chief drawbacks to the district is the weakness of the soil, especially that overlying the sandstone. Laid down to grass, the herbage does not hold for more than four or five years; it becomes mossy, and the finer grasses disappear. This would probably be greatly obviated by top dressings, occasional dusting with white clover seed, and by penning the mossy land with sheep supplied with roots and cotton cake.

The general well-being of the Devonshire estates gains by the comparatively small number of tenants holding less than ten acres. They are too frequently the most poverty-stricken of the population, are often dependent on their neighbours for working their tillage, have seldom capital to buy stock, and frequently have their grass consumed by beasts tacked out by larger farmers, who usually pay in oatmeal and potatoes. Many portions of the Black Mountains were fifty years ago occupied by small holders, who, although they had been in occupation twelve to fifteen years, and had got much of their land fairly reclaimed, were ruined by the potato failure of 1846 and 1847, and migrated to America.

Some of this land has reverted to its former condition of heather and furze. The Trappist monks of Mount Melleray, near Cappoquin, seven miles from Lismore, have held from Sir Richard F. Keane for about thirty years 750 acres of mountain-side. It has been intelligently and diligently cultivated, but is poor, thin land, full of springs, and on a cold clay subsoil; it seems to swallow up almost any amount of manure, and is not now worth much more than 10s. per statute acre. In the hands of most tenants it would speedily revert to its original state. Other portions of this Knockmeildown range, Sir R. Keane informs me, are of somewhat better, drier sort, on a clay slate, which when broken through allows the more rapid drainage of the superabundant rains of this dripping locality. This lighter land is more easily reclaimed at a cost of about 10*l.* an acre, grows fair oats, potatoes, and turnips, if not too frequently recurring, and makes useful upland for sheep and young cattle, worth, within an altitude of 700 feet, about 16s. per statute acre.

Of such hill and mountain ranges thousands of acres unreclaimed and partially reclaimed extend throughout the South and West of Ireland. Owing to the poor and precarious returns of potatoes, reclamation of mountain and bog has not recently paid. As a rule, very small returns are got for upwards of two years. Where draining and liming have to be done—or, in the case of a mountain side, large boulders and stones have to be removed—reclamation frequently costs 12*l.* to 15*l.* per acre. Small tenants without other occupation or resources, set to such work, would require alimentation for three years before their labours would furnish food for their own support. By adjacent occupiers small portions may be gradually brought under cultivation at leisure times. Near Tallow, Mr. Currey, jun., introduced to me a small tenant who, he remarked, has 'a mania for reclamation.' His farm extends steadily up the hill-side; heather and stones are diligently stocked out, and, as the land is dug and the work done at intervals of other engagements, the industrious occupier estimates his labour at about 6*l.* per acre.

Although generally well housed, often rent free, the condition of the labourer is susceptible of considerable improvement. Those living in cottages on the farm receive 3*s.* 6*d.* to 4*s.* per week; turn out at 6 A.M. in winter, at 5 A.M. in summer; have breakfast in the farm kitchen, usually of potatoes and milk; have the same for dinner, varied, perhaps, by occasional stirabout; continue work until 5 P.M. in winter, and 7 P.M. in summer, and return home to supper. Besides these wages, they have three barrels, or about 15 cwt., of coals, and make something by feeding a pig and some poultry; while the women of the family have occasional work among the root crops or hay at 6*d.* to 8*d.* per day, and in harvest earn 1*s.* 6*d.* to 2*s.* One of their chief grievances is the high price of 5*l.* to 6*l.* per acre charged by the farmer for the use of land manured and prepared for the potato crop, the cottager finding and planting his own seed.

The smaller owners in this part of county Waterford are not very prosperous, and their condition does not particularly encourage the manufacture of yeomen or peasant proprietors. When the present Duke of Devonshire came into possession upwards of twenty years ago, he sold some land at Dungarvan and Youghal. In both places the people continue to regret the change of ownership. At this time one tenant bought a farm of sixty acres; but ownership has not stimulated him to improvement, and a few years afterwards he was anxious that the Duke should repurchase the land. Kilcockan parish, between Lismore and Youghal, was in great part disposed of in the Landed Estates Court thirty years ago. It was bought, some of it by occupiers, some of it by shopkeepers and attorneys. Rents have been raised, and there is not much appearance of prosperity. Newtown, for several generations the fee-simple property of a family of the name of Nason, after the famine of 1846 was cut up and sold; the family residence is in ruins. At Lower Curryglass, a few miles east of Lismore, a good farm of 500 acres, belonging to a family who have been obliged to leave it, bears sad evidence of neglect; the good old deserted manor-house, the farm buildings, and a dozen cottages in the village are falling to pieces. Contrary to what might be anticipated, some of the smaller proprietors in this district have been strenuous supporters of the Land League, although it is to be hoped that they repudiate the destruction of the cattle on the land of Mr. Grant, which in November were stabbed, and some of them drowned in the river. Mr. Grant had come under the ban of the League for evicting a dissipated bankrupt tenant, whose debts, to the extent of 200*l.*, he had paid, and who would have been reinstated if there had been the remotest prospect of reformed habits or of getting clear of his difficulties. Such acts appear to justify the statement 'that Irishmen don't know what they want, and won't be satisfied until they get it.'

CHAPTER VII.

ESTATES BETWEEN CORK AND KILLARNEY.

Messrs. Hussey and Townsend, of Cork, Kilkenny, and Killarney, have the supervision of eighty-eight estates, upwards of 3,000 farming tenants, and annually collect rents to the value of a quarter of a million sterling. They have, therefore, large and varied experience of estate management, and courteously furnish me with the following particulars :—
So recently as the end of November the Lady Day rents had been well paid up; old arrears had been reduced; on two estates in the Court of Chancery 6,000*l.* had been collected with only a few shillings in default. Dairy farmers prospering had been particularly well able to pay rent and other claims. More recent rent collections unfortunately have not been so satisfactory. Tenants generally have earned the money, but have not been allowed to pay it over. Some have tendered Griffith's valuation, and called subsequently with the balance; others have had two separate receipts—one for Griffith's, and the other for the residue. Occasionally, by pressure or cajoling one or two leading tenants have been persuaded to settle, and the others have followed suit. Where rent payments have been refused or postponed, the money, sometimes laboriously earned, is understood to have been melting away. Not one-fifth of the tenants under Messrs. Hussey

and Townsend's jurisdiction have leases; many hold their land merely on parole. With uncertainty as to prices, with intensifying American competition, and the anticipated State intervention which in some easy, beneficent manner is expected to hand over the land to the occupier, few tenants now trouble themselves about leases. The highest-rented estates are those that have been put up in anticipation of sale, or bought by speculators and the rents subsequently screwed up. High rents are not, however, the cause of Ireland's agricultural trouble. Unpalatable as the fact doubtless is, many of the low-rented estates are badly farmed and the tenantry in low water. On the higher-rented the struggle for existence has brought out extra industry and energy, and led on to fair success. Illustrations crop up frequently, and the following is an apt one:—Mr. W. R. Gould Adam, of Kilmachill, has a small estate on the north side of a hill rented at 20s. an acre; the rents are paid up, the tenants doing well. On the southern aspect of the same hill, with better land at the devoutly desiderated Griffith's valuation, which is 16s. 4d., the tenants are invariably hard up, some of them two years in arrears. Assuredly Ireland is a country of paradoxes and enigmas. Practically, Mr. Townsend assures me, all tenants have free sale, averaging five years' rent. Now that butter brings over 1s. per lb., dairy farms are naturally most keenly competed for.

With so many diverse sorts of property the management is necessarily rather varied. The larger proprietors as a rule are most liberal and helpful to their tenants. From estates heavily mortgaged, held by life owners, by clergymen or by old ladies, allowances for improvements are small. Where improvements are not effected or initiated by the landlords,

Messrs. Hussey and Townsend remark that 'they are seldom done at all.' The most useful, practical measures benefiting Ireland are said to be those facilitating the borrowing of money for agricultural improvements. There has often been considerable difficulty in overcoming the prejudice and 'the rest and be thankful' spirit both of landlords and tenants, and inducing them to take adequate advantage of these loans.

On Sir George Colthurst's Ballyvourney estate, twenty miles south of Killarney, under the auspices of Mr. Hussey, 6,455$l.$ has been expended since January 1879 in draining, building, and roadmaking. In timber and slates 2,330$l.$ has been laid out in eight years. The economic value of many holdings has been doubled, although the rent has only been increased to the extent of 5 per cent. on the judiciously expended outlay. For labourers and smaller tenants remunerative work has thus been found in winter and dull times. Although thus improved and helped, and their holdings put in the fair way of profitable use, the tenantry, obeying the arbitrary behest of wild agitators, object to pay anything beyond Griffith's valuation, and fail to recognise the fairness of meeting their share of the percentage charges. Sir G. C. Colthurst's Blarney estate, four miles from Cork, extending to nearly 3,000 acres, was well farmed for some years by his kinsman, Sir John Jeffries, who improved the amenity and shelter by planting. Some of the land rents at 50$s.$ an imperial acre; the average is about 30$s.$, or one-third over Griffith's valuation. Several of the tenants are very successful dairy farmers, too busy and prosperous to trouble themselves with political agitation, managing their herds and farms economically, and securing fair results in their winter dairy by the use of roots, hay, grain, and a daily allowance to each cow of 4 lbs. of mixed cake and corn.

Anxious to meet with an actively improving, energetic Irish tenant, by advice of Mr. Robert Townsend I visited Mr. J. Hegarty, of Mill Street, a station midway between Cork and Killarney. In the township of Mill Street rents generally have been moderate. Many farms have been held at 2s. 6d. an acre. The tenants, nevertheless, careless and thriftless, have not prospered. They have ruinously divided and subdivided their holdings; many are reduced to the condition of paupers, and Canon Giffen, the resident priest, informs me that some of the small farming tenants absent themselves from church because they cannot pay their dues. Such idleness and apathy obviously increase poor rates, which in Mill Street Union are 5s. 10d. in the pound. In fairness it must, however, be remarked that it is 2s. less than it was some years ago, and the valuation of 26,000l. is less than half the actual rental.

Mr. Hegarty farms 800 acres, belonging to Major Wallace's trustees, originally in twelve separate holdings, for several of which he had to pay the tenants he superseded seven years' rent. Much of the land was taken in hand three years ago. Part of it is held on lease for forty years, some of it for fifty; but a portion is held only from year to year. Griffith's valuation is 239l., which testifies the unimproved state in which it was thirty years ago, and, indeed, remained until Mr. Hegarty took it in hand. The rent now paid is 595l. 10s. In good earnest and with sound judgment the improvements have been devised and carried out. Fully 3,000l. of his own money has been expended; 1,000l. has been granted by the Board of Works last year under the

Distress Act, and will be repaid in thirty-five annual instalments of 3*l.* 6*s.* 8*d.* per cent., while 700*l.* bears 5 per cent. during thirty-five years.

Immediately outside the extending village of Mill Street, which during the last few years has been in great measure reconstructed by the exertions of Mr. Hussey, Mr. Hegarty has substantially built with stone, and slated at a cost of 1,000*l.*, a goodly set of farm premises, including barns, stabling, tying-up for forty cattle, and a cottage. Concrete is usefully employed, not only for the floors and for coping for the walls, but also for the water troughs. The fields are well laid out in six or seven acres, many of them divided by double rows of thorn quick, nearly 2 feet apart, between which is planted a row of privet. Pipe drains put in fifteen years ago, having become broken or displaced, are being superseded by more substantial stone drains. A mill-race on a higher level, soaking twenty-five acres, and causing its steady retrogression, has had the leakage intercepted. The land is heavily manured and enriched by eating off big crops of roots with sheep, and is laid down to grass, which looks very promising.

Two miles from Mill Street Mr. Hegarty has another farm of 300 acres in process of reclamation. A good set of buildings and rick-yard are placed on the mountain-side, which yields splendid green-stone for buildings and fences, on the top of which furze is planted for shelter. On the lower ground thorn quick is grown on clay and turf banks, thrown up 3 feet high. A road two and a half miles long has been made at a cost of 150*l.* per mile; the expense, chiefly borne by the county, was aided by 50*l* from Major Wallace's trustees. Parallel roads, connecting his six- and seven-acre fields, are made by the tenant. The miserable mud and thatch cabins, the last two of which still remain, are giving place to well-built, comfortable cottages. To prevent flooding of the newly improved lands, the pretty trout stream which runs in the valley has been straightened for several hundred yards. The burning of the heather and grubbing up stones are the first stages of the reclamation. Four-feet drains, generally 10 yards apart, stoned 18 inches from the bottom, cost 7*l.* an acre. Including enclosures, stocking, levelling, digging, and working diagonally with the plough, other 7*l.* or 8*l.* is expended. Including buildings and roads, the total cost of bringing the wilderness into cultivation is 20*l.* an acre. Twenty to twenty-five acres are taken in annually. To hasten disintegration of turf and peat, a good deal of lime is used, is burnt on the estate, and costs 6*s.* per ton. Potatoes are grown usually on 5-feet beds, each of which carries three rows; much of this year's crop yielded three tons. There follows a second crop of potatoes or swedes—the latter eaten by sheep—then oats, succeeded by grass. Until cultivated for a few years, the land has a strong tendency to revert to its original wild state. Reduced to fair working order, every hundred acres of tillage employs four labourers and four horses. With tradesmen, and those reclaiming and draining, Mr. Hegarty usually employs sixty people; but during last winter he had generally 100 at work. Wages range from 7*s.* to 10*s.*, but out of this the men have usually to pay house rent. Throughout the district 3*l.* is considered a fair amount of capital per acre; but Mr. Hegarty declares that he cannot get along without 5*l.* The business of the farm embraces dairying, with the rearing and feeding of cattle and sheep.

Mr. Hegarty thinks that farming might be much improved if landlords, or their agents, if practical men, went more among the tenants, talked with them, and encouraged them. Government loans might advantageously be extended; the money should be available for all agricultural improvements, and should be obtainable at 5 per cent., principal and interest being repaid together in thirty-five annual instalments. Much useful labour might thus be provided, greatly improving the hard lot of the labouring population, while a solid basis would be secured for subsequent profitable farming.

Throughout the wide district between Cork and Killarney the farms range from thirty to fifty statute acres. Very few tenants have leases; many have no agreements whatever. Small endeavour is made to effect any improvements even in the way of ditching or cheap draining, which might amply repay the outlay within three years. With other sensible men Mr. Hegarty deplores the action of the Land League. Non-payment of rent being generally approved, the obligation to meet other debts is notably weakened. Although there is more money than usual in the hands of the farming community, shopkeepers are not so promptly and willingly paid as formerly. Want of security checks the improved business which should have set in after a good harvest. The Land League agitation generally originates with the publicans, small shopkeepers, and bankrupt farmers rather than with the actual land occupiers. For peace and protection many pay their subscription to the League and allow their names to be enrolled. The intimidation and 'Boycotting' now so widely had recourse to render it dangerous for either farmers or tradesmen to make a stand against the mob. With Sam Weller it is regarded expedient to shout with the biggest crowd. Mr. M'Swenny, a neighbour of Mr. Hegarty's, has also taken advantage of the Board of Works loans, and is draining and otherwise improving 150 Irish acres, which two years ago he leased at 17s. an acre from Mrs. M'Carthy, who, although she had a lease for ever at 2s. 6d. per acre, had farmed in a most miserable and unprofitable manner.

CHAPTER VIII.

LORD BANDON'S AND LORD KENMARE'S ESTATES.

LORD BANDON'S estates extend to 40,941 acres, which Sir Richard Griffith valued at 19,215*l.* The portion of the property about Bandon, twenty miles west of Cork, is in the best farmed and most prosperous condition, and now contains few holdings of less than 10*l.* annual value. Thirty miles further west, around Bantry Bay, on the other section of the property, the holdings are small, many of them not exceeding 5*l.* of annual value, and the tenants are badly off. The rental varies considerably, and ranges from 10 per cent. to 20 per cent. over Griffith's valuation. As constantly happens, the highest-rented farms are not always the dearest. Many of the tenants are without written agreements; most hold from year to year; a few have leases, and all are allowed to assign their possessory interest, which usually represents five years' rental, or is about one-fifth of the value of the fee-simple. There is reasonable anxiety to secure good tenants and to dispose of farms vacated to neighbours, and thus consolidate the smaller holdings. The sale of the tenant's interest is usually made through the agent, and payment of the way-going occupier's just debts is thus secured. No eviction has occurred for three years. Where suitable or substantial houses or buildings are put up, Lord Bandon furnishes timber and slates. On Saturday mornings, when at home, his lordship attends at the office and sees tenants or labourers who have demands or complaints to make.

On the outlying portions of the estates, around Enniskean, an irregularly-built, tumble-down village, ten miles west of Bandon, I found a good deal of undrained land, farm premises not always in superior repair, fields small, and fences crooked and badly kept. Joseph Fuller holds 121 statute acres, pays 20*s.* an acre, which, being Griffith's valuation, he is thoroughly satisfied with. Unassisted he has done twenty-five acres of draining ; states that since 1863 he has laid out nearly 700*l.* ; takes pains to remark that this money was never made by farming ; but admits that much of the land which he and others have reclaimed, formerly worth 2*s.* an acre, becomes in five years, with an outlay of 10*l.*, worth 20*s.* an acre. The best bogs and lower lands pay better for reclamation than the barer, hungry, stony mountain-sides. William Appleby, of Castletown, farms seventy-five acres at 18*s.* In 1840 his farm kept three poor cows and a lot of snipe, and even in the driest summer it was impossible to walk or ride across it. With some help from the landlord it has been drained, is now sound and healthy, and profitably carries twelve good cows, eight two-year-olds, and two horses. Benjamin Schofield, Knockinady, has 150 acres, besides a useful mountain-farm, lives in a dilapidated house, with rough and ready, not over-clean, surroundings. Like so many of his class, he is regardless of appearances, and unwilling that his landlord should suppose him to be well-to-do. Mr. Schofield, nevertheless, farms well, helps his good root crops with three or four hundredweight of superphosphates, and has about one-sixth of his land in tillage. His cattle are useful, but of a somewhat miscellaneous character; forty sheep were lost last year from rot, and more sold at a sacrifice. Lord Bandon, he remarks, has never helped him; but, without an agreement or lease, he has every confidence that he will not be disturbed or dealt with unfairly.

A very superior tenant is old Mr. Daunt, of Derry Grey East, whose father, with a lease for two lives, or sixty-one years, built the substantial house, mill, and farm premises. His land, comprising 200 acres and rented at 20*s.*, is in nice condition; he dairies eighteen cows, rears and feeds out his young stock; in a capital dairy the milk stands in pans two days and a half before skimming; the butter, slightly salted, goes to Cork, generally averaging 1*s.* per pound. Michael Bryne, of Ballineen town, has fifteen acres, keeps a cow and a few sheep; he built his cottage, 'knocked the place out of the mountain-side,' and was at first charged 3*l.*; but now, after an interval of twenty-five years, has to pay 9*l.* for his holding—an advance which provokes complaint.

Lord Bandon has lately done a great deal on the western coast portion of his estate, long held by middlemen, and, as usual in such circumstances, subdivided and impoverished. During 1878 and 1879, with a loan from the Board of Works, he has expended 1,500*l.*, chiefly on draining and roads, which were sadly wanted, crops and manure having frequently to be carried long distances in baskets on the backs of horses, donkeys, and even women. This useful, timely labour last winter kept many families out of the workhouse. 100*l.* worth of champion potatoes distributed gratuitously in spring have this autumn produced capital crops.

At Newsistown, near Bandon, several tenants three

years ago bought up their occupation of about forty acres each. Twenty-three years' purchase was paid; as yet they are not particularly well satisfied with their bargain, and two or three have appealed to Mr. W. R. Doherty, Lord Bandon's agent, to take over their holdings. Mr. B. Daunt, near Desert, is making better use of his opportunities. Six years ago he took a lease for sixty-one years of his farm of 140 acres, which belongs to an English clergyman. He pays 20s. an acre, which is considerably over Griffith's valuation, has in every way improved the place, and keeps more than double the stock that his predecessor did. Although he had to pay down 1,100l., which was mostly for the good-will, reasoning as an English or a Scotch tenant would do, he prefers to lease thus for a long period a good holding at a moderate rent rather than to expend fully three times the capital in buying the fee-simple. Men who thus in a business-way look at the land question are not at present very numerous in the South of Ireland. Were there more of them, there would be less clamour either for the 'three F's' in their entirety or for peasant proprietorship.

Lord Kenmare has been a kind and considerate landowner, united to his people by strong ties of race and creed, residing during a great part of the year on his estates, ready with purse and influence to advance the interests of his neighbourhood. On his mansion and on the town of Killarney, since his accession to the property in 1871, he has spent 100,000l. At his own expense he has erected a town-hall and improved and beautified Killarney. That it is not all that might be desired is not his lordship's fault; small owners and middlemen, occupying on long leases, have at present possession of many sites, and object to be bought out. A great deal has been done for the farming tenants. They have had the offer of leases for forty-one and thirty-one years at moderate rents. When middlemen have been removed, the occupiers in possession have not been disturbed; their rents, indeed, have frequently been reduced; within the last twenty years 10,000*l.* of arrears have been written off. From last year's rents 10 to 20 per cent. was deducted. During the last few years of distress 15,000*l.* has been borrowed for draining and other improvements; regular work has thus been found for labourers; on such outlay in many instances no percentage has been charged. Since 1870, 300 labourers have been comfortably housed and provided with gardens or allotments varying from a quarter to half an acre, at rents ranging from 20*s.* to 60*s.* annually.

Unmindful of all this consistent liberality, ungrateful for the great efforts to improve his poorer neighbours, popular prejudice had been roused against Lord Kenmare; it has been impossible to collect rents; threatening letters have been sent to him. Mortified with the apparent fruitlessness of his humane endeavours, he has been compelled to leave Kenmare Castle.

His agent, Mr. Hussey, who for twenty years has been earnestly and intelligently labouring to improve Irish agriculture, to bring more capital to bear upon it, to render it more profitable, and has besides most energetically striven to elevate and house more decently the labouring population, has also brought down on himself the odium of the powers that be. For months he has had to travel armed and guarded by a couple of constables; now he has thought it discreet to leave the county. It is sad that the friends and benefactors of the Irish tenantry are thus ungratefully estranged and their career of usefulness arrested. Very serious must be the widespread loss of employment which results from the persistent withholding of rents and the driving away of landlords. Besides the inconvenience and loss to owners and those dependent upon them, the labouring population and shopkeepers must be notable sufferers. And the wretched cause of all this heart-burning agitation, lawlessness, and widespread misery is the eviction of a few worthless and hopelessly bankrupt tenants.

The distribution, acreage, and Government valuation of the Kenmare estates are as follows :—

	Acres	Valuation
County Cork	22,700	£3,497
County Limerick	4,826	5,724
County Kerry	91,080	25,252
	118,606	£34,473

The Kenmare estates are not highly rented. The Limerick and Cork portions are let at little over Griffith's valuation; the tenants have larger holdings and are generally more industrious and painstaking; recently they have gladly accepted offers of Board of Works money for improvements. On the Kerry section of the estate, with about 2,000 occupiers, since Griffith's survey was made thirty years ago, extensive improvements have been effected, many of them at the cost of the landlord. During the last twenty-five years 71,000*l.* has been expended in substantial works. As old leases have dropped, some increase of rent has been made, and the roll now averages one-third over the Poor Law valuation. Between the farming of the yearly tenants and that of the longer leaseholders there is not much difference. The latter, however, recently paid up their rents rather better; but a few years back some of the old middlemen, although occupying on very moderate terms, were in hopeless difficulties. Among both leaseholders and yearly tenants industry, energy, and the economical application of labour are generally wanted. Few tenants accept the long leases freely offered to good men; and even at $3\frac{1}{2}$ per cent. many refuse to take up money to drain bogs which in summer cannot be safely crossed, and which in three years might have their value doubled.

If neglectful bankrupt landlords are to be bought out, which would certainly be desirable in the interests of the community, provision must likewise be made for the quiet dismissal of neglectful and bankrupt tenants. On the Kenmare estates efforts have been made to remove these cumberers of the ground. Every facility is given to the tenant for the sale of his possessory right. A yearly tenant receives usually two or three years' rent; but a leaseholder generally makes double that amount.

From the estate books I have been courteously furnished with the following illustrations:—Jeremiah Crowley, of Aghalee, had forty-three years' lease or one life, whichever ran longest, of his 162 acres; his rent was 82*l*.; Griffith's valuation 97*l*. 10*s*. He received for his good-will 1,000*l*. Timothy Cornes, paying a yearly rent of 35*l*., or 3*l*. under the Government valuation, enjoying a lease of forty-one years, for which he had paid a fine of 80*l*., sold his interest for 850*l*. The possessory interest in Lemuguila, rented at 25*l*., Griffith's valuation 23*l*. 10*s*., although only a yearly tenancy, was bought in 1871 by John Barry for 120*l*. Daniel Crowley held a farm on an annual take at 33*l*. 8*s*. Mr. Hussey, on account of various improvements in 1878, determined that he should pay 36*l*. He demurred, and accepted 334*l*. to clear out; within a week the present tenant came forward, cheerfully paid the amount, and goes on at the enhanced rent. Such premiums obtained by way-going tenants are clear evidence that the rents are moderate, and that the tenants have fair security and reasonable fixity of tenure.

Mr. A. H. Herbert, of Muckross, has nearly 50,000 acres in counties Cork and Kerry, extending west of Killarney. Much of it was originally in such poor plight that Sir Richard Griffith estimated its value at 10,547*l*.; but by intelligent, judicious outlay its value has since tripled. Handsome, artistically constructed houses have been placed in the midst of the farms, which range from fifty to 200 acres; good buildings have been added; picturesque cottages are set down where needed. The fences are straight and tidily kept. The fields, of good size and symmetrical shape, are well cultivated. The tenants, although said to be higher rented than their neighbours, are farming better and are evidently prospering. Mr. Herbert's unwearied endeavours to secure cleanliness and energy have no always been gratefully received. He was wont frequently to visit his tenants, to walk over their fields with them, to keep them up to the mark, to see that pigs were not lodged in the parlour, or that manure heaps were not allowed to accumulate at the front door. Occasionally he would beg a brush, and with his own hand proceed to sweep down offensive cobwebs. On the top of a hill with an operaglass, at four or five o'clock on a spring morning, he would turn out to see which of his tenants made the earliest start, while to the laggards he would forward a bundle of nightcaps. He took much trouble in developing emulation among small farmers and cottagers, and gave premiums for keeping the houses and gardens tidy. When the railway was made, and the coach traffic consequently diverted, finding a great falling off in the cleanliness and smartness of the roadside houses, cottages, and gardens, he made complaints, and was repeatedly met with the excuse, 'Shure, now that no one comes this way, we thought your honour would not be so mighty particular.'

CHAPTER IX.

TRINITY COLLEGE AND THE KNIGHT OF KERRY'S ESTATES.

The wild and picturesque scenery of Dingle Bay presents magnificent and varied attractions for artists, tourists, and sportsmen, but there is not much to interest the agriculturist. In the bottom of precipitous valleys are patches of cultivation; cabbage and potato gardens here and there hang on the picturesque sides; along the coasts are dotted the huts of small crofters—who eke out a scanty subsistence by occasional fishing—and the more imposing quarters of the coastguardsmen, who tell me that since Mr. Plimsoll's humane measures came into operation their occupation has been materially lightened and the wreckage along this wild coast reduced to one-fifth of what it formerly was. After stormy weather the beach is still abundantly strewed with seaweed, which is laboriously conveyed inland in baskets on women's heads, on the backs of donkeys, or, where its destination is more distant and the roads permit, in little carts. Along the mountain-side are scattered mud or stone cabins, thatched with straw or rushes, seldom in good repair or tidily kept, affording in one end accommodation for one or two little Kerry cows and the pony or donkey, while the other is occupied by the family, often including the pigs and poultry. Around the cabin a few small fields are sometimes enclosed by the stones laboriously got out of the land; sparse crops of oats, potatoes, and turnips are grown. There are frequent evidences of more extended tillage and of the imperfectly cultivated land having reverted to its normal condition of heather and furze, interspersed with poor grass. The soil varies considerably. In the valleys, enriched with the denudation of the higher ground, is often a deep, useful loam. On many of the hill-sides the granite rocks are very thinly covered; elsewhere a sticky marl rests on cold yellow clay or on bog. Within the narrow compass of an acre are often several descriptions of soil. These conditions, with about forty inches of annual rainfall, are not particularly encouraging for arable farming.

Of this unpromising description are thousands of acres belonging to the Marquis of Lansdowne, Lord Ventry, the O'Connells, Trinity College, and other landlords. The population, fortunately, is thinly scattered; repeated seasons of famine have caused their removal to more hospitable regions. Yet some would-be philanthropists declare that these wastes should again be peopled; landlords are blamed for neglecting their heritage; yeoman and peasant proprietors, it is urged, would bring the wilderness into cultivation; the magic of property, it is averred, would turn the barren places into gardens. Experiments made on the small scale are not, however, very encouraging. Numbers of plots once cultivated, as already stated, presumably from the small profits derivable from them, have been allowed to revert to their original state. Landowners have always been thankful to allow any tenant to take in bog or mountain, and with the security of a long lease his outlay could not be confiscated. According to position and quality the unimproved land varies in annual value from 1s. to 5s. per acre. To fence it, drain it, and keep it tilled for a few years necessitates an outlay of 10*l.* to 15*l.* per acre. To select those portions which would afford fair prospects of repaying the outlay requires considerable care and practical judgment. Considerably more than half the wilder mountain-sides and upland bogs of this Dingle Bay district must still remain as they now are—worth from 1s. to 5s. an acre as summer grazing for the hardy Kerry cattle, for mountain sheep, and for goats. Reclamation of bog and mountain can only be carried out with the willing, active co-operation of industrious tenants. For the landlord himself to undertake such work, unless for the making of a farm which he is to occupy, would be money thrown away. From what I have seen of many of the tenantry in the South-west of Ireland, I reluctantly conclude that the initial outlay would not be followed up or the improved condition properly maintained.

Trinity College, Dublin, owns nearly 9,000 acres near Dingle Bay, with the town of Cahirciveen, which now boasts of 2,000 inhabitants, is fairly prosperous, and lies thirty-six miles south-west of the railway and of the town of Killarney. The chief portion of the College estate fringes the coast for twelve miles between Cahirciveen and Portmagee, extends back several miles over bog and mountain and among more fertile valleys, and includes several hundred acres on the opposite side of the bay, on the island of Valentia. The property illustrates the evils of middlemen. Until within the last fifteen years it was held on long leases, renewable at intervals by the Knight of Kerry and the family of Daniel O'Connell, whose birthplace—an ivy-covered, castellated house—lies in ruins hard by the water's edge, a mile east of

Cahirciveen. Between the occupying tenant and the owners were often three or four intermediaries. With such divided responsibilities, as might be supposed, nothing was done for the estate or for the people. Excessive rents were often screwed out; subdivision and underletting were unchecked; the population increased beyond the capabilities of the land for its support; excepting a little precarious fishing there were no resources beyond those of the undrained, partially reclaimed, half-tended soil. The neglected, dilapidated, pauperised condition of the estate was forcibly described by Mr. T. C. Forster in *The Times* in 1845.

When the leases of the middlemen lapsed and the College took possession in 1865 it had a most difficult task to pursue. Without harshness, it got rid of or removed some of its surplus population. There are now 492 tenants; of those renting land 102 pay under 20*s*. of annual rent; sixty-three under 5*l*.; while thirty-one pay 20*l*. and upwards. Excepting one farm still on an unterminated long lease, all are let from year to year. The agreements are chiefly verbal; there are no restrictions as to cropping or sale of good-will; but endeavours are made to prevent subletting and subdivision. Griffith's valuation stands at 3,223*l*.; the actual rental is 3,529*l*. Complaints regarding excessive and unequal rents were met by a revaluation of the estate in 1869, pressed for by the tenants and made by Messrs. Brassington and Gale, of Dublin. This valuation had the effect of lowering the general rental; where rents were reduced tenants, of course, were delighted; where they were advanced, as they were in a few instances, there was grumbling—sometimes continued even to the present date. Yet the grumblers do not relinquish their holdings; they care not to realise five years' rent for the way going premium which at any time they might receive; several of the loudest complainers I find readily manage to make, when they sublet their summer grazing, double the rent they pay to the College. Frontage for any houses built or remodelled in the main street of Cahirciveen has been charged by the College at 1*s.* 6*d.* per foot. This is inveighed against as excessive; but its moderation is attested by the fact that private owners for similar advantages obtain 2*s.* 6*d.* per foot, while some College tenants make a like profit on the improvements of their undertenants.

To improve the neglected population, schools have been established and are supported by the College; those at Portmagee, where eighty-five boys and ninety-three girls were in attendance, appear particularly well managed—the children read fairly, answer questions promptly, many of the drawing-books show artistic aptitude, and the boys in the higher standards examined upon agricultural subjects make good answers. Roads and piers have been made; while at Cahirciveen has been built a butter market, costing 1,000*l.*; a fish market, costing 300*l.*; a pier, to which the College contributed fully 100*l.*; sewers, at the expense of 300*l.*, have been put down, but as yet are little used by the householders. The proposal of the College that a good supply of water should be introduced into the town from the adjacent mountains for the present has been rejected by the veto of the principal people, who refuse to contribute to this important work. The paving of the sideways, which are in a bad state, has not been carried out owing to the county surveyor having made so low an estimate for the work that no contractor is willing to undertake it.

These are no small improvements to have been effected by the College in fifteen years at a cost of 11,000*l*., or with an outlay representing about 20 per cent. of the moderate income of the estate. The bursar of the College and the agent, Captain Needham, courteously placed at my disposal the books, from which it appears that the expenditure since 1865 may be divided as follows :—Buildings, 7,208*l*.; roads, 1,853*l*.; drains and fences, 513*l*. Moreover, 1,000*l*. has been advanced on loan to tenants for improving their holdings, interest at 5 per cent. being added to the rents, or, in some cases, a charge of 1*s*. 7*d*. per pound is made, which repays principal and interest in twenty-one years. With 5,000*l*., borrowed last year from the Board of Works, more roads, fences, and main watercourses, all much needed, are being undertaken, the drains tapping great bogs and providing outfalls for the field draining, which is being encouraged.

But the tenants are not yet generally alive to the necessity of draining. On holding after holding fields are wet; in the soaking weather of the south-west large areas are frequently reduced to the state of quagmire, and throw up a sparse, poor, cut-throat herbage. Yet the open ditch was sometimes conterminous, or perhaps one field off; very often, from carelessness, was overgrown with rushes and allowed to stand brimful, saturating a good many perches of adjacent soil. One small farmer, to whom I pointed out the folly of this neglect, said he could not do ditching unless he were paid for it. The ditch certainly needed clearing below his holding. The usual excuse was that there is no security for tenants' outlay; but presently it would be admitted that the tenant and his father before him had occupied the holding, and that he did not know that the rent had ever been raised. Like many of his class, he conjures up the spectre of possible confiscation, and will not exert himself to undertake even cheap improvements which one good crop would repay. Improvements effected by tenants, which are neither so frequent nor so extensive as could be desired, are never taken advantage of. Only two tenants have been evicted during the last ten years—one owing five, the other three years' rent—and both have been reinstated. In spite of the liberal help given last winter in finding work, in distributing meal to the value of 500*l.*, in furnishing last spring champion potatoes at a cost of 270*l.*, and in deducting 20 per cent. from the rents of 1879, recent rents are fully twelve months in arrear. How much of this non-payment depends upon absolute inability and how much on the pressure of agitation it is difficult to say.

Outside the town of Cahirciveen, going west, is a forty-acre farm, rented at 48*l.* a year, for which I am told a few years ago the tenant, Mr. Lynch, gave a premium or bought the tenant right for 145*l.* Although close beside the town, this holding is water-soaked and neglected ; the occupier has a prejudice against draining, and rushes and poor starved grass disfigure his pastures. Several contiguous holdings are nearly as bad, are only very imperfectly drained ; the tenantry will not undertake such a primary improvement themselves, and most demur to pay the 5 or 6 per cent. which the landlords reasonably charge if the work is done by them. Well-tended fields and garden-plots here and there testify how much might be made of these starved poor subjects. The Rev. Thomas Hallaran, the rector of the parish, most zealous for the well-being of the people, and desirous that they should make the best of their farms, last spring obtained a loan of 100*l.* from the Board of Works, and, at a cost of 8*l.* per statute acre, thoroughly drained about four acres of his glebe; three-quarters of an acre of this drained land, previously scarcely worth 10*s.* an acre, having been well ploughed and manured, yielded a return of thirty-two tons of red and yellow mangel—a very strong encouragement to his neighbours to go and do likewise. He assures me that he does not know any portion of the British islands better suited than this coast land in soil and climate for the ready production of vegetables. Besides potatoes and cabbages, which are the only garden-stuff grown, Dingle Bay might furnish admirable varied supplies of fish for the English markets. There is now weekly communication by steamer with Cork, and such facilities could readily be increased.

By the roadside, two miles from town, J. Sullivan has thirty-five acres, held by his father and grandfather, and the place appears as if it had the while undergone very little change. Two generations have passed away since the house and premises were put up at a cost certainly not exceeding 50*l.* The rent was then 10*l.* a year; but twenty years ago it was raised to 13*l.* 10*s.* Around the house there seem to be about twenty acres in nine small fields, with wide clay banks, which, I am informed, are useful for shelter; and fifteen acres further off towards the mountain. All of it lies well for the much-needed draining, which would certainly double its value. The tillage comprehends about an acre of oats, about the same of potatoes, and a few chains of swedes. The stock consists of six Kerry cows, worth 5*l.* to 6*l.* each, three yearlings, three calves, two or three pigs, and a mule, which is quartered in the end of the dwelling-house, separated from the family by a low partition. With the help of about ten sacks of meal, the six cows produce in the season eight firkins, of eighty pounds each, of butter. A bull-calf a week old is worth 5s., a heifer three times as much; two or three pigs are reared and fed; poultry realise 3s. a couple; eggs at present (December) are sold at 5s. per long score of 120. Here, as in so many other holdings, considering the work done, there is great superfluity of labour. Besides Sullivan, an active man of sixty, are two girls about twenty, and a grown-up son, whose services might very well be dispensed with.

Mrs. Shea, of Direen, has eighteen acres, for which she pays 3l. 12s., keeps two cows, two or three young things, with pigs and poultry. Although her land is wet, and part of it boggy, she does not think that draining would do much good. Like her neighbours, she cannot understand that if she doubled her produce, as she could do by draining, she could well afford to double her moderate rent. She and some of her neighbours sometimes take in a cow or two, charging 20s. for the season's grazing. Nearer Portmagee is a larger, better farm of sixty acres, rented at 40l., with a good house, built by a former squire, who spared no expense in squaring and improving fields—advantages now reaped by Mr. Charles O'Connell, who dairies about twenty cows, some of them of shorthorn character, and makes about 7l. or 8l. per head, or double what his neighbours realise for the season's produce of the little Kerries. Mr. O'Connell also holds some mountain grazings, paying, not according to acreage, but 10s. to 20s. for the run of each beast.

Eight miles west of Cahirciveen, at Donnybrook, is a

colony of cabin-holders, who had squatted under the lax *régime* of the Knights of Kerry, occupying two to five acres, for which they pay from 5s. to 50s. of annual rent, and half their share of county cess. They are miserably housed; many of the cabins are awfully dilapidated, but the children look bright and healthy, and mostly go to school; 100 attendances qualify for examination and participation in the Government grant. A few of the more prosperous keep a Kerry cow; some boast of a goat or a donkey; the majority have only the pig and some poultry, and some have not the capital to secure even these helps. From their portion of land, on which many have lived for generations, without any increment of rent, and without interference from their landlord or his representative, almost their entire sustenance appears to be derived. There is no sufficient or regular work for these men. Several assure me that from the larger farmers, or any other source, they have only from thirty to fifty days' work in the twelve months, earning from 1s. to 1s. 6d. per day. Peat from the bog costs little, but, at the moderate price of 1s. for a donkey-cart load, scarcely pays to cut. A trifle is occasionally made by fishing, or a little winter food is thereby provided, but even this handy source of aliment is not sufficiently taken advantage of. As might be anticipated, destitution was last winter rife among these cabin-holders, who are grateful for the timely relief afforded them from the Duchess of Marlborough's and the Mansion House funds.

Jack Macarthy may stand as an exemplar of these cabin-holders. He has two or three acres; he does not know exactly the quantity, but he pays 35s. Like other holders of less than 4*l.* of annual value, he has no poor-rates, but is charged 2*s.* for county cess. Occasionally he has a few days' work at 1*s.* 6*d.* per day at the building of the quays which the College has been putting up on the sands, or still more rarely for some farmer. He complains that it is hard to find food for his nine hearty but hungry children and 'a sop for the old folks,' who live in a hovel abutting on the low-roofed, one-roomed cabin. He affirms that he cannot raise enough of potatoes, swedes, or cabbage. And no wonder; for going over his four fields, I found only one dug, a wide and irregular, untidy six-foot strip of grass and weeds extends round it: 'Shure, for a footpath, your honour.' The plot contiguous to the garden lies in inferior grass, from which a little hay is sold at 40*s.* per ton. If dug and manured even with the seaweed which is washed up within 300 yards of his hovel, a profitable garden might be made. But to do this entails too much trouble, even for a man who professes that he cannot find employment and has a dozen people dependent on his exertions. Two other adjacent plots nearer the beach are useless for want of a few short drains run into the watercourse which bounds the holding. Many of Macarthy's neighbours make equally indifferent use of their opportunities. Instead of being occupiers at the moderate rent of 10*s.* or 12*s.* an acre, would these easy-going mortals exhibit more energy and activity if they were converted into peasant proprietors? As already stated, the soil along the coast where these cabin-holders have planted themselves is good; the climate is also favourable for gardening. With intelligent, painstaking cultivation double the present produce might readily be raised, and the modest requirements of these people fairly supplied.

The Rev. Thomas Hallaran, the Church of Ireland clergyman of Cahirciveen, informs me, that, in spite of the apathy of many of the tenants, some have a little money; they are seldom so poor as a stranger unused to Irish rags and squalor might suppose them to be; some of the best have a certain pride, and would not admit that they are in difficulties; they are reported to be helpful and kind to each other; country people coming into the towns and villages walk into any house, ask and receive the use of the kettle, infuse the tea they bring with them, and produce their own bread and butter. When the surplus glebe lands were disposed of, the seven larger and six smaller holders all bought at twenty two and a half years' purchase. Some paid up in full; others are taking advantage of time settlements. The condition of these small suburban farms has progressed.

Sir Maurice James O'Connell's estate of Everard, although occupying a great breadth of poor land, extending to 18,752 acres, and in 1840 valued only at 3,050l., furnishes some of the most thriving tenants who come into Cahirciveen. It affords good illustration of prudent management; 'self-help' is encouraged; subdivision is stringently prevented; any tenant against whom two years' arrears accumulate is compelled to clear out, being either removed entirely or dropped into a smaller holding.

Sir Maurice FitzGerald, Bart., Knight of Kerry, owns two-thirds of the island of Valentia, embracing 5,372 acres, valued by Sir Richard Griffith at 2,207l. Twenty years ago he bought out several old holders. With money borrowed from the Board of Works he has squared the irregular riband-shaped holdings; and built on the partially reclaimed or unreclaimed lands substantial houses, some of them of two stories, costing from 80*l.* to 120*l.*, which are not always as much appreciated as the old thatched cabins, of which some miserable specimens still remain, especially on that portion of the island belonging to Trinity College. Whether for houses, draining, or reclamation, and no matter what benefit accrues to the cultivator, Irishmen have an unutterable aversion to the 'per cint.' The farms average about thirty acres—more are under than over that amount. To avoid claims for compensation, and especially on the newly-acquired portions of the property, several thirty-one years' leases have been granted; but yearly tenancies are the rule. Although the Knight discountenances free sale, believing that it locks up the capital of the incoming tenant, and virtually adds to his rent, he pays any way-going tenant for unexhausted improvements. But, although there is grumbling at high rents and no profits, there are few changes. Rents during twenty years have risen a little, and are generally double Griffith's valuation. The cultivated lands are let at from 15*s.* to 20*s.* an acre; the furze, heather, and mountain at from 5*s.* to 10*s.* Rents are due in May and November, and six months' grace is given in their collection. Now that the League has extended its teaching to the island, and compelled all in self-defence to become subscribers, many of the tenants affirm that they will not pay more than Griffith's valuation. Hitherto they have complained less of rent than of the office regulations forbidding sale of crops and consecutive corn-growing; but these must be sentimental grievances on an island where there is no profitable sale for bulky agricultural produce. Contrary to office custom, some land rented at 20*s.* an acre is sublet to labourers or to the quarrymen at from 40*s.* to 50*s.* an acre.

During the last twenty-five years a good deal of draining has been done; ferruginous deposits have blocked many of the pipes sometimes used, and stones, readily got, are accordingly now preferred.

Mr. James Bremner, a Scotchman, who, as steward to the Knight of Kerry, and now as tenant of Keelbeg, has lived in the island for twenty-five years, occupies 117 acres, on a lease for twenty-one years, and pays 110*l.*; his poor-rates are 9*l.*, his county cess 12*l.* A five-course rotation is followed, the land lying two years in grass; oats are the only cereal grown; for turnips, which he was the first to introduce into Valentia, he uses from 3 cwt. to 5 cwt. of Lawes's superphosphate, has the plants thinned by hand, and hoed by girls at 8*d.* per day. His farm men receive 1*s.* 6*d.* per day and 2*s.* in harvest; the wages have doubled in twenty-five years. The people require much looking after; piece-work is unknown. Much encouragement is secured in busy times by an extra 1*d.* or 2*d.* per day. Were all the land on the island farmed as Mr. Bremner's is, the produce would be greatly more than doubled. Those portions bearing furze and briers pay particularly well for reclamation. Beyond potatoes for themselves and a little hay for their small herds, tenants too generally do not trouble themselves with the great bulk of their holding, which is left in a state of nature; and without constant, systematic cultivation, the thin, light soils retrograde. With such supineness no wonder that in bad seasons distress prevails somewhat widely. Last winter 1,200*l.* was distributed in charities; but it is generally understood that some of the recipients were gentlemen with savings, or even with deposits in the hands of their bankers. The great drawback to Valentia farming is the difficulty and expense of marketing. The thirty families of the telegraph staff and the hundred people employed in the slate quarries do not consume all the agricultural produce; and the ferry, a mile across, is sometimes tempestuous, and prevents the transference of live stock to the markets at Cahirciveen.

CHAPTER X.

ESTATES IN DOWN AND ANTRIM.

SIR RICHARD WALLACE'S estate at Lisburn has an historic interest in connexion with the early establishment of tenant-right. In the archives in the office is a record that Sir Fulke Conway, who had come over in the reign of Elizabeth and received some of the escheated estates of the O'Neills, settled on them, and in 1620 granted leases of ninety-one years to several of his Welsh retainers. One, it is mentioned, had 300 acres of cleared land for 50*l.* of annual rent; another had 600 acres for 100*l.* Here is the germ of that security of tenure which is one of the two cardinal points of the Ulster custom. Baron Conway, of Ragley, was confirmed in his Irish holding by James I., who, departing from the Elizabethan policy pursued in Munster of giving the land to a few great owners, divided Ulster among a smaller resident proprietary, brought in Scotch and English settlers, encouraged them to plant and improve, and took especial care to settle and secure under-tenants. The hardy Scotch settlers appear to have prospered best. Pynnar, in his Survey in 1618, quoted in Mr. R. Barry O'Brien's recent volume on the Parliamentary History of the Irish Land Question, thus reports:—' Many English do not plough or use husbandry, being fearful to stock themselves with cattle or servants for those labours. Neither do the Irish use tillage, for they are also uncertain of their stay. So, by those means, the Irish, using grazing only, and the English very little, were it not for the Scottish, who plough in many places, the rest of the country might starve.' (P. 162.)

This and other evidence led Mr. R. Barry O'Brien to conclude that the English tenants shortly became dissatisfied with their location; the Irish, it had been determined, on account of the possibility of war, were to be excluded from these 'fat' lands reserved for the strangers; encouragement, accordingly, seems to have been given to the Scotch settlers to purchase the goodwill of their way-going English neighbours. Thus, probably, originated, between 1617 and 1620, the second prominent feature of the Ulster custom— namely, the tenant's right to sell the goodwill of his holding. The custom grew and extended over the north of Ireland, and has recently developed analogous customs in other provinces.

By the Land Act of 1870 the Ulster custom has acquired the force of law. Securing the tenant fixity of tenure so long as he pays his rent and the right to sell the goodwill of his holding, it has brought to the cultivation and equipment of the land a large amount of tenants' industry, energy, and capital. The good farming and prosperity of Ulster owe much to its highly-valued custom. Endowing the occupant with a possessory interest, which is now frequently double the value of the fee-simple, it has secured thrift and loyal support of law and order.

The Ulster custom has, however, its shortcomings. It is by no means an unmixed benefit even to the tenant. He pays dearly for his desiderated security. The premium on entry frequently reaches 30*l.* to 40*l.* an acre. This investment, charged at 4 or 5 per cent., often more than doubles the rent. If, as too frequently happens, the capital has to be borrowed at 7 to 10 per cent., independently of any payment whatever to the landlord, it constitutes a very full rent. So much of the tenants' capital being thus locked up, diminishes the amount available for the profitable cultivation and stocking of the land. The money sunk in the possessory interest is of course recoverable if the tenant sells. But if a sale becomes necessary, as is apt to be the case in times of agricultural depression, competition is narrowed, and the price of the tenant-right is considerably reduced. A large capital is invested on a small area of land, it lies comparatively unfruitful, securing the right of the farm instead of being more profitably used in its remunerative cultivation. Weighted with these disadvantages many Ulster tenants declare that they cannot pay their way. In times of keen competition for land they have been tempted to give perhaps 40*l.* an acre for their holding. At 5 per cent. this represents a rent of 40*s.* The landlord's interest or rent for his fee simple is probably 20*s.* From the lenders of their borrowed money the tenants know they can expect no rebate; their major rent of 40*s.* must be paid; but they complain loudly of the landlords' exorbitant claims, and clamour for Griffith's valuation or for deductions of 10 to 25 per cent.

Under the Ulster custom the landlord has hitherto felt perfectly secure of the willing payment of a fair rent, but throughout even the orderly northern province agitation has now extended, and on many estates rents are refused or payment deferred until it is seen 'what will turn up.'

Against landlords and agents, tenants sometimes have just cause of complaint. Building, draining, and farming improvements effected by tenants have led to unjustifiable revaluations and enhanced rents. In reclaiming bog or mountain, 15*l.* to 20*l.* an acre has sometimes been sunk by the occupier. Land worth one or two shillings an acre has been raised to more than ten times its original value. Help has seldom been accorded by the landlord. Before there has been anything like an adequate return for the outlay, at the death of the tenant or on a change of tenancy the rent is advanced. The improver or his family has no appeal; the enhanced rent proportionally diminishes the value of the tenant-right and the fair restitution for improvements. Reasonable landlords as well as tenants admit the necessity of some legislation which shall prevent such misappropriation and which will secure his improvements more permanently to the improver.

The evils of absenteeism, in many ways hurtful to Ireland, are just now widely expatiated on; the years are reckoned during which such territorial magnates as the Marquis of Hertford regularly withdrew from his estates 50,000*l.* to be spent abroad; the paltry sums are detailed which are devoted to the benefit of many estates and the neglected people struggling upon them. Happier pictures are drawn regarding such landlords as those of the Downshire family. The big Marquis is still gratefully remembered as being especially zealous in helping his people with purse and personal exertion, and in the famine time of 1846-48 is reported to have repeatedly said that 'money must be found to aid those who required it, even if he required to mortgage part of his estates.'

In counties Down and Antrim Sir Richard Wallace has 64,156 acres, distributed as follows among nearly 4,000 tenants. Of agricultural holders, 623 are paying under 5*l.* of annual rent, 671 under 10*l.*, 438 under 15*l.*, 283 under 20*l.*, 377 under 30*l.*, 264 under 50*l.*, 131 under 75*l.*, 47 under 100*l.*, 30 under 150*l.*; only 16 exceed 200*l.* The average size of the farms is twenty-five statute acres. The tenantry are hardworking and careful. Of late years only the larger holders have been able to realise any profits. The rental averages 18*s.* 9*d.* per acre for the better cultivated land, and 9*s.* for the rougher mountain pastures. Regarding proximity to good markets, and putting tenant-right out of consideration, the farms I saw appeared moderately rented. Since 1830, mainly from the falling in of old leases, there has been an increment of 1*s.* 6*d.* an acre. The present rent roll is 57,870*l.* for farming tenancies, and 3,500*l.* for accommodation lands and building sites. It is 2,500*l.* under Griffith's valuation. The value of the tenant's interest has advanced much more rapidly than that of the landlord's. Tenant-right sold previous to 1845 at from 5*l.* to 8*l.* per acre now realises fully triple that amount. This enhancement does not always depend upon increased equipments. The buildings do not keep pace with the times. A good deal of wet land demands attention. Many farms are not nearly so clean or in such good manurial condition as they should be. Several holdings recently disposed of, and where everything is in a state of dilapidation, are, nevertheless, bringing 20*l.* an acre. Competition, not only among farmers, but among successful shopkeepers, maintains the demand for farms, and especially for those of a small size. Previous to 1878 there were not more than twenty changes in twelve months, but recent bad times have somewhat increased them.

Arrears of rent, usually amounting to three or four years, is the only cause of ejectment, and, even when the decree is obtained, six months are allowed during which the tenant can still make his arrangements for settlement. Before, however, he is seriously crippled or his holding much deteriorated, he usually wisely conveys to the landlord or agent his intention to sell. Notice is forthwith sent to the adjoining holders, who usually have the preference. Arbitration settles any dispute as to price. If no neighbour desires to purchase, the tenant-right is sometimes put up to public auction. Only once in ten years has objection been taken to the nominee of the tenant. A previous agent, in the Marquis of Hertford's time, endeavoured to limit the value of the tenant-right to 10*l.* an acre; although even under his *régime* it sometimes sold for 16*l.* No attempt is, however, now made to control the price, which has sometimes reached 30*l.* an acre, or 33 per cent. more than the landlord's share in the holding. The new tenant's name is substituted for the old one in the office books. No deeds, titles, or conveyance are used, no fees are paid; between landlord and tenant there is no contract, lease, or agreement. Unfortunately, however, the incoming tenant has often to borrow a considerable portion of his purchase-money from loan societies or usurers at from 7 to 10 per cent. The banks seldom make advances on tenancies-at-will. In ordinary changes of tenants the landlord obtains no accession of rent, although occasionally he may have contributed to the increased value of the holding.

On this estate, between 1845 and 1860, 20,000*l.* was

expended by the landlord, chiefly in draining, main watercourses, and roads. Since 1870 thornquicks and trees have cost 500*l.*, and the cost of fencing has been partially borne by the landlord. In aid of the sufferers from a flood of Lough Neagh, 700*l.* was contributed by Sir Richard Wallace; while last year seed potatoes to the value of 1,000*l.* were purchased for the poorer tenants. Few cottagers hold direct from the office. The cottages generally have been built and are owned by the farmers, are usually in a wretched tumble-down state, and are rented at 2*l.* to 3*l.* per annum. Some cottagers have bought up their tenant right of house and garden, which sometimes extends to half an acre. Bearing a landlord's ground rent of 10*s.* to 20*s.* a year, the tenant right of such a cottage, costing, perhaps, 25*l.* to build, sometimes reaches 40*l.*

The country around Belfast is diversified with a succession of hill ranges and rich valleys, containing useful arable and some grass land. Almost as diversified as the surface is the management of various estates, the treatment of tenants, their rents, tenure, and prosperity. Neither landlords nor tenants are at present satisfied. Landlords complain that rents are not so certain or well paid as formerly, that land investments are not realising 3 per cent., that friendly relations with tenants are disturbed. Tenants complain that their profits are shrunk, that enhanced rents are reducing the value of their tenant-right; that their security, much greater than in any other part of Ireland or in England or Scotland, is, nevertheless, insufficient to insure cheerful outlay for improvements and profitable high farming In the present excited, expectant state of matters, neither party appears to care about the long leases, which in many instances should prove satisfactory to both. In the widespread dissatisfaction, even the Ulster custom is grumbled at. Landlords who would improve their estates—and of these a few still survive—complain that their outlay is liable to be appropriated in enhancing the value of the tenantright. Since the passing of the Land Act of 1870 it is generally stated that landowners, feeling they have less control over their estates, demur to lay out anything. Tenants, on the other hand, affirm that their interest to improve is seriously checked by the fear of enhanced rents. With such want of confidence improvements certainly in many quarters are arrested, and the capital needful for successful farming is not forthcoming. Although farming for twenty miles around Belfast compares favourably with many parts of the south and west of Ireland, a great deal of land is not made the best of, and there is obvious want of draining, improved fences, and more tidy, clean, and thorough cultivation. On small as on large farms are corners, waste places, wide, uncared-for fences and banks, which, if made use of, would add greatly to the returns, and, if duly attended to on some farms I have walked over, would amount to more than a 10 per cent. reduction of rent.

While some of the larger estates have been handed down from generation to generation since the days of Cromwell, the smaller estates in Ireland appear more liable to change hands. The squireens, remarkable for hospitality and good fellowship, too frequently wasted their resources; their establishments were carelessly and extravagantly administered; horses and hounds, cock-fighting, and electioneering brought many to ruin. Repeated subdivision has also reduced other yeoman families. This has been the case even in Ulster, with its greater admixture of race, its manufactures, and its better markets. Mr. Hugh M'Caul, of Lisburn, who has a great repertory of information on many subjects, informs me of the sad downfall of many good old families. Hawkins M'Gill, a retired London merchant, who acquired property in county Down about the middle of last century, distributed several hundred acres of reclaimed, useful land among favourite tenants at 6s. an acre. Fifty years later these farms had become subdivided to fifteen or twenty acres; and now not one of the families to whom the land was originally demised survives.

Between Lisburn and Belfast, Lord Donegall, a hundred years ago, let several thousand acres on leases for ever at 2s. 6d. per acre. Some of the awards were for 1,000 acres. Jack Sayers, the last of the jolly sporting squires who rode and racketed in these pleasant valleys, could not raise money to meet the moderate annual payments. At Lower Malone are about forty freeholders with long leases, each occupying fifty acres or upwards, charged on an average 5s. an acre, or one-fourth of what the land might be let for, and instead of making money, many are drifting steadily into debt and difficulty. Such frequently recurring facts are disheartening. Earnestly as land is sought for in Ireland, like some other blessings, when it is got it is sometimes most carelessly and wastefully used.

Smaller holders are not usually more careful of their heritage. Sometimes unable to live at a nominal rent of 1s. or 2s. 6d. per acre, they have sold out, and, subsequently occupying as tenants at 20s. to 25s., have occasionally made extra exertion and prospered. On Lord Arthur Hill-Trevor's property at Glencoe I met with several illustrative cases. Tom Finlay had a small farm in perpetuity at 2s. 6d. an acre, failed to make it answer, too readily obtained reiterated advances upon it, and several years ago became so involved that he was obliged to sell out. David Jamphery had thirty acres, was without a family, but the land, untended, went from bad to worse, and was bought by David Grey. A family named Blen had twenty-five acres in perpetuity at 3s. an acre; whisky, as usual, was the destructive power; money was borrowed until no more could be had, when two years ago the farm was sold for about 900l., and the buyer, David Shaw, appears to be making it answer. Yeoman and peasant proprietors are assuredly not indigenous and successful in all parts of Ireland.

Fortunate in being introduced to Mr. George M'Auliffe, of Belfast, the most experienced estate agent in the north of Ireland, I visited with him several estates between Belfast and Carrickfergus, and obtained considerable information regarding estate management in Ulster. There has been generally more contentment and prosperity on some of the older and larger estates than on the small, and those more recently acquired. The value of the tenant-right is usually a fair measure of the attractions to the tenant, which mainly consist of low rent, good buildings, land in fair cultivation, convenient markets, and unrestricted sale. On the Marquis of Londonderry's estates no revaluation occurs even at the close of the thirty-one years' leases, which have been common; good markets are conveniently handy; 60l. and even 70l. per acre has been given for tenant right; the rents range from 20s. to 25s. One element in the prosperity of the 1,500 tenants of this fine estate is the small number of tenants who pay under 10l. of annual value. On the Downshire estates the same care in preventing subdivision, the help conceded to tenants in hard times, and the liberal management have also conduced to general prosperity. Demands have, however, been recently made for reductions of rents, although many of them remain at the figures they stood at forty years ago, and when almost every description of agricultural produce was upwards of 50 per cent. lower than it now is.

Rents vary considerably on different properties and in different parts of the same property, and, owing to differences of tenure and other modifying circumstances, do not always represent the actual value of the holding. A farm well managed for twenty-five years will present a most favourable contrast to one which during a like period has been mismanaged or neglected. Occupiers of thirty to 100 acres are almost invariably doing better than those who are farming either on a larger or smaller scale. The man in Ireland, as in America, who makes the most money by arable culture is he who with his own family does the chief amount of the work. All farmers have somewhat recovered from the disasters of 1879. The bank agents in the north of Ireland inform me that the deposits in their branches in agricultural districts have increased as the year advanced. But now that farmers are acquiring more business education, bank deposits are not a fair criterion of their prosperity; for, scorning the 1 per cent. given for short-period deposits by their banker, they invest in railway, foreign, or other stocks, or make advances to their less prosperous or more speculative neighbours.

The Ulster custom, Mr. M'Auliffe assures me, prevails in its integrity on most estates. The occupier sells his right sometimes without any consultation with the office as to price or selection of his successor. This perfect freedom is most in favour with the tenantry. The man in possession or the outgoing tenant is in an enviable position; but as much cannot be said for the incomer, who has to pay so dearly for his privileges. On some estates the landlord receives notice of his tenant's intention to sell, and has a *veto* on the nominee. Occasionally the amount given for the tenant-right is limited to three, five, or seven years' rent; and, in conformity with the provisions of the Land Act of 1870, payment is, besides, made for any permanent, suitable improvements, paid for by the tenant on entry or subsequently effected by him. On a few estates tenant-right has never been recognised; buildings, draining, and other improvements have been mainly done by the landlord or paid for by him. Some such estates sold recently have brought upwards of thirty years' purchase. As no premium is charged for entry, there is no difficulty in letting such holdings at 20 to 30 per cent. more than those on which a high tenant-right makes the entry so expensive. On the Red Hill Estate, near Carrickfergus, extending to 4,000 acres, no tenant-right obtains; but the farmers manage successfully and as prosperously as their neighbours who enjoy the full privileges of the Ulster right. It was the existence of these varied systems that induced Lord Cairns, when the Land Act of 1870 was under consideration, to insert the alternative expression, 'custom' or 'customs.' Some authorities, and especially those who have not paid for their Ulster right, are desirous that all tenants alike should have the full advantages of free sale. Under such a system the owner who had bought his land and the tenant-right upon it would obviously be a loser to the extent of the value of that tenant-right. With as much justice might the English landowner who bought an estate free of land tax, tithe, or rent charge, or who had redeemed these charges, be asked without adequate remuneration to submit to their reimposition.

Mr. M'Auliffe has had ample experience in the sale of Church lands and bishops' leases, which in this district were generally in the hands of well-to-do middlemen with *toties quoties* leases, paying fines at intervals of eighteen years and charged small annual rents. At about twenty-five years' purchase these middlemen have sometimes bought up the bishops' leases, usually paying and closing the transaction at once. A high value, however, has sometimes been placed on the annual rents, and the fee simple is left in the hands of the Commissioners. The occupying tenants frequently continue to hold as formerly, and in a few instances are buying from the first purchaser, and will thus become perpetuity holders at small annual rents. Where purchasers are not hampered with borrowed money, they are generally prospering.

Lord Donegall, besides 10,000 acres in Antrim, has 2,275 acres, valued at 26s. an acre, close to Carrickfergus. The tenants had long leases, which lapse in twenty-two years. On the death of the present owner, now an octogenarian, this estate passes to some distant connection. In anticipation of giving up or having their rents raised, the houses and other buildings, the fences, gates, and even the cultivation are already allowed to retrograde. Many of the small owners who abound on this estate, in their fear of laying out an unnecessary shilling, are evidently in a fair way of ruining themselves.

Mr. Dobbs, of Castle Dobbs, three miles north-east of Carrickfergus, has a well-managed, well-farmed estate of 5,669 acres ; the Government valuation is 5,065*l*., the actual rental very little higher. There have been no changes for thirty-five years. The Ulster custom exists in its entirety. On the tenure of three lives, two of which have lapsed, a handsome imposing house, which cost 12,000*l*., has been built, and, with 120 acres of capitally managed land, is now held by Mr. S. Archer. The residue of the lease, I am told, was sold several years ago for the moderate sum of 1,300*l*. On the coast towards Larne is a valuable compact estate belonging to Sir James M'Garel Hogg. Buildings and land are in capital condition ; much is done for the tenants ; abundant employment is found for men and horses in the adjacent lime quarries ; a half-year's rent not long since was excused, but another such concession is again asked for. The Island Magee, about a mile from the mainland, is at present in joint ownership of the Duke of Manchester, Mrs. Leslie, and Lord Donegall. Like some other Irish estates, the titles appear to have been somewhat indefinite. In disputing in the Courts at Dublin the power of the late Duke to grant a lease, it transpired that his own and Mrs. Leslie's portion of the island were only held on lease, and shortly revert to Lord Donegall. The island farms are remarkably well managed and productive, and range from twenty-five to thirty acres ; a few reach 100 acres ; the rents average 25*s*. to 28*s*. ; recent sales of tenant right have realised 50*l*. and even 60*l*. an acre.

The Right Hon. the Earl O'Neill, of Shanes Castle

Antrim, has 64,133 acres, valued by Griffith at 37,000*l*. The agricultural rents are 42,000*l*., or 12 per cent. over Griffith's valuation. Including head rents and royalties the total income of the estate is 44,937*l*. A general reduction of rental was granted in 1841; since then few advances have been made. During twenty-five years the income has been augmented by 2,000*l*., and this includes the rental of several houses built since 1855, and a slight increment made on lands relet at the termination of leases which were granted last century or in the earlier years of the present century. Some lands leased in 1823 have, however, been recently relet at the same values. No interference is attempted with the sale of the tenant-right, which ranges from ten to fifteen years' rent. The tenant-right of fifteen acres, rented at 17*l*. 10*s*. ten years ago, sold for 60*l*., and has since changed hands at 160*l*.; a lot of thirteen acres, paying 20*s*. an acre, has been bought for 325*l*.; a lease of seventy acres, at 20*s*. an acre, granted in 1859 for a period of thirty-one years, or for the lives of the Prince of Wales, the Duke of Edinburgh, and the Duke of Connaught, has made 1,400*l*. Excluding villages and townpark holders, there are about 450 agricultural tenants whose rents are less than 10*l*. a year, and about 1,500 whose rents range from 10*l*. to 50*l*. The large majority are yearly tenants holding without any special covenants or agreements. The occupations average twenty acres, rented at about 15*s*. an acre. On main drains, outlets, and mearing watercourses, Lord O'Neill expends annually about 500*l*. Little assistance is given to tenants either in building or draining. Notwithstanding injunctions against subletting, some under-tenants enjoy more than double the rents obtained by Lord O'Neill. One farmer secures a profit of 50*l*. a year by subletting a portion of his holding of thirty-four acres. Another with forty acres similarly makes a profit of 50 per cent. Another with a total rent of 12*l.* sublets a house and three roods of garden ground for 10*l.*, retaining for himself nearly ten acres which hence cost him 40*s.* a year. Excepting those employed on the home farm, the cottagers appear worse off than the tenants. They are miserably housed; their cottages, belonging to the farmers, are charged at 1*s.* to 2*s.* per week. Gardens are small or wanting; employment is irregular; wages 9*s.* per week; but a trifle is earned by the more thrifty by eggs and poultry, and occasionally by weaving. Even in Ulster the condition of the agricultural labourer is unsatisfactory; he is generally poorly paid. In winter he often has difficulty in obtaining work, while even at other seasons his employment is not so certain or constant as it should be.

From the rents of 1879, all tenants paying more than Griffith's valuation received deductions ranging from 10 to 20 per cent., involving to Lord O'Neill a sacrifice of 4,000*l.* Nevertheless, there is much grumbling and a demand for a continuous general reduction. Satisfactory as it might be for the tenantry, such an arrangement represents an enormous sacrifice to the owner of an encumbered estate. Three-fourths of the income of Shanes Castle, as of so many other Irish estates, is absorbed in settlements and other payments which must be punctually discharged, and abatements to tenants or outlay on improvements have to be borne entirely by the one-fourth which comes to the owner.

CHAPTER XI.

THE LONDON COMPANIES AND IRISH SOCIETY'S ESTATES.

WHEN James I. ascended the throne in 1603 he found Ireland, as it has often been since, in a state of distress and anarchy. In Ulster the escheated lands of the O'Neills and other disaffected chiefs he bestowed on English and Scottish subjects, while further to plant loyal and Protestant people among his warlike Celts and to recruit his exchequer he applied to the Corporation of London and offered the London companies tracts of land in county Derry. Twelve of the guilds responded to the King's request, and according to their means took up considerable estates. Sir Thomas Phillips was sent over to arrange the distribution, and for his trouble was told to pay himself with a portion of land, which he took at Limavady, a few miles below Derry. About the same time (1609) the Irish Society was founded to promote loyalty, Protestantism, and education, was allotted large tracts throughout Ulster, and retains to the present date a considerable estate around Londonderry and a smaller near Coleraine. From official statistics it appears that 584,327 acres of agricultural land valued for poor rates at 234,678*l*. are at present held by trustees of charitable institutions and other public companies throughout Ireland. This includes about 155,000 acres with a valuation of 90,275*l*.

held chiefly in county Londonderry by the London companies.

These public companies have been the subject of much discussion. It has been averred that they neglect and mismanage their estates, harass and overcharge their tenants, squander their income, and that their disestablishment is desirable. As absentees they are stated to withdraw from the country a considerable amount of money, which, under other ownership, might be spent in it. As corporate bodies without hearts, it is urged that it would be no hardship to compel them to sell to their tenants. Some have already sold. The Goldsmiths, Haberdashers, Merchant Taylors, and Vintners have disposed of their estates. The Grocers more recently sold considerable portions to their tenants. The Fishmongers, Mercers, Drapers, Salters, Ironmongers, and Skinners are still holders. Until recently the lands of the companies were let to middlemen, who sublet to the actual occupiers. The leases of the middlemen having expired, the companies have taken direct control and are devoting themselves to judicious improvements.

The Mercers' Company's estate is situate in the half-barony of Coleraine and barony of Loughinshollin ; the agent, Sir William R. Holmes, resides at Kilrea, the chief town on the property, possessing a population of 600. The acreage is 21,024, divided among 1,200 tenants, 700 of whom pay under 10*l.* The Government valuation is 11,549*l.*, the actual rental 11,769*l.* When the company recovered possession in 1831 by the lapsing of the lease with the Stewart family, who had long held the estate, the rental was 9,205*l.* ; on the representation of the tenants that rents were too high, reductions were made bringing the total to

8,498*l*. In 1853 two valuers, acting independently, went over the estate ; the mean of their estimates was 10,654*l*. The rental was, however, settled at 10,111*l*. In 1875-76 two other valuers again went over the estates, and, acting independently, both brought out valuations exceeding 14,000*l*. The company, anxious, however, to give the tenants fair advantage of the improvements which had generally been effected by themselves, fixed the rental at 11,769*l*. Deducting allowances, the average yearly receipts are 10,000*l*. Where the holdings exceeded 30*l*. of annual value leases for thirty-one years were offered, with a covenant restricting the tenant-right on the basis of the sliding scale of the Land Act of 1870. But the tenants objected to the advanced rents and also to the leases. They would not be taxed for their own improvements ; they would not submit to any limitation of their tenant-right. In 1876 litigation was resorted to ; fifty-three tenants were taken as test cases ; the Land Court decided for the company, awarding 820*l*. in costs, the greater portion of which the company subsequently forgave. The irritation thus produced has passed away, and the tenants are fairly satisfied. Comparing their condition with that of their neighbours on adjacent properties, they have no cause to complain ; their right of sale is unrestricted, excepting that the incoming tenant has to be approved by the agent. The company annually expends on schools donations to ministers, maintaining embankments and main watercourses, assisting building, draining, and other improvements, 3,456*l*. ; agent, clerks, and expenses of management in Ireland absorb 1,878*l*. Taking the whole period since 1831, when the Mercers recovered control of their estates, they have spent upon them considerably more than half the income. This is a great deal more than is done or can generally be afforded by private owners.

The Salters' estate is in the barony of Loughinshollin, the chief town being Magherafelt, with a population of about 2,000; it reverted to the company in 1853 on the fall of the lease of Sir Thomas Bateson. The acreage is 19,281, the Government valuation 17,718*l*., the rental 14,852*l*. Since 1853 the guild has expended in improvements 34,776*l*.; donations, schools, additions to ministers' salaries, office expenses, amount to 22,083*l*.; the building of the court-house at Magherafelt cost 1,803*l*. The majority of the tenancies range from thirty to sixty acres; the tenants are industrious and prospering. The company several years ago endeavoured to limit the tenant-right to 10*l*. an acre, but, finding much opposition to such a course, they now give unrestricted right.

The Skinners' Company, centring in the town of Dungiven, lies in the baronies of Kennargah, Yorkeeran, and Loughinshollin. The lease vested in the Ogilby family since 1800 terminated in 1872. The acreage extends to 44,334 acres; all is high-lying land; nearly half of it is rough mountain; the tenants number about 1,200; the valuation is 13,114*l*., the rental 13,387*l*. The company have increased the rental, but since coming into possession have laid out annually in improvements 4,730*l*.; in donations, schools, and clergymen, 1,000*l*.; in establishment charges, 1,000*l*. Towards making a railway which will greatly benefit the neighbourhood they have guaranteed 5 per cent. for twenty-three years on 20,000*l*. For most of these particulars regarding the Mercers', Salters', and Skinners' estates I am indebted to their solicitor, Mr. B. H. Lane, of Limavady.

The Ironmongers' estate, near Ballymoney, county Londonderry, was let on lease for a term of sixty-one years and three lives from November, 1767, to Mr. Josias du Pré. The last life died in 1840, when the company resumed direct possession and admitted as tenants all holders, excepting cottiers. The estate is now 11,373 statute acres; the rental 6,973*l.* 9*s.* 8*d.*; the Government valuation bearing date 1859, 7,471*l.* 3*s.* The land was valued at 6,272*l.* 14*s.*; the houses at 1,198*l.* 9*s.*, which includes 190*l.* for Messrs. Barklie and Co.'s bleach works; 46*l.* has since been added for the agent's house, which is held rent free. Mr. Edmond Stronge, who ably represents the guild, informs me that the number of tenants has been gradually reduced by consolidation. The estate custom gives ten years' rent to any tenant who desires to part with his farm, and receives the same from the incoming tenant, those adjoining having the preference. Excluding twenty-one who hold at nominal rents, there are now 378 tenants; of these fifty-nine pay under 5*l.* of annual rent, 104 under 10*l.*, sixty-five under 15*l.*, forty-seven under 20*l.*, fifty-eight under 30*l.*, thirty-two under 50*l.*, six under 75*l.*, two under 100*l.*, one under 150*l.*, two under 200*l.*, and one over 200*l.*; two other tenancies are not strictly agricultural. There are few leases, the tenants, it is stated, preferring to hold from year to year; a revaluation is made every twenty-one years. The company wisely prohibits subletting or subdivision, reserves the right to retake lands for planting or other improvements, preserves game, forbids the removal or sale of sand or gravel, prohibits the keeping of goats, which, unfortunately, are fond of browsing down the thorn quicks, forbids the planting of two consecutive corn crops, and the sale of straw or growing crops. These restrictive clauses, not very common in the North of Ireland, and the revaluation every twenty-one years, are seriously grumbled at. Grants have been made for building and repairing school-houses. For farm buildings, slates, roofing and flooring tiles have been given, and draining pipes supplied. Thorns are furnished for hedges, and skilled labourers employed to assist the tenants in dressing them. Allowances are made for pumps and iron gates, for draining roads and bridges ; lime is granted for manure. About fifty acres of waste has been planted in different parts of the estate. Extensive brick and tile works have been established, were worked by the company until 1873, and are now let. For repairs of roads the landlords supply broken stones, the tenants draw and spread them. For twenty-one years to September, 1873, bricks, draining, roofing, and flooring tiles to the value of 4,943*l.* were given free to the tenants. From that date to September 1880, independently of schools and charities, 2,617*l.* has been expended on draining roads and hedging. Considerable sums are, moreover, lent to tenants, repayable by instalments, with interest at 5 per cent. The company's 13 schools are all vested in the National Board. They give 12*l.* a year to each first class master or mistress ; 9*l.* to those of the second class. The amount given under this head in 1880 was 179*l.* 15*s.* 30*l.* a year is awarded in prizes ; an annual exhibition of 25*l.* is given at the Magee College, Derry, for which tenants' sons only are eligible. The company contributed 200*l.* towards the Parliamentary expenses of the Derry Central Railway ; they gave 52*a.* 1*r.* 30*p.* land free, which, at 25*l.* per acre, represents 1,311*l.* 17*s.* 6*d.*, besides guaranteeing interest at 5 per cent. for twenty-two years on 5,000*l.* worth of shares.

The Fishmongers' Company, on the death of George

III., who was the last life in the lease held by the Beresford family resumed possession of their estates, which lie in the baronies of Keenaght and Tirkeeran, in the union of Newtown, Limavady, and have since been zealous and liberal landlords. Under the intelligent management of the late agent Mr. A. Sampson, great portions of the estate liable to frequent floods were dried by cuttings and embankments; the good alluvial deposits left from the great lake which in olden times occupied the fertile valley of the Roe have thus been available for improved cultivation; roads have been made, farms squared, and tenants helped with their buildings and reclamation. Towards houses put up by the smaller upland tenants 40*l.* has been contributed by the company, for which an annual addition of 20*s.* is made to the rent. A grant is regularly awarded for cottage building and repairs, and is expended at the discretion of Mr. W. C. Gage, J.P., the much-esteemed agent. Mainly through his exertions Ballykelly has been made a model village, which might contrast favourably with any in England. The cottages are well built, comfortable, and nicely kept; plants in pots are ranged in many windows; flower gardens and trim hedges are in front—amenities indicative of tidiness and thrift seldom seen in Ireland. Good vegetable gardens, well stocked, are set aside for every cottager, who pays according to accommodation, for house and garden, from 2*l.* to 5*l.* a year. A common is provided for the cows belonging to the villagers. Of this privilege thirty families now take advantage, paying 42*s.* for the summer, 21*s.* for the winter grazing of each cow. Other cottages throughout the estate are let with the farms. In the village are a church and Presbyterian chapel: a capital school, where the labourers' children have gratuitous education, and the farmers pay 8s. a year, and where all books and appliances are found; besides a post-office, saw mill, and flax mill—all maintained for public benefit, mainly at the expense of the landlords. Whatever might be said by other residents on the estate, the neatly-dressed, tidy labourers, and their wives, with the well-shod, clean, wholesome-looking children of Ballykelly would certainly protest against any change of landlords.

The agricultural tenants number 370; the largest farm is 500 acres; more than half are under seventy acres. The estate comprises 20,540 imperial acres; Griffith's valuation is 9,595*l*. 12*s*. the actual rental is 9,507*l*. 5*s*. 9*d*. During twenty-one years, the accession to the rent-roll has been 1,600*l*. All tenants have leases for twenty-one years, at the termination of which revaluation is made; but in such valuations tenants' improvements are always allowed for.

William Leech had sixty-one acres of heath, for which he paid 40*s*. It came out of lease in 1851. The company, who, by a deputation of their members, triennially inspect their domains and make note of what is done, which is more than is effected by some absentees or even by some resident proprietors, were so pleased with Leech's improvements that they gave him another twenty-one years at the same figure, and in 1872 charged him during his third lease 6*l*. 10*s*. for a holding which would be cheap at 20*l*. All fences were made by the company, and they contribute to the keeping up of all mearing or march fences. Building is undertaken for any tenant on payment of 4 per cent. on the outlay; but the tenantry, generally, being well-to-do, usually prefer to carry out their own improvements, often, however, receiving grants of slates. For buildings put on one farm at a cost of 1,000*l.* 15*l.* a year is charged. Tenant-right is not restricted; it has doubled in value in twenty-five years; it is generally disposed of through an auctioneer, and makes twenty-three or twenty-four years' purchase. J. Douglas, a peasant proprietor, recently bought the tenant-right of a farm rented at 40*l.* for 1,130*l.* Ferguson, anxious to secure twenty-two acres rented at 14*l.*, paid 800 for the entry. Now that times are worse and money scarcer, he could not sell on equally good terms. R. Dunn, required to part with half an acre for enlarging a graveyard, made and received his claim of 30*l.*, being at the rate of eighty-six years' rent for the tenant-right alone, the company granting it to the parish free of rent for ever. Solicitous for the moral well-being of the people, 120*l.* is annually granted in aid of the salaries of the clergy on the estates. Schools cost on an average 800*l.*, but owing to extra buildings the outlay in 1879 was 1,188*l.*

One of the worshipful company's tenants must be taken as an exemplar of the whole. Mr. Arthur Gibson rents 138 imperial acres, for which he pays 194*l.*; he has a lease for twenty-one years, but complains that he is liable to be raised when the lease is renewed. He would gladly buy the fee simple of his farm at twenty-five years' purchase on a fair rent, but cautiously premises that his present rent would be too high an estimate. His tenant-right would realise fully 30*l.* an acre. Buying the fee simple at twenty-five years' purchase would, therefore, represent fifty-five years' purchase—a very handsome value for a purely agricultural holding. Mr. Gibson has followed his father and grandfather in the occupation of Broighter. By them and by himself all the buildings have been done, the handsome house erected, as well as the ample ranges of stabling and stalling, in which seventy-seven feeding cattle are now tied eating oat-straw, about 36 lbs. daily of the superior swedes, of which the yield exceeds 30 tons an acre, and further helped along by about 4 lbs. each of mixed meals. Only three milch cows are kept. The cattle are bought in, occasionally as yearlings, chiefly as two year olds; when fat they are sold in the byres, and usually go to Liverpool. Under the supervision of the sons everything seems carefully and tidily arranged; the large amount of well-made manure is heaped mostly under cover; ricks and rickyard are clean and smart, as they seldom are in Ireland; a six-course rotation is pursued, the grass seeds remaining down during three years; the only notable extravagance is the keeping of nine horses, four or five being sufficient to work the deep, good loam, which never misses a crop, and is grateful for Mr. Gibson's judicious, liberal treatment.

The rich valley of the Roe is liable to excessive floods, and owes its prosperity entirely to expensive embankments of the river, kept in order only by constant supervision. On the lower part extensive tracts of slob have been reclaimed from Lough Foyle by a Scotch company, and by Messrs. Brassey and Wagstaff, who built a sea wall 18 feet high, three miles in length, which keeps back the tide of Lough Foyle, while the draining of the district is secured by steam pumps forcing the water over the sea wall into the Lough. On many other rivers this sort of reclamation may be greatly and profitably extended. On the other side of the Roe are the estates of Sir Frederick Heygate and Sir Hervey Bruce. On the estate of the former, 5,500 acres, occupied by about eighty-five tenants, a sum exceeding 80*l*. is annually advanced by the landlord in clearing and maintaining the system of drains and watercourses. The larger main drains are kept in order at the cost of the landlord, while the smaller are superintended by committees of the tenants who allocate the amount to be repaid by each. On the mountain sides cultivation has reached the height of 600 feet, beyond which crops do not ripen in this climate. The higher reaches, 600 to 1,200 feet above the Lough, are wisely devoted to Scotch black-faced sheep.

On the townland of Crindle, Myroe, two miles from Sir Frederick Heygate's, are eight small holders with perpetuity leases averaging twenty acres each, labouring, as is often the case, under the serious disadvantage of having their plots scattered in rundale. Their houses are poor, and some of them in bad repair. 'No straw to spare in 1879' is the excuse for some rain coming in; but the cultivation of the good land is tolerable, the swedes are excellent. In the pastures and in the hedges thistles and ragweed are, however, much too abundant. Among these perpetuity holders lives Mr. William Moore, who rents about 100 acres from various landowners, pays for most of it 42s. an acre, appears well to do, but avers that without road contracts and other such outside help his farming would not pay. This gloomy view, like many other such statements, must, however, be accepted with some reservation, for Mr. Moore forty years ago began the world without capital, is now prosperous, with money lent to some of his less industrious, improvident neighbours, and most of it derived from farming. In this and adjacent townlands he tells me that there were wont to be considerable freeholders who wasted their substance and have long disappeared.

The Marquis of Waterford had a large estate around Limavady; considerable portions have recently been sold to Mr. Alexander, to Mr. Tillie (whose shirt factories prove an enormous boon to Londonderry) and to others. A few occupying tenants of twenty to fifty acres bought their holdings at twenty-eight to thirty years' purchase on their moderate rental, but, hampered by borrowing the money, have not yet improved their position. The purchase of the fee simple by an occupier with tenant-right worth 25*l.* an acre appears like buying his property twice over. Fifty pounds an acre is a heavy investment on an ordinary agricultural holding; even at 4 per cent. it makes a rent of 40*s.* an acre, which an ordinary tenant would generally regard as exorbitant. Lord Waterford's rental in the county is still 3,700*l.*, being a trifle over the Government valuation. Sale of tenant-right has always been allowed, subject to the agent's approval of the new tenant and his right to put in any person who will pay the *bonâ fide* price for the farm. Evictions are unknown, but if a tenant gets into poor circumstances he sells and pays his debts; or if he drops three years behind and refuses to sell, proceedings are taken against him, a sale of his tenant-right is made, and, after deducting the rent, the balance is handed to him. The large interest which the tenant under the unrestricted Ulster custom has in his holding, sometimes exceeding considerably the interest of his landlord, may be gathered from the appended table (pp. 130–131), obligingly furnished by Mr. B. H. Lane, solicitor, Limavady. It sets forth many of the sales of tenant-right which have been made in that district since 1873. Tenants who thus have an interest in their holdings valued at 25*l.* to 30*l.* an acre are virtuall copyholders or co-partners with their landlord, and with justice are entitled to representation on the proposed County Boards.

Mr. Donolly Thomas M'Causland, Drenagh, Limavady, has an estate in the county Londonderry containing 13,000 acres. The annual rental is 6,257*l*. The Government valuation of the land in the hands of the tenants is 5,500*l*. Mr. M'Causland resides very constantly upon his estate, takes an active, personal interest in its management, farms several hundred acres, and pays for wages on his demesne 1,000*l*. a year. The land, both in his own occupation and that of his tenants, is very well farmed. The holdings average thirty to forty acres, the rents are about 20*s*. an imperial acre, but somewhat higher near the town.

One of his most improving tenants, Mr. James Caskay, informs me that, although many manage to farm with a capital of 3*l*. or 4*l*., he cannot get on without 7*l*. He pays 100*l*. for his seventy-seven acres; poor-rates are 1*s*. 2*d*., county cess 1*s*. 3*d*. in the pound. Tenants' houses and offices, draining and fencing, are generally made by the landlord, who has expended during the last twenty years an average of 500*l*. a year. On advances to tenants interest varying from 3*l*. to 5*l*. per cent. per annum is charged. Expenditure for the general benefit of the estate, such as arterial drainage boundary fences and repairs of river banks, are made at the landlord's expense, and without any interest being charged. But the tenants besides make improvements, and when leaving are paid for them as well as for unexhausted manures, clover and grass-seeds sown the previous year, and, in addition, have three years' rent in lieu of tenant-right. Mr. M'Causland pays these allowances himself to the outgoing tenant, and disposes of the farm, sometimes dividing it among adjoining occupiers, shifting into it a tenant from a smaller holding, treating this smaller holding in like manner, or giving the lands, if arrangements of this kind be impracticable, to some one connected with the estate. Mr. Caskay, the tenant above alluded to, on entering his seventy-seven acres seven years ago, for three years' rent to his predecessor and for tillages paid 400*l*. With unrestricted tenant-right his payments would have been more than doubled. His farm being already equipped with buildings, reclaimed, and in fair cultivation, does not now require any considerable outlay for improvements; the restricted tenant-right consequently is no hardship, and as he enters, on the same terms he would leave. Only one person not a tenant or connected with the estate has been inducted into an agricultural holding within the last twenty years. Within this period on this estate upwards of fifty transfers have occurred, many of them being promotions from smaller to larger holdings. There have been no evictions except in four cases for nonpayment of rent, and in each upwards of four years' rent was due. There is no stated time for revaluations, but no readjustment is made under twenty years. Indeed, several rents have not been changed for upwards of thirty years. The rents are punctually paid.

This limited tenant-right occurs on other estates in this quarter. Major Scott's 2,500 acres in the barony of Keenaght, under the auspices of Mr. Michael King, of Dungiven, have been admirably laid out in convenient square fields, and improvements effected by the landlord. As in England or Scotland, improvements being undertaken by the landlord, the outgoing tenant is fairly paid by receiving five years' rent in the event of his moving. Entry is thus much easier for the incomer. On Mr. Young's estate in the barony of Ennishowen, as long as memory extends, five years' rent has been allowed to the way-going tenant, with the value of any improvements which he has effected, and which are determined by arbitration.

A detached portion of Mr. M'Causland's estate at Tamneyrankin, in the half barony of Coleraine, was last year sold on account of its subdivided condition and the difficulty of getting a numerous and troublesome tenantry to agree to squaring. The small fields belonging to each farm are in rundale or separated from each other, mixed most annoyingly with those of neighbours, necessitating complicated rights of way. Among the twenty-one occupiers on these 417 acres is one man of capital; the others have had to borrow half the purchase-money, which was agreed to be paid over before the purchase was completed, and a very wasteful, untidy arrangement of holdings runs much risk of being indefinitely perpetuated. When Government creates its peasant proprietors, it is to be hoped that efforts will be made to square or arrange the holdings so that they can be economically fenced and worked, and that provision, moreover, will be made for the construction of main drains and roads, the necessity of which is seldom appreciated by Irish tenants and small owners. Indeed, in the most unreasonable way, they often oppose the making of roads and drains across their farms even when they are of undoubted benefit to them and might be made at public expense.

King James, failing to induce his English and Scottish subjects freely to take up the escheated lands of Ulster, applied, as already stated, to the Corporation of London, and granted in 1613 a charter of incorporation to the Irish Society, conveying to it large grants of land for plantation of colonies. These lands were in great part reconveyed to the London companies. For their own purposes the Irish Society reserved the city of Derry and some 4,000 acres adjoining, the town of Coleraine with 3,000 acres, together with the fisheries of the Foyle and Bann, the soil of those rivers and the Culmore lands, containing 720 acres, which latter were to be enjoyed by the Governor of Culmore Fort, a nominee of the Crown. As recently as 1861, the Crown relinquished their right to appoint the governor, and sold their interest in the Culmore lands to the society. A great deal of slob land within the last fifty years has been recovered from Lough Foyle. As regards the town property, fully nine-tenths are let in perpetuity at nominal ground rents, and building leases of the remainder are granted for ninety-nine years. Most of the agricultural lands are let on lease for thirty-one years and upwards. The tenancies at will have not in many cases been revalued for thirty or forty years, and the society has lately agreed that no revaluation shall be required until at least twenty-one years have elapsed since the last valuation. The agricultural holders have tenant-right, limited only by the out-going tenant obtaining permission to sell, and his proposed successor being approved of as a solvent respectable man. Twenty to twenty-five pounds an acre is frequently given for the tenant-right of holdings changing hands. Long leases have wonderfully developed the property, and raised on some holdings of 200 or 300 acres houses costing 2,000*l.*, with barns, stabling, and covered yards. The rentals generally speaking are about 12 per cent. below the Government valuation. At 4 per cent. money is advanced to those who desire to make improvements. South-west of Londonderry the society has set out nicely-squared farms of twenty acres, and built smart, good houses and offices sufficient for holdings of double the area, which would probably have proved in every way more economical. Some capital cottages have also been built.

The total rental from all sources amounts to a little over 15,000*l.* per annum, which, after deducting the working expenses, is all employed in public improvements, education, and other works of usefulness on the estates or connected with the district.

The Hon. A. C. C. Plunkett, J.P., the society's zealous agent, informs me that in 1877 40,000*l.* was contributed to the Derry Bridge; 30,000*l.* has been paid towards the Bann navigation at Coleraine; 1,000*l.* to the cemetery; 500*l.*, continued for five years, goes to the waterworks. The handsome school buildings at Coleraine have cost 10,000*l.*, and their maintenance will involve about 1,000*l.* a year. The Foyle College, Derry, receives 1,095*l.* annually; the M'Gee College and Londonderry Academical Institution have grants of several hundred pounds; public improvements in the towns connected with the estates took last year 3,600*l.*; charitable contributions make a total of fully 1,000*l.* The Irish Society's estates appear to be made the best of, and their resources are worthily and widely employed.

The property is managed and controlled by a court of assistants elected annually by the Corporation of London, of which the governor, Sir Sydney H. Waterlow, Bart., M.P., and the Recorder, are the only permanent members, all the other members by the terms of the Charter being ineligible for immediate re-election after two years' service. This is said to be a blot in the constitution of the society.

Sales of Tenant Right in the Limavady District of Londonderry from 1873 to 1880.

Date.	Seller.	Townland.	Acreage. a. r. p.	Rent. £ s. d.	Buyer.	Amnt. £	Landlord.
1873, Dec. 3	John M'Loskey	Leek	41 0 0	19 10 0	James Feeny	435	Wm. Cather
1873, Aug. 15	James M'Ateer	Ballyhargan	8 0 0	3 3 0	Henry Deany	60	Mr. Wray
1876, Dec. 7	John Aull	Ballyscullin	2 1 18	1 15 6	Joseph Aull	31	Sir F. W. Heygate
1878, Feb. 11	Wm. Carlin	Ballymoney	10 0 0	6 5 0	James Kane	127	John M'Curdy
1878, Jan. 23	Jas. Douglas	Boveva	22 0 0	20 0 0	Wm. Laughlin	108	J. S. Douglass
1878, Feb. 19	Dennis Brolly	Gortnaghymore	12 0 0	9 0 0	Michael Doherty	106	John Quigley
1877, Jan. 31	Wm. Stewart	Termaquin	23 1 26	17 15 2	Robert Simpson	270	Samuel Pollock
1878, Feb. 15	Alex. Lytle	Gortgarn	16 3 9	10 0 0	Geo. Stewart	200	Lord C. Beresford
1877, Sept. 1	Paul Kane	Killywill	14 0 0	10 10 5	Wm. M'Kinney	290	Rev. Maxwell
1877, Dec. 14	Ed. Hampsy	Boley	5 0 0	6 6 0	Jas. Murray	105	Ditto
1876, Nov. 16	Robt. Ogilby	Tullyvery	14 0 0	13 8 9	Wm. Mullen	360	Ditto
1876, Aug. 31	Roseau Divine	Faughanvale	23 0 0	13 0 0	James King	500	Ditto
1878, Jan. 4	John Hargan	Muldooney	18 0 0	9 10 0	Michael Carten	210	Major Brown
1877, Jan. 24	James Kane	Margymonaghan	137 0 0	64 10 0	Edward Conn	650	Sir F. W. Heygate
1876, Mar. 23	Jas. Hutton	Derrynaflaw	54 0 0	19 8 8	Jas. Fallows	406	Mr. Loyle
1875, Feb. 25	Wm. Latten	Drumballydonaghy	9 0 0	11 3 0	John Patchell	183	Ditto
1876, Jan. 27	Tho. O'Hara	Killywill	6 0 0	4 4 0	Wm. Mullan	180	Rev. Maxwell
1878, Jan. 4	Robt. Kane	Ballymoney	9 0 0	4 12 0	Thos. Murphy	120	John M Curdy
1879, Jan. 17	Henry Donaghy	Mulkeeragh	26 0 0	14 0 0	John Steel	520	Michael King
1879, Dec. 9	Wm. Millikin	Straw	30 0 0	23 11 0	William Dale	425	John Semple
1879, July 2	Patrick Carten	Tartnakelly	25 0 0	5 5 0	Michael Bryson	140	James Ogilby
1878, Mar. 5	Henry Deany	Feeney	13 0 0	9 13 7	Jas. M'Kendry	275	J. C. F. Hunter
18-8, Nov. 6	Sarah Atkinson	Broharris	33 1 14	41 5 0	James Thompson	880	Fishmongers' Company
1879, Aug. 27	William Steel	Ballymore	7 0 23	8 0 0	James M'Clelland	120	Henry Tyler

IN COUNTY LONDONDERRY.

Date	Name		Townland		Tenant	A. R. P.	£ s. d.	Acres	Landlord
1879, Feb. 6	Pat. Heaney	..	Drum	..	John M'Losky	34 0 0	14 9 4	450	Miss C. T. D. Nesbitt
1879, Dec. 16	James Mullen	..	Killywill	..	Jas. Donaghy	9 0 0	5 11 4	151	Rev. Maxwell
1879, Feb. 7	Samuel Young	..	Drumraighland	..	Wm. Hopkins	10 0 0	4 4 0	160	Robert Ogilby
1879, Dec. 26	Wm. M'Closkey	..	Kilunaght	..	Henry M'Closkey	18 0 0	10 10 0	270	Captain Bruce
1879, June 28	Thomas Young	..	Killywill	..	John Hara	6 0 0	2 17 9	90	Rev. Maxwell
1879, Sept. 5	John Miller	..	Drumraighland	..	James White	(Ho. & Grdn.)	0 0 6	54	Robert Ogilby
1879, Nov. 13	John Donaghy	..	Cool	..	John Baird	26 1 30	12 0 0	400	Fishmongers' Company
1879, Apr. 26	Susan Tower	..	Glack	..	Robt. Ferguson	26 0 0	14 15 0	775	Ditto
1879, Apr. 3	Thomas M'Closkey	..	Gortnaghy	..	John Quinn	7 3 0	3 13 0	59	Michael M'Cartney
1879, Apr. 15	Margaret Heany	..	Drum	..	James M'Cully	17 0 0	7 4 8	254	Miss C. T. D. Nesbitt
1879, Jan. 18	Eliz. Rosborough	..	Ballyhanedin	..	Edward Rea	46 0 0	25 10 0	360	Fishmongers' Company
1880, Jan. 22	Jas. Stewart	..	Turmacoy	..	John Hopkin	24 0 0	18 10 0	540	Ditto
1878, Dec. 24	Henry Mullan	..	Lenamore	..	Peter Conway	127 0 0	28 18 0	340	Marquis of Waterford
1879, Feb. 22	Ed. Rea	..	Ballymoney	..	Henry M'Closkey	28 0 0	14 12 0	320	John M'Curdy
1878, Nov. 14	John L. Horner	..	Burnfoot	..	James Connor	17 3 24	16 0 0	307	John Semple
1880, Mar. 4	Wm. Connor	..	Magheramore	..	James Holmes	35 0 0	13 9 0	366	James Ogilby
1879, Apr. 9	N. M'Keanery	..	Gortgarn	..	Neil M'Kennery, jun.	16 2 0	11 0 0	156	Marquis of Waterford
1879, Feb. 28	Nancy Heany	..	Templemoyle	..	John M'Intyre	8 0 0	5 10 0	122	T. Heany
1880, Feb. 13	John Kelly	..	Coolagh	..	Joseph Mackay	20 0 0	18 4 0	480	R. P. Maxwell
1880, Jan. 19	John M'Kinney	..	Boley	..	John Jamieson	20 0 0	16 2 10	360	Ditto
1880, Jan. 3	Jos. Ferguson	..	Killybleught	..	John Quigg	17 0 0	20 0 0	200	Jacob Jackson
1880, Feb. 23	James Ross	..	Killylane	..	Edward Coyle	54 0 0	41 0 0	805	Fishmongers' Company
1880, Feb. 24	P. Hampson	..	Gortnaghy	..	James Kane	8 1 7	7 0 0	100	Adam Wray
1880, Mar. 25	Robt. M'Elree	..	Moneyshinare	..	Robt. Jno. Nelson	70 0 0	60 0 0	970	Rev. M. M'Causland
1880, Mar. 26	Michael Kane	..	Terrydreen	..	William Evans	24 0 0	6 0 0	172	J. B. Beresford
1880, Jan. 13	Jane Magill	..	Moyse	..	Joseph Neely	43 0 0	15 15 0	310	James Ogilby
1880, Aug. 31	Jas. M'Greelis	..	Tyrglasson	..	Hugh Miller	8 2 0	3 15 0	200	Fishmongers' Company

CHAPTER XII

ESTATES IN DERRY, ENNISHOWEN, AND TYRONE.

Sir Samuel Martin, one of Her Majesty's Privy Councillors, has 1,000 acres in the parishes of Corticaw and Drumhoe, three miles from Londonderry, formerly belonging to the Goldsmiths' estate, twenty years ago one of the most ragged, irregular, hopeless-looking properties that could well be conceived. Judging from the old maps, it was largely occupied with irregular, straggling, crooked, wide fences, with accommodation roads which were seldom passable, with rights-of-way; while a good deal of what is now the best land was, excepting for a few weeks in summer, quaking bog unsafe to ride or even to walk over. In this unpromising form it was placed in the able hands of Mr. Michael King, who forthwith gave all the tenants notice to quit—a proceeding which, in the present state of feeling in Ireland, could scarcely have been attempted, which the Land Act of 1870 would make it difficult to effect, but which might still be beneficially repeated on some estates. A few small people were entirely bought out, but the great majority were reinstated as nearly as possible in their improved holdings, which some of the old people—of course strong opponents of such sweeping reforms—declare they could not have recognised. Old devious fences were levelled; dangerous pits filled up; drains 3 feet to 4 feet deep put in 21 feet to 24 feet apart; great main watercourses were laid out; the fields, thrown into parallelograms, were divided by turf mounds topped with sheltering thorn-quick. In one section, out of 45 small enclosures, three good-sized ones were made; intersecting roads were fenced and stoned; a belt of plantation has been carried a mile over some irregular ground along one boundary. Where special advantages were conferred on an individual farm addition was made to the rent, but the rents generally were very slightly increased. They average less than 20s. an acre, and are about 12 per cent. over Griffith's valuation. Notwithstanding so much having been done by the landlord, the Ulster custom and right of sale is conceded to the tenants. One of the principal, Mr. Gillfillan, has 170 statute acres, pays 170l. of rent, keeps six horses, nineteen cows, and about fifty other cattle, but no sheep, pays his labourers 8s. to 9s. a week, with a house, small garden, and portion of worked potato ground; has his land clean and in good condition, rests it three years in grass, takes generally two consecutive oat crops, then swedes and potatoes, followed by oats, and again down to grass. In food for man and beast and in profit for the occupiers Sir Samuel Martin's estate now produces four times what it did twenty years ago; indeed, some of the bog-land has been increased eight or ten times in value.

The peninsula of Ennishowen, lying between Lough Foyle and Lough Swilly, extending north about twenty-five miles from Londonderry, and varying from eight to twelve miles wide, has been a proscribed district ; processes could not be served ; military and extra constabulary were recently introduced; but at Buncrana fair, on December 31, and in the hovels of the small tenantry, I saw no evidences of malicious intent. A considerable number complain, however, of repeated advances of their rents. They plead that they dare not break up the superabundant bog, stock the heather and huge boulders out of the mountain side, or otherwise make improvements without risk in a year or two of the reclaimed land being charged as cultivated land, its rent being probably increased three or four fold. Mr. McGlinchey, who held under lease at 14*l.* 10*s.*, is recorded to have made improvements variously estimated at 600*l.* to 800*l.* When last year other tenants had their abatement he was passed over, and told that his rent should be 42*l.* 'Would any man reclaim bog or build houses after that robbery?' warmly exclaims my informant.

Instances are cited of men with good coats and hats met at market by landlord or agent, and told that such evidences of prosperity show that they can bear another rise. A new coat of thatch or a fresh whitewashing of the house has often, I am assured, brought a revaluation. Even if such cases are only occasional and exceptional, they shake confidence and paralyse enterprise. Better results, it is to be hoped, will ensue when, under an improved Land Act, the fair rents are fixed by a representative Land Court for twenty-one or twenty-five years, and when even at the termination of that period any enhanced value will be secured to the tenant, unless it results from advanced price of agricultural produce, from money expended by the landlord, or from unearned increment, such as the opening of a railway, the growth of a neighbouring town, or other such conditions determined independently of the tenant.

Some of the Ennishowen landlords have been unreasonable, despotic, and sometimes short-sighted. The late Daniel Todd, before dividing and selling his estates, raised the rents to 30 and even 70 per cent. over Griffith's valuation, small regard being given to the source from which the enhanced value accrued. One section of this estate, close to Buncrana, bought by an Englishman, with a rental of about 1,500*l.*, is understood to be 50 per cent. above Griffith's valuation. Under accumulated arrears, from which they cannot extricate themselves, some of the poorer mountain tenantry are hopelessly dragged down; help is refused to the good work of furnishing Buncrana with the much needed water-supply; no efforts in bad times have been made to provide work for the unemployed; the opportunity has been missed of utilising a fine bed of clay, and the promising brick and tile works have been transferred from Buncrana to Burnpool, where Mr. H. Brassey with mere foresight was glad to develop an industry which would help his irregularly employed people.

Captain McClintock has a rental of about 1,700*l.* Combining against enhanced rents and refusing lesser reductions tardily offered, his tenants have recently settled up, receiving all round a deduction of five shillings in the pound. In the town of Buncrana houses and cottages have been built on leases of sixty-one and ninety-one years, but the agricultural tenants have no leases; their cultivated land averages about 16*s.* an acre; nothing is done by the landlord; but the unlimited tenant-right is worth about twenty years purchase; 25 per cent. was allowed from the rents of 1879 for the distress and a like amount in 1880 on account of the agitation.

Colonel Todd Thornton's tenants hardly average 8*l* of annual rent; they received 20 per cent. from the gales both of 1879 and 1880. Most are Roman Catholics, whose sacrifice of time and money, not only at markets, but on holidays and at wakes and funerals, contributes to impoverishment. Among Colonel Thornton's small holders about Kinnigoe occur the invariable concomitants of subdivision and destitution. The splitting up of small holdings is most difficult to prevent. It is done in defiance of landlords' orders and threats of eviction. The usual apology is, 'The boy or girl would marry, shure; the priest gave his blessing, and we must do something for them.' It appears to be worse among the Roman Catholic population, who in this, as in other matters, are rather more difficult to manage than their Protestant brethren, who, perhaps, being more amenable to reason and less banded together, here and elsewhere, seem to be selected as the first recipients of ejectments.

Sir Robert Bateson Harvey has a nice estate, worth 3,000*l*. a year, lying towards the mouth of the lough, near Dunrea. It is moderately rented, liberally managed, assistance being given to all who will help themselves, and no percentage is charged on any such outlay. But, with unreasoning ingratitude, no distinction is made between such an indulgent owner and the most exacting of land-grabbers, and Sir Robert's rents are withheld until a 25 per cent. reduction is promised.

Mr. W. T. Hanna, of White House, Carrigans, six miles from Londonderry, twenty years a resident in the United States, exhibits abundance of the energy and enterprise which Irish tenants generally so sadly want, took up a few years ago his father's holding of twenty-nine statute acres, and began in earnest his thorough improvements. He has rented and similarly improved adjacent lands, has built a handsome dwelling-house with good farm premises, made roads, converted twenty-nine small, irregularly-shaped 'parks' into four shapely, well-enclosed fields, grubbed up furze, blasted with dynamite many tons of precipitous rock, filled up pits, levelled and subsoiled. To illustrate the mighty changes effected on the old furze and rock, an acre is left in the rude, wild state, worth perhaps 1s. a year for the occasional grazing of a goat. The improvements in some of the fields reached 50l. an acre. The landlord very soon put in his claim for a share in the tenant's dearly-earned profits, to which he had not contributed; the rent was raised first to 8s. and then to 25s. an acre.

As is ever the case where arable culture is successfully carried out, occupation is found for extra labourers. Good cottages of three rooms are provided, like the rest of the work, by the tenant; gardens of one rood and a half are enclosed, two tons and a half of coal are yearly furnished to each man; for the principal labourer a cow is kept gratuitously. With free house, coals, and potato-ground in the field proportioned to the family requirements, the labourers are engaged by the year and have 8s. to 9s. per week. Similar improvements, not so rapidly or thoroughly done, have been going on throughout this neighbourhood during the last forty years. On the opposite side of the river the furze and brambles then came down to the water's edge; now they have receded some miles back to the mountain crest, and the reclaimed land is set out in farms, generally of twenty-five to sixty acres, devoted to oats, swedes, potatoes, and grass, which usually remains down for three years; when lying longer the land is liable to revert to furze and bent.

Another model farmer, a near neighbour of Mr. Hanna's, is Mr. Alexander, who holds 170 statute acres at 23*s.*; has expended 2,300*l.* on his commodious house and substantial buildings; has made the hungry gravel hills fertile, and, in addition to successful general farming, has recently gone in for gardening, and disposes annually of 60*l.* worth of strawberries. Under the Church Act Mr. Alexander bought thirty acres at twenty-three years' purchase, which, like his other land, is thoroughly well managed. What these gentlemen have done, others with like industry and enterprise may do. But, unless with a long lease or with fixity of tenure and some arrangement, also, as to fixedness or only slow or remote increment of rent, it is scarcely to be expected, especially in such times of unrest, that tenants will undertake costly improvements. I was shown in this district great tracts of cleared bog, some of it lying by the side of the public road, at present looking like sustaining a goose an acre, but capable of being made as good as much of Mr. Hanna's or Mr. Alexander's land. The tenants, however, prefer to hold it at 1*s.* to 2*s.* an acre, rather than improve it and have the rent raised in a few years to 20*s.* or more.

The Duke of Abercorn's estates in Donegal and Tyrone extend to 69,937 acres, and, including 1,050*l.* for lands in hand, realise an annual rental of 40,284*l.*, which is about 5 per cent. over Griffith's valuation. Between Griffith's and the actual rent there is a divergence in different parts of the estate; in the manor of Cloghogal the rent is 1 per cent. over the valuation; in the manor of Derrywoon it is

16 per cent. over; the Donegal estate averages 12 per cent. over; throughout the manor of Doncheng the yearly rent and valuation are alike; in the manor of Strabane the rent is $4\frac{1}{2}$ per cent. under the valuation. Rents are little above the figure at which they stood forty years ago, when some of the old leases lapsed. Since 1870, leases, which would be granted to larger tenants, have not been asked for. The agricultural tenants number 1,194. On several of the townlands many of the holdings do not reach twenty-five acres; on others, doubled up as opportunity has offered, they average fifty acres; several in Tyrone measure 200 acres. Rents vary from 10s. for the mountain-land to 30s. for the better, older reclaimed lands. The farms are generally well squared, with shapely fields fairly fenced, the buildings, especially on the larger holdings, being good. All buildings have been erected and other improvements effected and maintained by the tenants.

Sales of tenant-right are usually made publicly by an auctioneer, who, after detailing the conditions, notes the bids offered. Between October 1876 and October 1880 thirty-five sales were made, ranging from eleven to fifty-four years' purchase. The particulars are appended. The highest bidders are said to be neighbouring tenants desirous to extend their holdings, to settle a son beside them, or to prevent the intrusion of a stranger. Whether from good seasons or improved security, it is difficult to say, but the price has advanced since the Land Act of 1870 came into operation. The landlord reserves a *veto* as to the solvency and respectability of the in-comer. The son or other relative, or another tenant on the estate, is preferred. Few evictions occur, and only for accumulated arrears. Sometimes after ejection notices are served the money is forthcoming from friends at home or in America. The following is a typical case :—J. O'Brian, holding two small farms, together rented at 48*l.* 10*s*., owes upwards of four years' rent, and, besides, farms badly ; his places are dilapidated, he will neither pay, sell, nor quit. An ejectment was served ; he put his holding up for sale in the usual way ; notwithstanding its unsatisfactory form he was offered 900*l*. ; he might have made 1,000*l*., but held on for 1,100*l*. and still remains. Another ejection is in preparation for him, and a little pressure may induce his acceptance of the proffered 1,000*l*., his paying his arrears, and making way for a more satisfactory tenant.

Until this year rents had been well paid. They are settled annually between Christmas and Candlemas. The tenants are generally well-to-do and thriving ; some complain of insecurity of tenure, of periodical valuations at intervals of twenty-one years or on changes of occupancy. Some holders of town parks, which on the deep alluvial around Strabane reach 60*s*. and even 80*s*. per acre, feelingly demur to land more remote than half-a-mile from any town being thus designated, and hence exempted from claims for disturbance.

Although farm improvements have always been done by the tenants, the landlord has not shirked his share of greater works. Major Humphries, J.P., the indefatigable agent, informs me that between 1846 and 1872 about 60,000*l*. has been expended in estate improvements.

From the Board of Works has been borrowed for drainage, embankments, bridges, &c. . .	£28,390
From private resources, for draining and other improvements	16,063
Ditto, for timber and slates	7,047
Ditto, for drainage and fencing since 1872 . .	6,075
	£57,575

In the better housing of his labourers the Duke has also recently expended 3,000*l.*; the cottages having three rooms, back premises, byre and pigsties, and a good garden. Work and wages are regularly found at Baron's Court for artificers and labourers, their payments for 1880 being as follow:—Demesne, 3,000*l.*: new farm, 1,000*l.*; old farm, 1,000*l.*; woods, 500*l.*; planting, 390*l.*; charitable subscriptions, 210*l.*

Here, as in so many other parts of Ireland, agriculturists are in a state of excitement, expectancy, and usually of considerable terrorism. Markets are early cleared; everyone gets home betimes; the constabulary assure me that there are fewer folks about at night and much less drinking; cases at Petty Sessions are falling off; the Land League Courts are said to settle some of the private differences. But rents are badly paid, arrears accumulate, some who have the money dare not pay it. Landlords and estate agents seldom stir from home after sundown or unarmed, and some have difficulty in getting their premises insured against fire. The agitation interferes with industry. Even on many good estates the tenants fall into the general state of idleness and unrest. Few improvements and less work are undertaken; very many stubbles still lie unploughed. The Land Bill is anxiously looked for. The small farmer appears to anticipate from it not only the 'three F's,' but all possible and impossible boons. Even the better class of tenants are delaying many arrangements to see what turns up. Leases arranged for stand over unsigned. Mr. M'Farlane, of Strabane, informs me that a relation who has 800 acres of mixed mountain and arable land at Plumbridge, eight miles west of Strabane, a few months ago had arranged to give his twenty-four tenants leases for 999 years on payment of a fine

Sales of Tenant Right on Estates of the Duke of Abercorn, K.G., between October 1876 and October 1880.

	Contents. Statute			Yearly Rent			Purchase Money		No. of Yrs. Purchase
	a.	r.	p.	£	s.	d.	£	s.	
Legnathraw, Mrs. Porter	100	1	39	91	4	0	2,630	0	28
Momien, Matthew Chambers	37	2	30	29	15	0	840	0	28
Cloghogal, John H. Moorhead	48	3	6	25	8	5	702	10	28
Drumicklagh, John Lynch	39	0	11	35	10	0	455	0	12
Ballylennon, Robert Colhoun	65	0	2	50	14	0	1,055	0	20
Momien, Edward Gilfillan	48	3	5	38	7	0	790	0	20
Ardagh, James Wright	60	2	28	23	18	0	400	0	17
Drumicklagh, Mrs. Dwine	35	3	0	31	2	5	350	0	11
Trentamucklagh, J. M'Clintock	41	0	0	30	14	0	655	0	21
Ditto, Alexander M'Clintock	68	3	23	30	0	0	565	0	18
St. Johnston, Joseph Roulstone	19	2	38	17	16	0	460	0	27
Ballee, Samuel Donnell	30	0	5	15	9	1	780	0	52
M'Crackens, Mrs. Chambers	40	2	21	37	19	0	1,005	0	27
Castlewarren, George Pollock	50	2	23	12	0	0	505	0	42
Stoneyfalls, Robert Entucan*	59	3	20	16	7	3	710	0	44
Ballee, Robert M'Cleery	71	2	35	56	8	9	1,100	0	19
Cavanalea, Edwin E. Graves	71	2	30	61	4	2	1,225	0	20
Tullyard, Andrew White	28	0	0	16	15	0	280	0	17
Druminaboy, Walter Lowther	100	3	35	77	10	11	1,730	0	22
Dunmore, Mrs. Rankin	33	1	10	29	11	0	350	0	12
Carrickgullion, Mrs. Stevenson	45	0	20	28	14	3	985	0	35
Castlemellow, Mrs. Smyth	30	1	15	19	3	0	401	0	20
Derrygoon, John Doak	14	3	22	12	15	0	365	0	30
Archill, Andrew Wilson†	34	0	36	15	12	0	560	0	37
Drumlegagh, Mrs. Maxwell	43	1	29	34	18	0	1,010	0	29
Envaugh, Cath. and Ann M'Crosson	26	3	7	12	8	0	220	0	19
Cavanalea, Andrew M'Ashee	17	3	20	10	3	0	240	0	24
Gartlogher, Robert Cumins	45	3	10	20	19	6	500	0	24
Trentauge, Joseph Alexander	149	3	37	62	9	0	1,600	0	25
Cavanalea, Thos. Cuthbertson	72	1	34	40	0	0	955	0	23
Dysart, Arthur Doherty	11	2	10	12	0	0	390	0	32
Gortileck, Henry M'Cay‡	45	0	17	15	11	4	810	0	54
Gilleystown, J. Jack	42	1	12	32	6	0	600	0	18
Woodena, Mansfield B. White	22	3	5	28	0	0	500	0	18
Ballymogany, ditto	18	3	20	21	0	0	420	0	20

* Leased, 28*l*., Government valuation.
† Sold 1880, 13*l*. 5*s*., Government valuation.
‡ Rent low, leased; Government valuation, 21*l*.

equivalent to eight years' Griffith's valuation and a fixed annual payment of that valuation. But they now prefer to wait until they see the expected Bill, which, like Mr. M'Farlane's lease, it is to be hoped will contain provision against subdivision. This Plumbridge property, like so many others, illustrates this ruinous tendency; in 1802 it was leased for three lives to seven persons; now it is in the the hands of twenty-four lessees, who, besides, have sub-tenants.

CHAPTER XIII.

THE SMALL OCCUPIERS AND OWNERS OF ULSTER.

SMALL holdings are in great part accountable for the shortcomings of Irish agriculture. Desirous to extend their political influence, many owners formerly favoured the multiplication of the forty-shilling freehold. The operation of the ballot has, however, lessened the importance of a long roll of small retainers. Under the supine rule of careless or indulgent landlords or middlemen subdivision and subletting were also extended. The Roman Catholic clergy gladly see the multiplication of their flocks. The dominant anxiety for 'a bit of a farm' and the scarcity of other occupations often lead to the cutting up of the holding among several members of the large families which are so common in most parts of Ireland. As sons and even daughters marry, in spite of office regulations, they settle in the paternal abode, have an acre or two set aside for them, sometimes have a cabin built for them. Under such conditions, no wonder that half the farms in Ireland are under fifteen acres and that one-fifth are under five acres. On good land near towns the owner of ten acres may get along fairly. His own labour and that of his horse or ass are probably occupied at odd times. But the small holder on second-rate soils, such as abound throughout the north and west of Ireland, has a hard struggle for existence. He cannot, even under good management, depend upon realising more than 2*l.* or 3*l.* profit from each cultivatable acre, which affords meagre sustenance for a family and for meeting occasional losses of stock and crop. There is very limited opportunity for extraneous earnings. The sparsely scattered farmers of fifty fairly cultivated acres work with their own families, have, perhaps, a lad in the house, and seldom need the help of their smaller neighbours, who, besides, are sometimes too proud to work near home for men of like position with themselves. In some localities, even in Ulster, the small farms are awkwardly circumstanced; the fields, of perhaps one acre, badly fenced, are sometimes scattered throughout the townland. Such a system of rundale has been adopted in order that each holder should have his proportion of land of different quality. It multiplies fences and roads, which often pass over neighbours' plots. The difficulties which lie in the way of re-allotting, squaring, or striping such inconvenient holdings are increased by fixity of tenure giving claims to tenants for disturbance. The Act of 1870 has retarded the desirable redistribution of such townlands.

Although Ireland is pre-eminently the land of small occupiers, it does not furnish so many small proprietors as Great Britain. The Census of 1871 enumerated 20,217 proprietors in Ireland in occupation of their own lands, but only half that number were holders in perpetuity. Some have fee-farm grants, others have perpetuity leases. Under the Church Acts of 1869 and the Bright's Clauses of the Land Act of 1870 upwards of 6,000 have been added to the roll of small proprietors. The longer established of the small holders have a somewhat diversified origin. Some have been squatters, acquiring their holdings from undisturbed possession. I have not met with intact specimens of the Cromwellian grants of 100 acres. They had long ago been split up by often repeated subdivisions. Landlords in former days in difficulties sometimes got ready money from their tenants, and in consideration fined down the rents. In this way throughout various parts of the north of Ireland, notably about Belfast and Carrickfergus, as well as near Londonderry, large portions of Lord Donegall's property have been devised in fee-farm or perpetuity grants, and these convenient lots in the hands of small holders willing to sell have often proved a great boon, especially in and about the growing towns.

To their agricultural owners these perpetuity farms have not always proved an unqualified advantage. With the rent fined down often to a few shillings an acre, the owners sometimes believed themselves relieved from the need of continuous hard work. Credit is, however, easily commanded; but thirty to forty acres of neglected or partially worked land will not support an idler, who is usually, besides, too proud or careless to find work for spare time. To get out of difficulties an acre or two is sometimes sold to more thrifty neighbours. Even if one generation passes without waste or division of the inheritance, the children growing up demand their share of the patrimony. One, sometimes several sons, marrying, bring their brides to the paternal fireside, and arrangements are made, either to partition the holding, or the young folks engage to pay the old people or the brothers and sisters for the portion they appropriate. To fulfil this engagement, money has usually to be borrowed, seldom on the best of terms; the interest on the loan amounts to a fair rent; and the perpetuity man thus becomes little better off than the yearly renter.

Fixity of tenure and permanent interest in his holding do not invariably develop in these small owners energy, industry, or prosperity. Their stake in the orderly well-being of the country has not always made them more law-abiding citizens. I am repeatedly informed that the poorest people in a townland are the small perpetuity holders, that the small freeholders paying head rents are the most numerous defaulters on the books of some estates. In the south with the multitude they have joined the Land League. The conditions which should elevate and improve these small holders are apt to be antagonised by stronger adverse influences. Their holdings, like those of their renting neighbours, are unprofitably small. They have difficulty in shaking themselves clear of prevailing idleness and apathy.

The history and condition of these small owners may be studied especially in various parts of Ulster. Occasionally considerable numbers are found together. There is an upward tendency of a few families, a decadence of more. Ignoring the Scripture warning, a few lay house to house and field to field. But this aggregation is slower than the disintegration. The number of leaseholders multiplies. Mr. H. B. Lane, solicitor, Limavady, gives me a list of perpetuity tenures in the barony of Limavady, which shows that in sixteen townlands of this union, about the years 1733 and 1734, the grantees were forty-five. About 100 years later, when these leases were renewed, the numbers of grantees amounted to 164, and have since again increased in an accelerating ratio. In Bollaghy ten holders are now crowded on eighteen and a half acres. The smaller leaseholders and owners, moreover, are particularly prone to cumber their tenancies with indefinite numbers of cottage occupiers, who are generally charged excessive rents.

Derryvane, on the borders of Donegal, five miles from Londonderry, illustrates the evils of subdivision and the poverty of small owners. One hundred acres, held in the early part of the century by one lessee, are now divided among five, and a younger generation growing up, further division is imminent. The land has been laboriously reclaimed from mountain side and bog, is cold and wet, not very grateful for good treatment, and will not hold grass for more than two years. The twenty-acre farms are held by a colony of Wylies. James Wylie was one of a family of ten ; had to give the other nine their shares when he acquired his twenty acres, for which he pays 4*l*. 10*s*. a year. He has nine or ten fields, grows seven or eight acres of oats, two of potatoes, two of turnips, the remainder is in grass. A second cut of grass made into poor hay is standing in small cocks in the fields (January 1). A horse, two cows, and the same number of calves or yearlings, sometimes with 'a slip of a pig,' make up the total of his live stock. Thomas Wylie has a similar farm, pays the same rent, appears to manage in the same manner. Richard Wylie I found comfortably in bed when I called for him at noon on January 1. He had not the seasonable excuse of having been indulging in any New Year festivities ; he was merely 'resting,' as most of his class do from November until the end of February. He is a hale man of sixty, with several smart daughters ; and is evidently somewhat better off than most of his neighbours. On his twenty acres he keeps a horse, three cows of mountain descent, which are now making five pounds of butter per week, sold at 1*s*. 3*d*. ;

in summer the three little cows produce fifteen pounds of butter. Other twenty acre plots are counterparts of these. The houses are stone and lime, of one storey, thatched, about 20 feet by 15 feet; a rough, wooden partition separates two rooms, there is no ceiling or lath and plaster; the small sash windows do not open, but this matters the less as a considerable number of the panes are broken and their place supplied by paper, a piece of board, occasionally by some rags; the floors are dirt bottoms not very level; tables, a few chairs, and a cupboard in the wall are the usual contents of the living room. One or more beds in the wall and a rough box or two, in which the holiday attire is stowed, occupy the inner chamber.

The most prosperous owner in Derryvane is William Brown, an adjoining perpetuity holder of 113 acres, for which he pays 20*l.* annually, who, marrying a Miss Wylie, had a claim to one of the twenty-acre farms, for which, however, he has paid 1,005*l.* With discretion, this amount should set up the lads and form a dower for the younger girls. A good bargain to these young people, it does not appear so for Mr. Brown. His capital, invested at 4 per cent., would represent 30*s.* an acre of rent for twenty acres of poor, cold soil, dear at 20*s.*, with buildings certainly not worth 50*l.*, and one wretched cottage letting rain in, and said by the tenant, a labourer, to be let to him with a garden of about one chain at 3*l.* a year. Mr. Brown believes his fee-farm neighbours to be worse off than regularly employed labourers. They have a hard struggle to get along; with large families, which most seem to have, and provision to be made for the younger members, the man who gets the farm incurs a burden which he can scarcely expect to clear off. Several families named Lynch, having among them 200 acres, for some years have been going down-hill, and are stated to be in difficulties. In good times any small extra earnings were squandered. The bachelors, of whom several of steady, frugal habits live on the adjacent townland of Sappagh, manage to hold their farms and their money together. Mrs. Swan, of Sappagh, has a fee-farm grant of ten acres, rented at 2*l.* 3*s.*, for which, without any house or buildings, she paid 200*l.* She has on the hill thirty acres under perpetuity lease for which she pays 6*l.* 10*s.* ; but this is let at 30*l.* a year to a tenant who is two years in arrear, and is, moreover, allowing buildings and land to get into a miserably dilapidated state. Like owners of wider domains, Mrs. Swan at present has no redress.

The adjacent townland of Drumhaggart presents a group of rather better farmers, holding fifteen to sixty acres on leases renewable for ever. Richard Wylie has sixty acres, for which the Marquis of Donegall's agent draws annually 25*l.* ; but on his entering a year ago he bought the place out of court at 400*l.*, which was borrowed from the bank at 5 per cent. Sober, steady, and newly married, he may probably do well. Joseph Wylie has thirty acres, half of what his father had, for which he pays annually 14*l.* 10*s.* ; a good manager and careful, he gets along fairly. J. M'Naughar, blacksmith, bought his thirty acres out of court at Strabane five years ago for 300*l.*, pays 14*l.* 11*s.* 10*d.* of head rent to the Marquis of Donegall ; has built himself a good, substantial two-storied house, improved the weak, soft bog land, and has evidently the industry and energy which will insure his prospering. On the crown of the ridge at Lenimore are two brothers Foster, each holding perpetuity leases of thirty acres at a rental of

6*l.*, but neither making any headway. Adjacent is an example of a more successful owner, Mr. John English, who holds here under fee-farm grant 100 acres, for which he pays 20*l.* His father and grandfather held the place under perpetuity lease, which twenty years ago was converted into a fee-farm grant, necessitating a payment of 60*l.* His predecessors, although enjoying permanent possession, had done little towards improvement; but during the last twenty years a new house and buildings have been erected at a cost of about 800*l.* The hard, greenstone boulders are got out of the arable fields; draining and reclamation, costing 15*l.* to 20*l.* an acre, have been undertaken; fencing with surplus stones has been well done. Notwithstanding small returns and uncertain prospects, Mr. English is still a land-buyer, and near Birdstone, three miles distant, recently acquired thirty acres in fee-farm grant, for which he gave 1,100*l.*, the annual rent being 7*l.*

A most favourable type of a small proprietor is Mr. George Thomson, of Ballyarnott, whose grandfather took a lease of 100 acres from the Marquis of Donegall, and thirty-two years ago did away with the lives, paid 5*l.* each on the two unexpired, 14*l.* for expenses, and has now a fee-farm grant for ever at his unaltered rent of 29*l.* His county cess is 25*l.*, his poor rate 4*l.* He has built a house good enough for 500 acres, and barns, stabling, and shedding, costing altogether 1,500*l.* During the past twenty-five years drains and fences have absorbed 600*l.*; water is brought to house and buildings; liquid manure is taken care of. The farm has not produced all the money required for such improvements, but as it could be got it has been laid out. Mr. Thomson is constantly about, working and superintending. Everything is in good form, and big crops are grown. Besides his own lads, three or four men are employed regularly at 9s. and 10s. per week, with free houses, gardens, coals carted, and portions of potato-ground laboured. It would be most satisfactory if such a stamp of owner could be widely created. But it is difficult to find the proper material and the favourable surroundings, to endow the would-be owner with the needful ready money and the judgment to use it, to secure a subject as good as Mr. Thomson's, worth double that a mile back at Derryvane, with a pleasant south aspect and within three miles of a good town which takes the produce and returns manure.

Eight miles south-west of Londonderry, between Newtown Cunningham and Letterkenny, Lord Wicklow sold in 1875 the estate of Dundruff, comprising 2,500 acres, to the occupying tenants, at twenty-seven years' purchase on the rents, which were not excessive. Since becoming their own landlords evidences of increased exertion are already visible; houses are repaired more thoroughly and substantially, fields are squared, fences tidied, cultivation deepened. The tenants' antecedents fairly justified such success; they had always been steady and industrious; they were holders on an average of forty acres; they had enjoyed full security of tenure, and been judiciously helped by their landlord.

Mr. John G. Bowen, Lord Wicklow's agent, informs me that between 1848 and 1852 when times were bad 2,000*l*., borrowed from the Board of Works, had been laid out in draining at Dundruff, while either wholly or in part timber and slates were given to tenants who built two-storied houses suitable for their holding. Fifty years ago sixty-three tenancies were recorded on this estate. Only four were yearly tenancies; one was held in perpetuity; one under lease for eighteen years, or for one life from November 1811; fifty-seven under leases for twenty-one or thirty-one years, or one life, whichever continued longest; the great majority lasting forty to fifty years, secured a desirable permanence of occupation. During the currency of the leases rents of course could not be raised.

	£	s.	d.
At the period of sale, November 1875, the yearly rental of Dundruff, deducting tithe, was	1,525	1	6
The rental November 1825	1,176	7	3
	348	14	3

Thirty-three per cent. is a small advance for fairly cultivated landed property to make in fifty years.

Near St. Johnston, ten miles south of Londonderry, are about eighty perpetuity holders with fee-farm grants on good lands, portions of the old Donegal estates, averaging fifty acres, paying head rents varying from 2*s*. 6*d*. to 5*s*. an acre, many of them having been in possession for two generations. With the exception of about half a dozen, all are well-doing, out of debt, generally strenuous upholders of tenant-right, but with small sympathy for the Land League.

In the union of Newtown Limavady are several townlands which strikingly exhibit the evils of repeated subdivision. One of the worst is Drumraighland containing 753 statute acres, leased in 1700 to five holders. In 1799 it was in the hands of ten lessees for three lives, renewable for ever. At the last renewal of the lease, in 1846, it had got into possession of forty holders, who, with subtenants, now muster seventy-five householders. Thirty-eight have under an acre; twenty-two pay over 5*l*.; only three pay over 20*l*. The total valuation is 300*l*. Some idea of the wretched, dilapidated state of the sixty-one hovels and other buildings may be gathered from the fact that their total tenement valuation is only 57*l*. 18*s*. In many localities their value would be determined by the mud and old thatch they might furnish for manure and the few stones they could contribute for road-making. The wonder is that many are not condemned by the sanitary inspector. Many of the occupiers are the tenants of subtenants; most are untidy in person as well as in their wretched hovels. The lanes leading to the parts of the village which lie back from the main road are narrow, and almost impassable in wet weather. The land is undrained, inadequately fenced, and imperfectly tilled. The crops are miserable. Adjacent fields, let sometimes to outsiders at 30*s*. an acre, when drained and properly cultivated, yield, however, good returns.

Hamilton, a poultry dealer, rents a wretched hovel and ten acres for 15*l*. His landlord's payment for this is 2*l*. 10*s*. James Miller is a direct leaseholder of a house of somewhat better stamp and eight acres, in seven fields, not over well-fenced, and in which any stock must be tethered or herded to prevent their straying. He grows four acres of oats and about one acre each of potatoes and swedes. The Moore family, who fifteen years ago had fifty acres at 2*s*. 6*d*. per acre, too fond of the national beverage, could not make both ends meet, sold a few acres from time to time, and are now cleared out. Hunter Miller is a better specimen, a mason, as his father was before him. His family for generations have been at Drumraighland; but he declares he has made much more by his trade than by his land, which he describes as 'poor and callow in seven parks.' 'Men with deeded land,' Miller remarks, 'seldom do much work. In good and bad seasons, they are up and down like the scales of a balance; but many that go down seldom rise much again.' He has recently sold one of his pieces at the rate of 45*l.* an acre, but adds that he has bought as good for 25*l.* A few labourers live among these perpetuity holders, and have a poor time of it. Although there is plenty of work which ought to be done, there is no money to pay for labourers. The chief employer is Mr. James Forrest, who has seventy acres of land from the chief middleman at Griffith's valuation, and works it most satisfactorily along with freehold and other land, and was most indefatigable in furnishing me with information regarding this locality.

Mr. James Ogilby, the most extensive immediate leaseholder, in order to encourage reclamation in this and adjacent parishes, charges for his cleared bog 2*s.* 6*d.* per acre for the first seven years, 5*s.* for the subsequent seven, and 7*s.* 6*d.* for the remaining term, usually of thirty-one years. But neither among the bankrupt, easy-going owners, nor even among the fairly industrious occupiers, does he find much response to his offer. Irishmen of this class have not much faith in remote returns; their bread must come back before many days, otherwise it will not be cast upon the waters.

The adjacent townland of Drumore, extending to 200 acres with a Government valuation of 220*l.*, in 1713 was demised to five tenants. When, a few years ago, the leases were converted into perpetuities, there were fifteen, and since then the sub-tenants have greatly increased. Upper Culmore, comprising 141 acres, 100 years ago held by two, is now in the hands of twelve leaseholders, and several yearly tenants have besides come in. Both these places are in a miserably dilapidated and poorly cultivated state. Owing to the dissipated habits of its male population, the leaseholders in Culmore are chiefly widows; and sixty years ago, from the same cause, a similar state of matters is said to have occurred. The townland of Moys, in the parish of Carnick, presents analogous illustration of pauperising subdivision; 857 acres in 1713 were distributed among five leaseholders. When recently converted into perpetuities, there were fifteen holders, with four times that number of occupying tenants. Excluding half-a-dozen, I am told it would be difficult from the remainder of the holders to raise 20*l.*

This unprofitable subdivision is carried to even greater extent in many parts of Donegal, and also in Mayo and Galway. The poorer the district, the more it is usually practised. It occurs equally among occupiers and owners. It is effected often in spite of landlord and agent, and in defiance of office regulations. The small holder, whose hard battle against poverty should have convinced him of the inadequacy of his farm to bring up even one family decently, is ready cheerfully to divide it sometimes into more than two portions. The new Land Act should enforce very stringent measures against subdivision. The tenant subletting or allowing another family to settle on his holding should render himself liable to eviction. The yeoman or peasant proprietor of twenty acres or lesser area, until he has paid off the last shilling of his Government debt, although at liberty to sell *in globo*, should not be permitted to subdivide. When his last instalment is cleared off it will probably be impossible to prevent the small owner from carrying out his own views as to the size of his holding. In devising in the first instance the farm, whether for occupier or owner, the State should endeavour to prevent its being, as it now often is, inadequate to support even a careful and diligent tiller. It might also give facilities for bringing into more profitable working the rundale and other faulty arrangements. One or two obstructive tenants now frequently prevent, to their own and others' disadvantage, the carrying out of needful roads and draining operations. In manipulating estates with the view of creating peasant proprietors, it will never do to perpetuate rundale and other unprofitable distribution of land. The experiment, if made on some of the poorer, remote western townlands, will have to start with the ejectment of every tenant. Despite prejudice or opposition, the holdings must be squared or striped, and roads and main drains must be formed. These salutary arrangements will require to be made before the new owners are inducted into possession.

CHAPTER XIV.

DONEGAL MOUNTAIN ESTATES.

LORD Lifford's estate of Meen Glas, five miles from Stranorlar, extends to 11,210 statute acres, but realises the small annual rent of 825*l*. It is a characteristic type of a Donegal mountain estate, largely made up of rock and heather, bog and lake, over which blow the keen, ozonised Atlantic breezes, and on which are annually deposited about 50 inches of rain. Lord Lifford's great grandfather, in 1787, leased 500 acres for three lives, or forty-one years, to four tenants for 8*l*. 9*s*. 10*d*. The lessees undertook to make ditches, reclaim and divide the mountain land into parks of six acres, with 4-foot stone walls, or with clay and turf banks topped with thorn quicks, and also engaged to plant oak and ash for shelter. When the present Lord Lifford came to Meen Glas, forty-five years ago, his great grandfather's lessees had made none of these promised improvements. Nothing daunted, he believed that something might be made of the place. He was encouraged by the declaration of Arthur Young, who had stated that large portions of this mountain and bog might be converted into well-cultivated farms. Meen Glas, the largest town-land but one in Ireland, and measuring 4,444 acres, was then let for 10*l*. a year for grazing; only three families lived upon it. Roads and watercourses were the first step towards reclamation. Assisted in further outlay by the Board of Works, he expended 600*l*. on four miles of road ; at his own cost during the famine years made other three miles, and with slight help from the county added two miles more of needful roads.

Thirty-three farms, varying from forty to seventy acres, were applotted. Towards house-building, door frames and doors, window frames and windows were given, with 5*l*. to 10*l*. in aid of workmanship ; slates were also offered, but among these cold hills the people, perhaps wisely, prefer thatch. The farms for about ten years were rented at 1*s*. These tenants, being without capital, as so many of the poorer class of farmers still are in Ireland, required help until food was grown. Lord Lifford accordingly employed them during half of each week in making roads through his demesne, planting, forming gardens, and building a mansion-house. Many got tired of the arduous reclamation, failed to drain, as specified, their acre a year, and left ; but newcomers hopefully took up their holdings. Reclamation, however, proceeds slowly, cultivated lands and even gardens formerly taken in have been found profitless and allowed to revert to poor mountain grass. The tenants now number 140 ; only twenty-two pay more than 7*l*. of annual rent. Leases have been offered, but are not cared for ; liberty is accorded to dispose of the tenant-right, which is worth four or five years' rent, or occasionally more. Even here, where land is abundant, subdivision has to be guarded against. Daniel Burn had six acres of old cultivated land and a good house built by the landlord, for which his annual rent was 3*l*. 13*s*. ; contrary to regulation, he sublet two acres, for which he was receiving 9*l.* His landlord offered to allow him to remain at the rent he was charging his sub-tenant; not complying with this request he was evicted, but by decree of the County Court received in compensation 60*l.* Another tenant had sixty acres of low-lying, better land: he cut off twelve acres, for which he was to receive 5*l.* a year, and pocketed a premium of 62*l.*; another portion of six acres he made over to another tenant at 3*l.* a year, and received a premium of 42*l.* 10*s.* Having thus realised upwards of 100*l.* in hard cash from his land-hungry sub-tenants, he complains to his landlord that his farm does not pay.

I visited several of Lord Lifford's mountain tenants. John Lough has about 200 acres, occupied since 1846; his rent is 6*l.* 11*s.* 6*d.*; he grows a few acres of potatoes and oats, worked entirely by the spade, but depends much more upon grazing than tillage; he generally keeps six cows and about twenty young cattle. The poor, late grass is not very suitable for dairying, and, if each cow brings up her calf, she does not produce more than a firkin of butter. The little mountain two-year olds are seldom worth more than 5*l.* each. But two of them disposed of every year meet rent and rates. A pony is generally used for turf-cart and other purposes. Although there is plenty of land for the money, the profits of the farm are said to be small, and the sons, discouraged, have one by one left for America.

Peter Munday has forty acres, has occupied for thirty years, pays 1*l.* 13*s.* 5*d.* of rent; grows generally two acres of oats, and potatoes sufficient to supply his household; keeps two cows and five or six young things, and during the summer manages to sell seven pounds of butter a week, for which he has 10*d.* a pound. He has a young horse, chiefly used for carting turf to neighbouring villages. All tenants paying under 7*l.* of annual rent have thirty perches of turf-bank without charge, which secure an ample amount of fuel for two fires. Munday and others who sell turf pay 9*d.* per perch for all they dig above their allotted thirty perches, and, although there is much grumbling, Munday, after considerable cross-examination, allows that his payment of about 2*l.* for the privilege of this extra bog-cutting enabled him to realise about 20*l.* for turf sold.

George Key has had upwards of twenty-five acres for twenty-three years, pays 30*s.* of annual rent; the landlord, as is invariably the case in Ireland, takes on himself all poor-rates where the rental is under 4*l.* The county cess is 5*s.* He has built a tidy house and some shedding; keeps three or four cows, which yield ten pounds or twelve pounds of butter per week during summer; grows three acres of oats, yielding about three quarters an acre; plants fully an acre of potatoes for home consumption, and a few chains of swedes. All the tillage is done by hand labour; indeed the soft, spongy bog would seldom carry a horse. On these smaller holdings sheep cannot conveniently be kept within the fences; but Key and other tenants occasionally have a few, which are shackled at home during the winter and are turned on to the mountain in the summer. Key is an industrious, intelligent man, and from his crops and live stock, including a couple of pigs and poultry, appears to make a gross income of 45*l.* to 50*l.* annually.

Lord Lifford's most prosperous tenant is a Scotchman, who rents 7,000 acres of mountain for 50*l.* a year. In olden times this was let at one-fifth of its present rent. It generally carries 1,600 sheep and 100 cattle; two men are usually in charge of the stock. The sheep at present are chiefly Scotch black-faced. The ewes and lambs run on such a pasture cost in May 25s. to 30s.; the sheep eighteen months old, in autumn are worth 20s. to 25s.; a year later their price ranges from 27s. to 30s. From small and lowland farmers a good many sheep are taken in at a charge of 2s. to 2s. 6d. for the summer's run; two-year-old cattle are grazed for 5s.; three-year-old for 7s. 6d.

The people of this district of Donegal during the last twenty years have considerably improved. Their clay huts are superseded by stone and thatch houses. They are more tidily and better dressed, but their English manufactured costumes are not so stout and serviceable as the old home-spun, which is now little seen, while the women's shawls and mantles of common British style are less picturesque and durable than the home-made red and blue cloaks of the last generation. The extensive begging expeditions undertaken every summer by many families when the potatoes were hoed and nothing much remained to be done at home have fallen into desuetude. Many of the small people, saving a few shillings from time to time, have money in the bank. Some lend to their less fortunate neighbours at 10 per cent., but the priests endeavour to limit the rates to 6 per cent. Self-reliance has grown with education, and if undisturbed by agitators, who promise impossibilities, the people would be fairly contented.

Residing very constantly at Meen Glas, Lord Lifford, by example and precept, has greatly contributed to the improvement of his neighbourhood and people. He has planted ful'y 200 acres of timber, which should ameliorate the climate. Exposed to high winds and on soft peat so deep that the roots cannot penetrate to the subjacent blue clay or mica schist, the trees at first grew with disappointing slowness. The climate or surroundings must have changed since those preadamite periods when forests grew and decayed, bottled up indefinite amounts of sunshine, and formed these wide tracts of bog. Indeed, in some places the trees have been a failure, and among the stunted survivors within the demesne thousands of rhododendrons have been planted, and, although at an elevation of 600 feet, flourish wonderfully in the congenial bog. Three hundred acres of farming-land are in hand, have been drained at a cost of 5*l*., trenched at about the same expense, and enclosed with the too plentiful stones at a further outlay of about 2*l*. an acre. Much of this land has been top-dressed with marl-clay, found in occasional beds, and curiously producing, where it is applied, a plentiful crop of rushes. When first reclaimed, a few full crops were obtained; indeed, so good was the grass that one field was let for the summer at 45*s*. an imperial acre. But, like so much of this pasture on the peat, after two or three years it becomes soft, mossy, and thriftless. Liming and bones have been tried without much permanent benefit. An important redeeming feature is the fact that turnips and swedes are readily grown, and, when fairly manured and cultivated, reach twenty tons per acre. The most economical manner of consolidating and raising the fertility of these soft, poor lands is by growing roots with such yard manure as can be spared, liberally supplemented with a mixture of phosphates and ammonia, and feeding them where they grow and in adjacent fields by sheep furnished with hay and cotton cake.

Under the fostering care of a kindly, liberal, landlord

disposed to help all comers, and willing to give long leases, land is here offered along the side of good roads at 5s. an acre. Settlers, however, are slow to come; improvements proceed tardily. Extending railway communication may, however, help to people the waste. Connected with the Londonderry and Strabane terminus at Stranorlar, a narrow gauge line, thanks to the efforts of Lord Lifford, is being constructed across the estate through the wild Barnesmore gap sixteen miles to Donegal. In bad seasons, when his people are poorly off, and now more recently, when they are unsettled by agitation, Lord Lifford has serious misgivings whether his own labours and outlay of forty years and that of his tenants might not have been better bestowed. Without trouble and expense, the hill-grazing might have been more profitably retained for sheep, cattle, and grouse, of which fifty brace have been bagged on the 12th by four guns.

In the West of Ireland are numerous estates of mountain and bog of this poor, unsatisfactory character. The Marquis Conyngham, for example, has stretching away beyond Meen Glas 122,000 acres, from which his total rental, including old cultivated and more favourably lying land, is about 16,000*l.* a year. In these wild wastes, among the brown heather, the rocks and boulders, diversified by tracts of red bogs 15 feet to 20 feet deep, it is hopeless to plant either small occupiers or peasant proprietors. Cheaply as such estates may be bought, they are not the sort which a Government Commission or any philanthropic association would secure for the occupation of yeomen and peasant proprietors or to afford profitable location for the crowded-out occupiers of other places. Much better results to all concerned will accrue from the application of capital and labour to the more promising subjects, which even in Ireland are not yet exhausted or fully utilised.

The Earl of Arran has 6,883 acres in Donegal, and fully four times that area in Mayo. On the Donegal estate are ninety-eight tenants paying 5*l*. and under of annual rental; eighty-nine paying 5*l*. to 10*l*.; twenty-nine, from 10*l*. to 20*l*.; nineteen, from 20*l*. to 52*l*. while one pays 84*l*. There are, besides, thirty-seven holders of town parks, and the town of Donegal contributes considerable ground rents. For eighty years rents have been gathered annually in December. Thus, collecting the year's rent in one amount must be more difficult, especially for small tenantry, than the usual English method of making two half-yearly payments. Poor rates range from 1*s*. 6*d*. to 1*s*. 10*d*. per pound; county cess is 2*s*. The Earl is virtually his own agent, and manages his business and estate very economically. In 1847 and 1848 some draining was done, but the levels were not always kept; the main outfalls have not been attended to, and thousands of acres now lie wet and starved. Some timber and slates were wont to be given to tenants who were disposed to build, but since 1870 the very moderate help formerly accorded has ceased.

Messrs. Brassington and Gale made a fresh valuation twenty-four years ago, but no advantage is said to have been taken of tenants' improvements. As is usually the case, many good managers had, however, their ardour for improvements cooled by a considerable rise, while the neglectful and careless remained at their former valuations, or, perhaps, enjoyed small remissions. When this new valuation came into force in 1858, it was understood that there would be no further enhancement for twenty-one years. It is complained, however, that whenever a farm changes hand by sale, the new comer has to pay 25 per cent. on the old rent, thus proportionately diminishing the price obtained for the tenant-right. These sales average ten to twelve years' rental; a small holding rented at 3*l*. 12*s*. 6*d*. made 120*l*.; 32 acres, with a rental of 30*l*. 10*s*., sold for 320*l*.; another, formerly leased at 20*l*., on which the rent was advanced to 32*l*. 10*s*., nevertheless made 340*l*.; at the Lifford Assize for forty-six acres, bearing about 20*s*. per acre of rent, 400*l*. was awarded. The highest prices in the district have been given by men recently returned from America, who have been anxious to settle in the old country. On Lord Arran's property there have been since 1871 twenty sales. Where the same holding has shortly changed hands no extra rent has been imposed on the second buyer; last year, owing to the reduced demand, tenancies changing hands had only 7 per cent. added to the rent.

Repeated advances of rent and the consequent reduction in the value of the tenant-right are stated by occupiers to arrest their improvements, and certainly little or nothing is done; many buildings are in a state of ruinous dilapidation; and, despite the teaching of the agriculturists whom his lordship was wont to keep for the praiseworthy purpose of instructing his ignorant smaller tenants, much of the land is slovenly and imperfectly cultivated. The Land League enjoys the confidence of the tenantry, and holds them back from the settlement of rents, which should be paid annually in December. From the purely agricultural tenants nothing has been received for 1880; although an abatement of 10 per cent. was offered on the rent of 1879, only half of it has been paid; while, in spite of an extra reduction being promised, some of the arrears of 1878 are still outstanding. Tenants, if they pay, are, or pretend to be, afraid of 'Boycotting.' The town parks, as is often the case, are a source of some controversy, and have led to ill-advised litigation. Where no houses or buildings are upon them, and they have not been used as occupation farms, the tenant rightly has no claim to payment for disturbance ; but on their changing hands, although there is no recognised tenant-right, money constantly passes between the out-going and the in-coming tenant, and it is obviously difficult for any landlord or for any legislation to prevent this.

Robert Hamilton rents forty-seven Irish acres from the Earl of Arran. His grandfather held it on lease for 7*l.*, and put up the house and buildings ; on the termination of his agreement his rent was raised to 17*l.* ; with a smaller intermediate increase, it was fifteen years ago advanced to 42*l.* ; Griffith's valuation is 28*l.* 5*s.* A pair of horses, three cows, five two-year-olds, and the same number of calves and yearlings are the present live stock. The tenant complains that bad seasons and high rent have gradually consumed his limited capital. Without much outlay, the buildings, fences, and roads might be much improved ; a few pounds expended in draining would evidently yield an immediate return ; more thorough cultivation and liberal manuring might add considerably to the tillage crops. The tenant's resources appear however to be exhausted, and, as he is an active member of the League, his landlord will probably be little disposed to extend the needful help. This is no singular case. Numbers of Donegal tenants, even on the lower, better land, for several years have been losing ground, and like their English brethren, have not now sufficient means to undertake needful work, or even to buy the required live stock. Among other circumstances against them is the cost of labour, which has doubled in twenty years. Labourers' wages are 7*s.* to 8*s.* a week; servant lads in the house receive 5*l.* a year; two years ago the wages of such boys were 50 per cent. higher.

Mr. Thomas Brooke, of Lough Eske, three miles north of Donegal, has recently sold some outlying estates, but still retains about 15,000 acres bringing in an annual rental of nearly 1,500*l.* Draining, fences, and roads are kept in good order. A considerable proportion is farmed by himself; 300 acres are under superior arable cultivation; about twenty-five labourers have constant employment, are well housed, have 1 to 5 acres of land at a nominal rent, most keep a cow, their money wages range from 6*s.* to 9*s.* per week, they are well looked after in health and sickness, and are evidently much better off than the smaller tenantry. Mr. Brooke's farming, intelligently managed, with adequate capital, yields fair profits, and his system more generally pursued might find profitable occupation for a portion of the surplus population and small holders, who very generally are unable to find employment for more than half their time, hence lapse into idle and careless habits, and are a loss to the State.

A mile down the bay from the town of Donegal by boat, but five miles round by car, is Bell's Isle, on which stands Mr. Arthur H. Foster's commanding castellated house and estate of about 3,000 acres. He has had no changes of rent and scarcely any of tenancy for forty years; has enjoyed the reputation of being a kind, indulgent landlord; has about seventy tenants, most of them paying less than 10*l.* of annual rent. To find work for the unemployed in 1847-48 he built a sea-wall and enclosed from the tide a considerable area of useful slob-land. Although the tenants have no tangible cause of complaint and are generally under Griffith's valuation, they have only paid one half-year out of the last four. Two months ago they conferred with their landlord as to the amount of abatement to which they were entitled; but, although admitting that they were not over-charged and that they had the money, they would not pay, and have not yet done so. Thousands of landlords in the West of Ireland are in a similar predicament. Unable to obtain a shilling even from well-to-do tenants, they have to meet rent charges, settlements, often interest on borrowed money, with rates and taxes.

Mr. Foster informs me that tenant-right is extending in this southern portion of Donegal. Despite the bad times, small holdings are still much in demand by the downtrodden labourers, whose precarious employment and the high price which they have to pay for their cabins, their potato-ground, and even for their milk and vegetables, make them keen competitors for the possessory interest in a few acres of land. Some of these small plots, when they change tenants, realise as much as fifty years' rental, while those of twenty-five or thirty acres do not bring more than ten or twelve years' rental.

On the light sand soil of Bell's Isle Mr. Foster was wont to grow 100 acres of potatoes, but finding labour less reliable and more expensive, he now restricts his area to fifteen acres; he grows about thirty acres of oats, a few swedes, and occasionally some rye and flax; he generally has sixty head of cattle; but on the 1,000 acres he keeps in hand rabbits are his most profitable crop. The sandhills, strips of plantation, and even the lawn swarm with them. During five summer months four men are regularly employed to trap, snare, and net. The produce chiefly goes to Birmingham and Manchester, at 2s. 2d. to 2s. 3d. per couple. The demand exceeds the supply; thousands of acres, of sand and other light soil, not worth 5s. an acre, extending along this and other Irish coasts, might similarly be devoted to this useful article of food. When fully stocked upwards of 3,000 couples are every year readily got from 800 acres.

Adjacent to Bell's Isle is the glebe of Drumholme, valued at 600*l.* a year, sold in 1872, some of it at twenty, some at twenty-five, and some at thirty-three years' purchase. The occupiers generally made over their right of preemption to two middlemen, who apparently have dealt fairly with their twenty-eight tenants. Six occupiers, the largest of thirty acres, took up their right. Three had to borrow the 25 per cent. of the total purchase-money which the Church Commissioners required should be paid down. Two at present express themselves dissatisfied with their bargains; one of these has already been endeavouring to dispose of his small estate. The 25 per cent. which he has sunk in the purchase he declares has absorbed more than he possesses, and he is left without capital for cultivation. This would be frequently a serious difficulty in the proposed conversion of impecunious Irish occupiers into thriving owners.

CHAPTER XV.

ESTATES IN DONEGAL AND SLIGO.

The Conolly estates were once the finest in the north-west of Ireland; one portion, between Bendrouse-bridge and Bellick, was seven miles long and two wide; the Ballyshannon and Parkhill properties were held direct from the Crown. The management was formerly of the old-fashioned, free-and-easy, feudal type; rents were low, they had not been advanced for fifty years, were irregularly paid, and never pressed for. On many townlands, especially round the coast, subdivision and subletting, and the introduction of squatters unchecked ran to a ruinous extent. Forty years ago Colonel Conolly vainly endeavoured to reduce this over-crowding and double up his small holdings. He is stated to have built 1,000 slated or well-thatched houses, or contributed 10*l.* to tenants who would put their cottages in decent order. The widows throughout the wide estate had an annual payment of 40*s.* or 50*s.* each, and rent was seldom asked from them. Throughout all his difficulties Colonel Conolly never withdrew these bounties. Under the able agency of Mr. Alexander Hamilton, on many townlands the farms were squared or striped. Tenants were never turned out, and, without charge, enjoyed the privileges of turbary and sea-ware. For 1*s.* a year as much turf as the family required was cut, and little restriction was placed upon selling turf. The estates mustered about 3,000 tenants. During the twelve years they were in Chancery and their interests well administered by Major Hamilton, he informs me that he never brought the sheriff either to execute eviction or seizure under process.

But horse-racing and gambling brought serious difficulties on the generous-hearted but improvident county family. Running the American blockade is said to have sacrificed a quarter of a million sterling, and large portions of the Conolly property have been sold in the Encumbered Estates Court. They have fallen into very various hands, and have been most diversely dealt with. In more than one instance efforts were made to dispose of townlands to the occupiers, but, as almost invariably happens, this was rendered impossible owing to the inconsiderable number of tenants able to pay down the required one-third of the purchase money. In a few instances previous rents remained untouched. Not infrequently they have been repeatedly raised, sometimes to much more than double their former figure. Consideration was not always shown to the industrious improving tenant. Disregarding the fact that he or his father had made the fairly productive land out of worthless mountain or bog, the full occupying value was put upon it. In the change of owners, careless, incompetent agents and unscrupulous, self-aggrandising bailiffs, who have caused many of the land difficulties in Ireland, sometimes managed to secure for themselves or their friends farms or portions of farms for which small or no compensation was given to former tenants. There being no agreements and few leases, these small holders had to submit sometimes to unfairness and hardship. Almost at any rent and under any conditions they cling to their holdings. Even with forty years of national schools they have not yet learnt the importance of short agreements, setting forth their obligations and rights. Clever enough in making other bargains, they show much unwisdom in those relating to land. Even where there was much over-crowding the new purchasers made few evictions. A tenant paying say 40*s.* of yearly rent if evicted and sent to the poor-house, with an average family of five, costs his parish about 15*s.* a week. Where many of the tenants are under the 4*l.* valuation, parochial relief is extensive and frequent, rates often reach 4*s.* to 5*s.* per pound, and largely fall upon the landlord. Of 730 tenants on one estate in this neighbourhood only fifteen reach 4*l.* of annual valuation and pay poor rates. Small tenants, although more squeezable than larger, and often charged relatively high rents, thus entail heavy charges on an estate, and, moreover, in bad times are uncertain in their payments.

Lettermacaward estate, occupying 5,500 acres in the barony of Boylagh, on Gweebarra Bay, was bought from Mr. Thomas Conolly, M.P., in 1867, by Charles Deazeley, M.D., of Pembroke. It comprised 239 tenants. The difficulty in satisfactorily dealing with such a subdivided property may be gathered from the fact that 161 of the tenants were rented at less than 2*l.* ; sixty-two ranged from 2*l.* to 5*l.* ; ten paid between 5*l.* and 10*l.* ; only five were over 10*l.* and under 20*l.* ; while only one was charged more than 20*l.* The estate was striped, which is the first stage of evolution from the ruder state of rundale. Several lots of about 100 acres of sandhills, rough pasture, bent grass, and rabbit warrens were held as common among ten to twenty adjacent tenants; the rents were moderate, in some instances less than 2s. an acre; buildings and any other improvements had been done by the tenants. Although rents have not been much advanced, the people do not prosper as they should do, and last year furnished a large contingent of applicants for the several relief funds. Mr. S. Teeven, a solicitor, bought 2,051 acres of the Conolly estate at about thirty years' purchase; immediately raised the rents; the tenants rebelled. The difficulty was settled by arbitration, but arrears accumulate. Mr. Ebenezer Bustard, seven years ago, bought 10,000 acres—a very fine tract of land. Although he has not raised rents, there has been some indiscreet management, and even before the present agitation payments were not well met. Possibly there was disappointment among some of the well-to-do tenantry that they were unable to buy up their holdings. Forty of them, I am told, were ready with a moiety of the purchase-money; but the others being unable to find the means, the estate was disposed of entire. Mr. Thomas Dixon, soon after his purchase, doubled his rental; his tenants last year, and again this year, demanded a deduction of 25 per cent.; they got 20 per cent., and some rents are said to have been paid. Several townlands of the Conolly estate, near Ardera, so soon as the new owner came into possession, had the rental doubled, some farms were tripled. Many of the rents on these townlands are exorbitant.

The Messrs. John and James Musgrave, of Belfast, have dealt more liberally with the four estates which they bought through the Encumbered Estates Court, the first of them a dozen years ago. They comprise 52,000 acres in the southwest of Donegal, including fishing hamlets and mountain farms, supporting a population of upwards of 8,000 persons. In dealing with their estates hitherto yielding a rental of only 4,200*l*., the Messrs. Musgrave present a striking contrast to the unconscionable rapacity and determination to get the most out of the tenants which has characterised so many purchasers in the Landed Estates Court. That portion bought from the Conolly trustees cost 27,000*l*.; the part leased in perpetuity was valued at twenty years' purchase, the remainder in yearly tenancies at twenty-nine years' purchase. On this, as on the three other estates, virtually no change of rent has been made. During twelve years to 1879 on the Conolly portion alone 12,000*l*. was expended in substantial improvements; one-half of this was for wages. Desirous to find work for the unemployed, within the twelve months ending Michaelmas, 1880, 5,000*l*. more was expended. The Murray-Stewart portion of the estate, bought in May 1879, is now coming in for its share of improvements. On the development of the Donegal property since it was acquired one-and-a-half the net income has been spent. On the several portions of the estate about 11,000 acres are let on fee-farm lease, the remainder partly on terminable leases, but the greater part is in the hands of yearly tenants. Most of the land is almost in a state of nature. The old system of 'rundale' has, however, been long abandoned, and each townland is divided so as to give every tenant a properly defined farm with the right to graze cattle and sheep on the mountain pasture of his townland in proportion to the size of his farm. The state of agriculture, however, is very backward, thorough draining and trenching being unknown. Much of the low-lying land consists of shallow bog resting on a gravelly subsoil. Advised by experienced agriculturists that the produce of the estate could be increased fourfold by sheep drains on the mountain pasture, and judicious draining and trenching in the valleys where the land is capable of raising root crops for winter feeding, Messrs. Musgrave have purchased from some of the occupiers their tenant-right in a tract sufficient to make a model farm, and are now engaged in considerable reclamations which give much useful employment, and when completed will, it is hoped, convince the tenantry of the advantages of a liberal scientific treatment of the soil. It is their intention also to introduce superior breeds of sheep and cattle, of which their tenants will have the advantage.

Much of this isolated country, formerly traversed only by donkeys with panniers, has been opened by good roads; a handsome hotel has been built at a cost of 5,000*l.*; money has been liberally contributed for the making of piers; 700*l.* was given towards the narrow-gauge line projected from Stranorlar to Donegal; 1,000*l.* was spent last winter in labour for the unemployed; of 7,800*l.* borrowed from the Board of Works, fully one-half has been expended in roads and draining; and, although yielding no enhanced rents, surely all this outlay must improve the condition of the tenantry? The expenditure has been judiciously and carefully made.

These are the sort of landlords that were expected to rescue the neglected, pauperised properties from the Irish Encumbered Estates Court. Here and there a few of them have made their mark and shown what judiciously applied capital can do even in Ireland. No Land Act will attempt to confiscate their improvements, or, without compensation, compel spirited landowners to confer on their improved yearly tenants perpetuity leases at the old rents of fifty years ago, or even at Griffith's valuation. In determining that difficult equation, a fair rent, while, on the one hand, the tenant's outlay is taken into account, on the other, the landlord's outlay, if adding to the letting value of the holding, must likewise be carefully considered.

The mountain farms, both on the Glen-Columbkille and Kilcar sides of Teelin Bay, with their patches of arable, range from five to eighteen acres; several are over 100 acres; the tenant-right is worth twenty to thirty years' purchase; one farm with a good house, rented at 6*l.*, in September last realised 205*l.* The townlands around Kilcar village furnish many fairly well-to-do tenants. In a pamphlet written for private circulation Mr. James Musgrave states that some districts, 'such as Teelin Bay, Tauney Bay, and Cashel, are densely over-populated, principally where people can supplement the produce of their farms by fishing. There is little actual subdivision of farms, but two or three families will sometimes live under one roof, and on the produce of one small farm. There is also another class located close to the sea, who came here some twenty years ago, when the herring and cod-fishing was good, and who squatted themselves on the lands held by yearly tenants. These people have no land, and now, when the fish have gone farther from the coast where they cannot be followed in open boats, and there is neither capital nor the skill to provide or manage the necessary deep-sea fishing-smacks, the condition of this class is at all times little short of famine. You may say, "Why not remove them?" I answer, "We could not, even if we wished, as they pay us no rent, and could only be dispossessed by evicting the tenants on whose farms they are, and if dispossessed we should not know what to do with them."'

To elevate and enrich the people in these remote districts, forty miles from railroads or good markets, Mr. Musgrave would introduce railroads and steamboats, would desire Government to advance money on sound security, and on the same principle as for ordinary agricultural improvements. Such facilities would reduce the rate of carriage, which is now 50*s.* per ton for ordinary agricultural produce transported from Carrick to Londonderry. Produce accordingly falls low—chickens are worth 3*d.* ; ducks 6*d.* ; geese 2*s.* ; cod-fish $3\frac{1}{2}d.$ Of such small value are poultry, and so meagre the demand excepting for breeding purposes, that so soon as their sex is known, cockrells and ganders are systematically knocked on the head. Local manufactures also deserve encouragement. A glove-knitting factory has been started, which is already paying wages at the rate of 1,000*l.* a year. The abundant water-power at the head of Teelin Bay is likely to be utilised in the establishment of a button factory and power-loom hosiery. Lastly Mr. Musgrave enjoins that the national schools undertake technical instruction in various trades, including farming —useful instruction which, he believes, will develop more industry and enterprise to be employed either at home or in some more productive sphere.

Trinity College, Dublin, were extensive landowners in Donegal and other counties. Under a recent Act they have now merely a head-rent varying according to a scale of prices. During last century they proved liberal landlords. Many townlands were leased, usually to middlemen, who sublet them to the immediate occupiers. Leases for twenty-one years appear to have been the full term that the college would then grant. The rents were often merely nominal. Before these leases had run many years, a renewal, on the same terms, was applied for. A fine, sometimes equivalent to the rent, was generally exacted; there was thus nineteen or twenty years' possession always to the credit of the tenant. About the beginning of the present century, the college began to increase their rents in the following manner :—Supposing the rent was 100*l.* a year, and the fine annually paid for the new lease 100*l.*, on applying at the end of the first year for a renewal the college would give twenty years at 100*l.* and the twenty-first year at 150*l.* At the next renewal, twelve months later, there would be nineteen years at 100*l.* and two at 150*l.* Sometimes, when ten years had thus passed, the rent would be raised to 200*l.* At first the tenants had a great pull, because, the fine and rent being equal, if the college refused to renew, they only got half their income for twenty years. When, however, the rent crept up and the fine remained the same, the tenants were in the power of the college, and rents were raised still more quickly. It is stated that no account was taken of the fact that houses, buildings, and all improvements had been effected by the tenants. The college never spent one sixpence, had no resident agent or bailiff, subscribed to nothing, and usually got from one-half to two-thirds of the gross rental. Fearing to have their interest on the estates, which many of them held for generations, confiscated by further accessions to rent, the lessees in 1851, joined the college in applying for an Act to convert the twenty-one years' leases into perpetuities.

This Act empowered the college to grant leases, without fines, for periods of 99 years, and also in perpetuity; tenants had the option of converting their terminable into perpetuity leases. The annual rent is directed to be ascertained from Government valuations or by arbitration based on the standard prices of commodities, and liable every ten years to variation with the varying average prices of agricultural produce. Exclusive of any rent-charge and interest on unpaid fines, the rent is estimated as follows:—Five-elevenths is represented and regulated by oats, one-eleventh each by wheat and mutton, two-elevenths by beef and butter. The standard prices thus paid for 112 lbs. of these articles were as follow:—Wheat, 8s. 4d.; oats, 5s. 6d.; beef, 41s. 1½d.; mutton, 47s. 1½d.; butter, 64s. 6d. The proportion of oats to other produce has been considerably reduced since 1851, and a schedule adapted for the present day would diminish the oats and increase the proportion of meat and dairy produce.

The regulation of rent by the valuation of agricultural commodities demands at present special consideration, as it is likely to be adopted as one of the few conditions which will alter, probably at intervals of twenty-one years, the rents of Irish tenants occupying tillage lands. In the neighbourhood of Ballintra, Trinity College have large estates, now generally let on these perpetuity leases, and bringing in probably 5,000*l.* a year.

The Trinity College produce prices were fixed on the average of 1848, 1849, and 1850, which, unluckily for the lessees, were the lowest years in the present century. Had the whole decennial period of 1840–1850 been taken, a fairer standard would have been secured. Prices, determined as they were by the averages of Dublin and Cork, represent much higher figures than are obtainable in West Donegal remote from markets and with imperfect transport facilities. Since prices and rents were thus determined in 1851 they have been raised about 20 per cent. in 1865, and 10 per cent. in 1875.

The subtenants, the actual cultivators, under these college leases enjoy unusual security, they were never liable to the periodical advances exacted from the middlemen, and their rents now do not rise and fall as those of their superiors do with varying prices. Without fines for the renewal of leases, it has been decided that these actual occupiers are entitled to fee-farm grants at the old rents. Many are now charged the same rents as they were in 1826, whilst their superiors are paying Trinity College in rent and fine just double the charge then made.

When the Act of 1851 was passed several of the middlemen preferred to run out their old leases. Where the rent and fine were equal or nearly so, they derived an advantage. Taking in illustration an estate where the annual rent and fine are each 100*l.*, and the gross rental 400*l.*, the profit rent would be 200*l.*, less agency, bailiffs and poor rates, probably amounting to 40*l.* a year. Running out the old lease the account would stand thus:

Gross annual rental	£400
Deducting college rent, and expenses	140
	£260

When the estate was thrown up at the end of twenty years, this would amount to 5,200*l.*

The tenant taking out his fee-farm grant would pay the college—

For rent and fine during first 10 years	£200
Charge of 10 per cent., making it perpetuity	20
Agency and poor rates, as before	40
	£260

During the second ten years his rent is further advanced 20 per cent., raising it to 260*l.* and with agency and poor rates bringing it to 300*l.*

Under the fee-farm grant, the profits would therefore be

First 10 years at 140*l.*	£1,400
Second 10 years at 100*l.*	1,000
	£2,400

As prices at present stand another rise of 10 per cent. is now imposed, reducing the annual profit on the estate to 80*l.*, and as this is the tail end of the 400*l.* gross it would not be worth full money. Such calculations indicate that no great profits have accrued to the college tenants who have converted their terminable into perpetuity holdings.

Major Hamilton, J.P., of Brownhall, holds one of these college estates for which his rent is 1,000*l.* a year; it has been in his family for over two centuries. On the handsome house, grounds, and plantations a great deal of judgment and taste as well as money have been expended, and the Major's energy and example, as well as his own good farming, have been of great value to his liberally-treated tenantry and to his neighbours.

Looking for other phases of land tenure, I come upon the Ballymagroty townlands, overhanging the road between Ballintra and Ballyshannon—100 years ago, I am told, held at 2*s.* 6*d.* an acre by one lessee. Thriftless and extravagant, he and his heirs gradually subdivided. On 534 acres, valued by Sir Richard Griffith at 317*l.*, there are now thirty holders with perpetuity leases, paying among them an annual head-rent of 57*l.* collected and brought in by the principal tenant. Many townlands are thus let to one man 'and company ;' all the tenants are individually and severally answerable for the rents, which are collected and brought to the office in one sum, the impecunious being often indebted to their better-off neighbours for an advance to pay their portion. The people here are Protestants ; the larger holders are doing best, but the smaller are rapidly recovering from their difficulties and debts incurred during the disastrous year of 1879.

Amid so many absentees, it is always gratifying to meet with an enterprising resident proprietor like Mr. Johnson, who has lived at Kinlough for nearly fifty years, and devoted himself to the intelligent management of his estate, which, if the rents were paid, should bring in 5,000*l.* a year. He has 640 tenants, a few paying over 30*l.* yearly, the great majority under 6*l.* Leases are not sought for. The rental of the drift clay and bog soil averages 6*s.* to 7*s.* per acre. In 1849 he borrowed 5,000*l.* from the Board of Works, and drained 2,000 acres, 3 or 4 feet deep, usually with 2 to 3 inch pipes. With the low rate of wages then current, and with home-made pipes at prime cost, much of this was done at about 3*l.* an acre. Not one shilling of interest or any sort of extra rent has been charged for this outlay ; but rents are as badly paid as where they have been repeatedly and excessively advanced. With other landlords in the poorer parts of Ireland, Mr. Johnson is fully alive to the difficulty of preventing suicidal subdivision. No man, he urges, can live as he should do on less than twenty-five to thirty acres. He would gladly remove all tenants whose valuation is below 10*l*. Here, as elsewhere, potatoes are the sheet-anchor of the small cultivator; if they fail, he is destitute. From want of care in selecting and changing seed, from persistently planting the small tubers, from lazily growing them continuously on the same soil, they have become more precarious and less productive. The most successful growers change the seed and the land, use lime, and are only now beginning to realise the importance of turning up their land roughly and exposing it to the winter frost. Tenant-right has not been recognised, but practically it matters not, for changes of tenancy are most rare. Notwithstanding his lifelong, unwearied efforts in their behalf, Mr. Johnson sorrowfully admits that his tenantry have not made encouraging progress. The obstacles to prosperity are the damp climate, poor soil, small holdings, and indisposition for continuous, steady work.

Similar results are met with even on the Hon. Evelyn Ashley's Malamore estates, where, in the hands of Lord Palmerston and subsequently of Mr. Cowper-Temple, a very liberal outlay was made, and all that money and enterprise could effect was done for the comfort and prosperity of the tenantry. The benefits of this continued, systematic help have, however, been greatly minimised by the hopelessly small holdings, and not infrequently by the indolence of the people. Rents, even at Malamore, are badly paid, and, despite large allowances made last year, 33 per cent. is the abatement demanded from the rent of 1880. The more that is done for some people, the less they are disposed to do for themselves. The Irish peasantry are capital traders, they are clever at making a bargain, are born orators, politicians, and agitators, but, unfortunately, they seldom have the steady capabilities which make good farmers. Yet agriculture, unluckily, is their main resource.

Desirous to visit some small owners, I drove from Ballyshannon, *viâ* Bandoran, which is now becoming a popular watering-place, through a wild and mountainous country to Manor Hamilton. In this district Land League terrorism has full sway; men suspected of paying rent are waylaid at night or dragged out of bed, stripped, unscrupulously seated in the embers of their own fires, and hackled among the abundant furze; clothes and other property are burnt or thrown into the rivers. So great is the general intimidation that the unfortunate victims dare not give evidence against their assailants. Two landlords accused of advancing rents were Boycotted; the stables of one have been burnt down. Close to the scene of this conflagration, five miles north of Manor Hamilton, is the glebe of Killasnell, in county Leitrim, extending to 300 acres, bought seven years ago by twenty-five tenants at eighteen years' purchase, on a moderate rental. James Devaney, the largest holder, has twenty-two acres; none have less than five acres, or grass for two cows; six were able to pay up the whole of their purchase-money; one expects to clear off in ten years; all express themselves satisfied, declare that they have 'good courage to improve,' or that 'they feel that by-and-by there will be no rent to pay.' Their cottages are whitewashed and tidy. Poor rates cost 1s. 1d.; county cess 1s. $\frac{1}{2}d$. The land is tolerably good, most of it being in grass and well watered; a great deal of waste, however, occurs from unnecessary crooked walls, wide ditches, and meandering watercourses, and it is impossible to get a wheeled carriage over the devious, narrow pathways which run from the main road half a mile up to some of the small farms. In the remote corner of the parish is the Glencar glebe of fifty acres, which was bought seven years ago, chiefly by the tenants, on a twenty-one years' rental. The land is good, was wont to realise 40s. an acre, and the embryo owners are doing well.

CHAPTER XVI.

SIR HENRY GORE-BOOTH'S SLIGO ESTATES.

ESTATES in Sligo present a large proportion of absentees, who withdraw large rentals from the country, who spend little in developing their inheritance, and relegate their authority to agents more or less competent, sometimes non-resident. Hitherto there has been small excuse for continuous absenteeism. The landlord now, with some reason, complains that the attractions of his estate are diminished; that he has no political power; that his right of sport is interfered with, hunting is sometimes interdicted, his game is destroyed by a few refractory tenants and by poaching intruders, and shooting on moor and bog, formerly productive, is reduced in value. The tenantry, moreover, are less trustful, friendly, and pleasant to meet, even if they are not positively evil-disposed. This rupture between landlord and tenant has, unfortunately, extended to the estates even of kindly resident proprietors.

In the best districts of Sligo the farms range from thirty to fifty acres. There is much more pasture than tillage. The subsoil is generally limestone and gravel. Even where drained, unless this primary improvement is followed up by tillage, the land is prone to grow rushes, and the grass becomes rough and coarse. Rents average about 20s. an acre, but lands are generally let according to the head of cattle they will carry, and range from less than Griffith's valuation to 100 per cent. over it. Although not excessive and seldom raised except in the case of estates that have changed hands, they are probably as much as can be afforded under the prevailing non-recuperative style of farming. Changes of tenancy are not common. They only occur among the smaller improvident holders. There are few evictions; tenant-right is not generally recognised; landlords have usually objected to it, on the plea that it swallows up the in-comer's capital and costs the landlord a fancy figure if he desires to double up several holdings or take farms into his own hands. Last autumn 50*l.* was paid for the possessory interest of a poor, swampy holding rented at 11*l.*; 40*l.* was offered for a tenancy at will rented at 7*l.*; for forty acres, moderately rented, 300*l.* was given. Landlords lay out nothing in improvements; the buildings erected by tenants are of a limited, pristine description, rough, not always very durable, frequently placed in the wrong spot, and their imperfections sometimes conveniently concealed by a liberal dressing of lime-wash. Leases are decreasing, and are seldom asked for or given, except to the larger tenants; but a few granted even since 1870 recognise a limited tenant-right.

The Land Act of 1870 here, as elsewhere, has certainly checked landlords' outlay, and has not proportionally increased tenants' improvements. It has not, as has sometimes been asserted, increased litigation; comparatively few appeals against exorbitant rents are brought under the cognisance of the County Court judge. Throughout Sligo there is a good deal of waste land, by some still estimated at 100,000 acres. But this includes the moor and bogs of the

Ox Mountains, where a considerable elevation interferes with successful cultivation. The improvements on the mountain undertaken upwards of thirty years ago by the Irish Waste Land Company, on the west of Lough Easky, I am told, have not generally proved remunerative. Reclamation, unless followed up by proper tillage, as already stated, rarely answers; the coarse grasses assert supremacy, and soft, boggy soils, unless fertilised with phosphates and mineral salts, and firmed by clay, sand, or cultivation, shortly produce only poor, innutritive herbage. In Sligo, as in so many other counties, by draining, by more liberal cultivation, by more careful collection and husbanding of manure, greatly better returns may be obtained from the cleared bogs already reclaimed and from pastures now wet, sour and neglected.

Mr. Owen Wynne has estates in the contiguous counties of Sligo and Leitrim; for many years they have been judiciously managed by Mr. J. M. Olpherte. Mutual trust and good feeling until last year have subsisted between the office and the tenantry, who have remained unchanged for generations. During thirty years the sheriff has only evicted six tenants for hopeless arrears. Rents are moderate; there are no periodical additions; they were reduced in the bad seasons, beginning with 1846, and were revised in 1855; on both properties they are under Griffith's valuation. The county cess and half the poor-rates are paid by the office. Reductions offered both in 1879 and 1880 have not yet secured satisfactory settlements. The tenants, however, are perfectly able, although not willing, to pay. Mr. Wynne has always acknowledged a limited tenant-right, generally of three years' rent, and paid also for any permanent improvements effected by the tenant. There was seldom, however, except on the pastoral holdings, which are the rule in this district, a *quid pro quo* for the payment, and he has discountenanced larger premiums, especially as the money was usually borrowed at 6 or 8 per cent., and thus tended to the impoverishment of the holder. A few leases for thirty-one years, and others for the life of the tenant, have been granted. Unless contributing to the price of the slates, no assistance is given by the landlord in buildings. Recent wet seasons have shown that large areas might profitably be drained. Mr. Wynne's Sligo rental is 5,600*l.*; from this there are deducted cess and half the poor rates, amounting to 570*l*. The Government valuation is 4,970*l*. The Leitrim estate measures 15,436 acres, the rental is 4,650*l*., the rates allowed are 550*l*., the Government valuation is 4,370*l*.

Sir Henry Gore-Booth, of Lissadell, on the sudden death of his father's agent, undertook the charge of the estates which he now owns, and managed them most successfully for ten years, inaugurating a very thorough system of accounts and book-keeping, which are sadly deficient on some Irish estates. Since his accession to the property in 1876, he has continued to direct the general management. Few owners or agents have such intimate knowledge of their tenantry, their holdings or their necessities. The people have been wont to come to Sir Henry as their adviser and friend, as their arbiter in family feuds, and as their depositary for wills and marriage settlements. He has a curious, carefully kept record of the troubles, disputes, and condition of his poor neighbours. In settling difficulties, his intervention has prevented much litigation, a pugnacious pastime in which even the poorer class of Irish are too fond of indulging.

The estate of Lissadell, on the coast, six miles north-west

of Sligo, and at Ballymote, fourteen miles south of the town, together measure 31,774 acres. Griffith's valuation is 16,774*l.* The actual rental is 15,000*l.*, putting a reasonable valuation on the house and demesne, where the planting and arrangements made forty years ago testify to the taste and judgment of the late Sir Robert Gore-Booth. His neighbours and tenants declare him to have been a model country gentleman, kindly hearted and liberal, ever ready to aid and improve his people, most zealous and helpful during the famine years of 1846–48, when it is said he spent 40,000*l.* in food and other assistance.

The present baronet does not think that the Land Act of 1870 has been altogether a success. With the increased security conferred on the tenant it enabled him to get more credit than was good for him; commodities not always needed or fitting were pressed on both man and wife; the necessity of payment seemed far deferred; and when bad times came other creditors were often more exacting than the landlord. The pauper tenant received handsome remuneration for being cleared out of his wretched hovel, his hopelessly small holding, his debts and difficulties. The better man, with a farm valued at more than 50*l.* of annual rent and who has probably expended thereon much more labour and capital, deserves recognition and some protection against disturbance. In some parts of the country the Act of 1870 has provoked disputes and litigation, sometimes increased by a certain class of lawyers; but no such annoyances have occurred in this part of Sligo. Frequent revaluations, or even the prospect of them, unsettle tenants and check the little enterprise they might otherwise exert.

On the Lissadell estate are 522 tenants, of whom 110

pay less than 4*l.* of annual rent, 352 range from 4*l.* to 20*l.*, while sixty are at 20*l.* and over. On the Ballymote estate are 454 tenants, 112 renting at less than 4*l.*; half of these, however, are town tenants; 264 pay between 4*l.* and 20*l.*, and eighty have a rental of 20*l.* or over. The tenants virtually have a fixity of tenure. An occasional experiment has been made of allowing tenant-right, but it has been limited to 10*l.* per acre. The system would, however, be of little advantage on these estates, inasmuch as few changes of tenancy occur. Payments are allowed for any substantial improvements made by the tenants. Rents are generally under the Government valuation, and have not been advanced for forty years. On two townlands, where the valuation was admittedly low, a 15 per cent. allowance was offered last year, but now 25 per cent. is demanded. There have been only six evictions in ten years of idlers who would neither work nor pay. A few of the larger holdings are let on lease; the smaller have no memorandum of agreement, and the Land Act now diminishes the need of any covenants. There is no notable difference as to the paying capabilities or prosperity of the small as compared with the larger tenants. On whatever sized holdings, the active and thrifty seem to thrive. Poor-rates are 2*s.* in the pound; county cess about 2*s.* 4*d.*

A great deal has been done, both by the late and present owners, to improve their property. Assistance has always been given in draining; lime and slates are furnished for building. As the old leases of middlemen fell in, townlands have been squared. That of Cloonagh has an area of 300 statute acres; its valuation is 159*l.* 15*s.*; its rental, 134*l.*; six years ago, when the lease expired, it was in 560 separate divisions or fields, many acres were unnecessarily occupied in fences, paths, and roads; the 43 occupiers, with a few cottagers living in small mud cabins, were crowded in hamlets; one man had his farm scattered in fifteen different places, another had his seven acres in twenty-nine divisions. The people themselves were alive to the need of a more economical distribution. A surveyor laid out roads and squared the plots, lotting them according to the numbers of holders, arranging as much as possible that a fair proportion of good and bad land went together. With Sir Henry's own assistance, a fair valuation, which has always given satisfaction, was put on the new farms. From 560 divisions the number was reduced to 43, conveniently grouped around new houses, for the building of which help was given. Assistance was also accorded for the removal of old fences, the making of new ones, and the cutting of main drains. Upwards of a mile of road was constructed, usefully employing the labour of the tenantry and of their available horse and donkey carts: this and all the other works were personally superintended by Sir Henry.

Doonfore townland, at a cost of 500*l.*, has more recently been similarly treated. It has an area of 470 acres, a valuation of 355*l.* 10*s.*; the rental is 370*l.*; the holdings range from four to six acres, charged at 12*s.* to 15*s.* an acre. Several good houses have been built by tenants receiving money from friends in America. The handy seaweed proves useful manure. Turf is brought from the bogs five miles distant. But for the employment Sir Henry gives in gardens, woods, and on his home farm, the population would be decidedly redundant. The townland of Carrigeens, containing 289 acres of useful, improvable, land, with a valuation of 224*l*. 15*s*. and a rental of 212*l*. 3*s*. 7*d*., two years ago was also squared, help being given to the holders in the making of roads, fences, and houses; eight to ten acres is the average of the farms, but one man pays 25*l*. a year; another, with forty-four Irish acres, rented at 33*l*., with a good house and buildings, bought out the previous tenant for 850*l*., obtained as a legacy from America. The pity is that half the population of these townlands could not be deported and their holdings doubled in size. Without fishing or work independently of their farms, the families, even on the best land, have not scope for reasonable subsistence and progressive improvement.

The following interesting statistics gathered by Sir Henry Gore-Booth in December 1872, will give some idea of the resources of his tenantry :—

	Valued at	Lissadell	Ballymote
	£ s. d.		
Statute acres	—	12,000	12,815
Griffith's valuation, including Ballymote town	—	£6,387	£8,796
Rental	—	£5,342	£7,490
Males	—	1,439	1,376
Females	—	1,388	1,409
Males emigrating during previous ten years	—	227	212
Females, ditto	—	166	172
Horses	17 0 0	219	172
Mules	4 0 0	15	11
Asses	1 2 0	186	268
Cows	14 0 0	1,453	1,206
Cattle, two-year-old	14 10 0	748	550
Ditto, one-year-old	9 10 0	761	518
Calves	4 0 0	998	828
Sheep	3 0 0	1,775	652
Lambs	2 0 0	899	586
Pigs	3 0 0	791	563
Goats	0 7 6	13	116
Dogs	—	238	350
Estimated value of live stock	—	£43,470	£41,215

The largest tenant on the Lissadell estate is Mr. Frank Barber, who began his farming career forty years ago with about ninety acres, mostly in snipe bog and a bit of rough pasture, remarkable for molehills. Drains were put in 3½ feet to 4 feet deep, the mains a foot deeper; a square culvert was built with picked stones in the bottom, and rougher stones, only too abundantly got out in subsoiling, were shovelled in to within 18 inches of the surface. On some land afflicted with springs deeper drains were run 5 feet or 6 feet through bog and shale into the more porous subsoil. Not a drain has ever given way, or caused the slightest trouble. On the reclaimed land potatoes are usually first grown, followed by oats and grass-seeds. Besides home-made manure, lime, sea-sand, &c., were freely used. After three or four years' grass, the lea was ripped up and cropped. Good cultivation and manure have banished rushes, rough grass, moss, and weeds. From ime to time more land has been taken in, and Mr. Barber now holds 450 acres. Great as was the expense of thorough draining, removing the numerous stones and boulders, and deeply subsoiling, the magnificent crops speedily repaid all outlay. So pleased was Sir Robert with the enterprise and success of his tenant, who at first held only from year to year, that he took 4s. 6d. an acre off his rent and gave him a lease for thirty-one years. When that expired, without any addition to the rent of 24s. 6d. an acre, he granted him, unasked, a lease for three lives. Responding to this most liberal treatment, Mr. Barber has built a handsome three-storied house, with barns, stabling, and shedding, which must have cost 4,000*l*. Part of the money has been borrowed at 4 per cent.

Judged by his own well-managed fields, on which his working acreable capital ranges from 6*l.* to 8*l.*, he may well remark that 'the country is not half farmed.' The ordinary tenants, he says, do not know how and will not try; he believes they are lazier than they were thirty years ago; those that will not farm as they should do he would turn out, deducting dilapidations; he cannot get much more than half the amount of work out of his people that he was wont to do; piece-work is rarely attempted; with all the complaints of poverty, he rarely can have women or girls either for turnip-thinning or hay-making. His chief remedy for Irish troubles is more steady work, and less idleness, whisky, tobacco, tea, and agitation. About one-third of Mr. Barber's land is in tillage. Although more capital is thus required than if a greater area were under grass, bigger returns are believed to be obtained. More adapted for the climate and soil, cattle are preferred to sheep. They are of short-horn character, and are partly bred and partly bought. Three to four pounds is generally earned for the summer grazing. The beasts are all finished off for the butcher either on grass or in the stalls. The winter keep of the twenty milch cows, eating about two tons of hay, is computed at about 2*l.*; the summer keep at 30*s.* During their nine months' profit the cows are expected to average about five pounds of butter per week.

The coast villages are generally miserable and poor; the double resource of land and sea seldom conduces to prosperity. With the alternative modes of livelihood neither seems to be made the best of. Cottagers often squat upon the small farms, and when the fishing or the potatoes fail add seriously to the destitution. These evils are exemplified at Ballyconnell, four miles from Lissadell and nine south from the pleasant watering-place of Grange. Ballyconnell belongs to Mr. Gethin and Mrs. Huddleston, both absentees, not known even by sight to their tenants. The valuation is 419*l.* 8*s.* There are 102 tenants and about ten cottagers. The population is said to have doubled within thirty years. About the famine-time the townland was inclosed and squared. The families appear large, averaging at least five or six in each one-room house, built of mud or rough stone, usually low and dark, innocent of lath and plaster; the thatch, liable to be ripped off by the wild Atlantic winds, is only held on by straw ropes placed at nine-inch intervals over the roof. The furniture is of the sparest and rudest description, consisting of one, occasionally of two, beds, a rough table, and a few benches; the donkey and any cattle, pigs, or poultry, of course, are housed with their master. Many of the older people, especially the women, cannot speak English. The people evidently are of mixed descent, but a few families partake of the distinctive Celtic type. The children, seldom shod, are not very regular winter attendants at school, but the last three months' average shows forty-six boys and fifty-nine girls, the latter usually attending longest. Children able to pay are charged one penny per week, but many are defaulters, and the non-payers increase.

Three or four acres appear to be the average extent of the holdings; of this area about one-half is cultivated, the remainder is a sandhill bearing benty grass, or bog, which towards the shore is frequently under water. Sometimes the tillage land is ploughed; more generally it is cultivated by the spade. Almost invariably under potatoes, the crop is poor and uncertain; oats ripen badly, and are knocked about by the high winds. A little guano is sometimes bought for manure. Not half the families have a cow; more have the easily-kept patient ass. Many of the holders have the use of the common, but declare it is poor, generally over-stocked, and always bare. The hay they have generally to buy in winter, on credit, costs 5s. per cwt. Those able to keep a cow do fairly well; the milk greatly helps the potatoes and Indian meal, which are the staple dietary. Home-grown potatoes and a little oatmeal are fairly plentiful from harvest until about March, when Indian meal has generally to be got, usually on credit, and is paid for in summer either by an extra take of fish, by the produce of the cow, or by the crop of oats. I am told that some of the land is charged at 40s. an Irish acre; the general complaint is that rents have been repeatedly raised, especially on those farming fairly; another grievance is the 4s. 2d. per 1l. imposed sixteen years ago for the privilege of cutting or gathering sea-ware, and charged indiscriminately to all tenants, whether they use it or not. Little is now made out of kelp or other seaweed. The charge for the ware has, however, been remitted from the rent of 1879, and the tenants resolutely declare that they will never pay it again.

One old woman, reputed the patriarch of the village, has about four acres, pays 7l. 13s. of rent for these and her one-roomed cottage, grows three-quarters of an acre of potatoes and a little piece of oats, and is mistress of a cow and a donkey. Thomas Carway has four Irish acres, for which he pays 2l. 10s. This seems moderate, but his father built the house, and drained, reclaimed, sanded, and clayed the poor bog, which could not previously feed a rabbit; 10s. a year was put on three years ago for making a watercourse, which, having since fallen in, leaves matters worse than formerly—half the holding, indeed, is under water. Fishing should help the livelihood, but it has recently been very unprofitable. A donkey and a pig are the live stock, with a few poultry, which, as elsewhere, are bartered for a little tea and tobacco. Pat Hart has four Irish acres of cut-away bog, over which the spring tide sometimes rises 5 feet, for which, with his house and small garden, he pays 2*l.* 10*s.* He was wont to make 7*l.* or 8*l.* from the summer fishing, but now seldom realises half that. He declares emphatically there is no employment; no gentry or large farmers to give an occasional day's work; no money to be earned to get to America, where many would gladly go if they could. Mike Hearty has a cottage and an acre of cut-away bog; he used to earn 10*l.* to 15*l.* by fishing, but asserts that he now does not make one-third of this. The boats are old: they do for weed-cutting, but not for following the fish 30 to 40 miles out, where they now often go. To succeed as fishermen new boats appear needful; new nets, costing 9*l.* to 15*l.*; new lines, costing 40*s.* Dan Micken has five Irish acres; pays 8*l.* 2*s.* 10*d.*, including rack money; grows an acre each of oats and potatoes; has a cow and his pigs comfortably quartered on the premises. Michael Conway is better off than some of his fellows; his father and uncle were noted makers of poteen, and the profits therefrom are expended on a better house, which cost fully 20*l.*, and a few extra buildings. His rent is 12*l.* 10*s.* 4*d.* He has about two acres of potatoes, which produce 6*l.* to 7*l.* an acre, and are mostly used for household consumption. About the same area is under oats, yielding six to seven sacks an acre. The produce of two cows, he estimates, should pay the rent, while the pair of calves sold in autumn will fetch 6*l.* The cattle, whether grazing on his own piece or on the common, must be herded, tied, or shackled, for the turf fences are low and full of gaps. On the common they are charged 3*s.* per head per month, but they are said never to do much good there. Michael Conway, jun., has six-and-a-half Irish acres; his valuation he believes to be 9*l.* 5*s.* ; his rent, 13*l.* 2*s.* 4*d.* ; his rates reach 1*l.* 4*s.* 8*d.* ; he generally boards out his cow and ass, which hence do not yield him as large profits as if they were kept at home. Although it is easy to recognise the life-long struggle for a bare subsistence, and the untoward surroundings which steep these and thousands of other small holders in perennial poverty, it is most difficult to carry out feasible plans which will effectually amend their condition and protect them from being occasionally subjected to absolute destitution.

CHAPTER XVII.

LORD DILLON'S ESTATES.

LORD DILLON'S estate, of nearly 100,000 acres in Mayo and Roscommon, mustering 4,000 tenants, two-thirds of them paying less than 6*l.* of annual rent, for upwards of forty years has been managed with admirable discretion and system by Mr. Charles Strickland, J.P., who succeeded his father. He has lived among the people, acting not only as the landlord's agent, but as their guide and counsellor. He has been their mentor in agricultural matters, and their arbiter in their settlements and personal disputes, which are constantly brought for his adjudication. For forty years a record has been kept of every man upon the property, his history and his family, and of every important transaction submitted for consideration or settlement. Middlemen and larger holders, who farmed out the land to the immediate occupiers, long held possession of this as of so many other Irish estates. Some of these leases fell in at various times during the last fifty years. As the old maps testify, the land was in rundale and wilderness; very small and only scattered patches were reclaimed. The small plots belonging to different small occupiers were scattered in the most indiscriminate manner. Each man usually had a piece reclaimed near his cabin, at some distance a plot of bottom land, and elsewhere a tract of bog. There were neither roads, fences, nor drains.

As the old leases expired Mr. Strickland had the land surveyed, and each man's claims specially recorded ; the site and condition of his house were carefully noted. Several houses had generally been placed together in small clusters. The area held by each occupier, the proportion of cultivated and bog, and its value, were carefully ascertained. In laying out the new divisions or small farms each occupier was given as nearly as possible the same quantity he held before, but all in one piece, including part of each quality of land—arable, bottom, reclaimed, and bog or waste—and each new farm or holding was valued and charged its own separate rent. Hundreds of little farms proportioned to the claims of the occupiers were thus symmetrically mapped out in stripes and carefully examined by Mr. Strickland. The man whose house was left standing was usually allowed to retain possession of it and take the farm on which it stood. If from one of his neighbours he had acquired a portion of reclaimed land, he would have to pay for it. The older cabins were pulled down and rebuilt on the fitting situation, assisted by the landlord. The wholesale redistribution and striping of the lands is not such a seriously expensive affair ; it required, however, much time and trouble, with no little tact and judgment, to balance rival claims and assess how much had to be credited for disseverance of a piece of good land, or what was to be debited for the new or improved house. Rent with entry charges and rebates being duly arranged by Mr. Strickland, the new holdings were allotted, and the keen little farmers, most jealous regarding their interests and rights, unanimously proclaim the great pains and labour bestowed on these troublesome little awards, as well as the justice with which they have been made.

But this redistribution, so important for economical cultivation and bringing into convenient juxtaposition the irreclaimed and the reclaimed lands, was only a small part of Lord Dillon's labour and outlay. Very many miles of roads were made; main watercourses were constructed; many miles of boundry mud and turf fences were erected, and help was also sometimes accorded to tenants with the subordinate fences dividing the holdings. In such an exposed country, furze, especially on the boundry fences, would be a great benefit. During the famine years of 1847, 1848, and 1849 thirteen stores were opened on various parts of the estate, and provisions sold at prime cost; the needy were freely helped. In favourable contrast to many other Irish estates there was consequently no serious destitution, no decimating famine fever, no great exodus of the survivors. The population numbered about 30,000 before the famine, remained about the same after, and has not varied much since. From 1848 to 1850 much was done in lowering river beds and improving main drainage; more recently a subvention of 15,000*l.* has been given towards bringing the railway from Kilfree Junction ten miles down to Ballyhaderreen, thus connecting this isolated district with Sligo and Dublin. The repayment of this Government loan now costs the estate about 1,000*l.* a year.

Ballyhaderreen is a poor, desolate-looking little town. But Lord Dillon, on whose property it stands, endeavours to improve it. In the ample market-square, shedding, under which the merchants meet their constituents, and lock-up stores have been erected at a cost of 2,000*l.* To the new

Court-House, erected by the county, Lord Dillon contributed half the outlay; and he has also greatly helped the funds raised for the building of the diocesan cathedral, convent, and commodious schools. Nine miles from Ballyhaderreen, Charlestown was founded in 1846, increases in importance as a well-attended weekly market and monthly fair, and already exceeds in size many towns dating from last century.

Lord Dillon's estate presents several interesting specialities. It has, as indicated, a very large number of small holders; about 3,000, or three-fourths of the total, pay an annual rental of 6*l.* and under; more than half pay less than 4*l.*; very few exceed 15*l.* Rates range from 2*s.* to 4*s.*, and county cess from 2*s.* to 2*s.* 6*d.* in the pound. The rates fall heavily in bad times, and Mr. Strickland would gladly have part of them contributed by those who benefit by the labour of the Mayo men.

The great bulk of the tenantry belong to the ancient Firbolg race, which constituted the Celtic aristocracy, which anteceded the Normans and Saxons, and in this district have very slightly mingled with them. These people are short of stature, spare, with small heads, prominent cheek-bones, large mouths, very dark, often curly, hair, rather sallow complexions, often with grey eyes. Three-fourths of the householders annually migrate to England. Before they go they generally sow the oats, plant the potatoes, and cut the turf, leaving the women and children to hoe and work the crops, manage the cow, calf, and pigs, and dry and bring home the turf. Most of the men are gone by the end of April, return towards the close of October, and bring with them from 9*l.* to 12*l.* Once a month, or oftener, many of the men now take advantage of the Post-office facilities and remit money to their families. Through the office at Swineford I am told that in one week last autumn the amounts thus forwarded reached 500*l*. It is generally stated that nearly 30,000 men annually go from Mayo and Galway to find several months' work in Great Britain. However idle and apathetic when at home, they work hard while absent, endeavour to get as much remunerative task-work as possible, and are generally careful and saving. Even the unmarried men return regularly for the winter. They rarely marry out of their own set. Some of them have lofty ideas of the dower to be given with their daughters; sometimes 50*l*. or even occasionally 100*l*. is saved for this purpose, impoverishing the family for years. At the time of the wedding half the dower is general paid down, and goes to settle the priest's dues and start the young couple. The other moiety is discharged when the first child is born; but Irish promises to pay, although readily made, are not always performed. The money not forthcoming, its non-payment occasionally leads to family feuds and litigation. The hard work of the absent breadwinners during summer is counterbalanced by the winter leisure; there is a good deal of loafing and smoking; reclamation and tidying up of the farm do not proceed so rapidly as they might do.

On this estate, exertion cannot be paralysed by suspicion of insecurity. Evictions are unknown. They would only occur for persistent non-payment of rent and subdivision. For forty years Mr. Strickland has followed out the principles embodied in the Land Act of 1870. The tenants have practically had fixity of tenure; all improvements have belonged to the improver. Tenant-right has been recognised, but changes of tenancy are very rare indeed—a fact which indicates the content and steady habits of those small occupiers, their devotion to the spot of their birth or early location, while it further demonstrates that they are not very highly rented. The arable land averages 8s. to 10s.; the reclaimed is from 5s. to 6s. per statute acre; the bog is not charged at all. Notwithstanding the convenient situation of the bog to roads and land already reclaimed, and the fact that every man is assured that he has full benefit from his reclamation, it is only slowly taken in. A great deal of the bottom land, which would pay even better for cultivation, is left untilled, or is tilled only partially or at rare intervals, reverting in the meanwhile to sedge and rough grass. Of the bog, the most diligent tenants do not bring in annually one rood. At this slow rate of progress many years must elapse before even the portions fairly reclaimable will be taken up. On this estate, although handy portions of waste bog might thus add to the limited area of the small holdings, there are no large tracts which would afford location for surplus population. Very many acres of the estate are of such a poor, rocky, intractable character, that they could not be profitably brought under cultivation.

Lord Dillon's rents are low; many have remained unchanged for over thirty years; in some townlands they are under Griffith's valuation. But the present agitation has unsettled the people, and makes them clamour for reductions. They had an abatement of 6s. in the pound in the bad year of 1879. Notwithstanding the full crops and better prices of the present season, their leaders demand the same handsome rebate. They refuse a proffered 15 per cent. Persuasion and intimidation are so widely used that many well-disposed occupiers having their rents ready dare not pay. The state of feeling is illustrated by a letter I have seen, received from the employer of a relative of one of the tenants. This man, working in one of the English seaports, is desirous to pay rent and arrears for his Mayo friends, but dare not send it to them—fears even to communicate on such a subject directly with his family, but when he learns the amount due will have it remitted in the name of his employer.

CHAPTER XVIII.

LANDLORDS AND TENANTS IN MAYO.

The O'Conor Don has paid much attention to Irish land questions. He has been an active member of many commissions; he has contributed a valuable supplementary report to the Irish Land Act Commission of 1880, he advocates simplifying all dealings in connection with the transfer of land; he urges the multiplying of owners in all parts of Ireland. He has not, however, much faith in Government reclamation and colonisation of waste lands. The fixity of tenure with which it is generally proposed to endow the tenant would, he believes, deprive the owner of his position without materially benefiting the tenant, and often to the detriment of subsequent tenants. Land, he considers, would thereby be more firmly tied up than heretofore, and would be more difficult of acquisition either by the saving labourer or the rising generation of tenants. He does not believe that fixity of tenure alone would long satisfy the great bulk of the people, and settle once and for all Irish land grievances, unless accompanied by low fixed rents. To secure such acceptable rents would necessitate their reduction on many estates, especially on those recently purchased. Can this be fairly done, he inquires, without compensating the owner, not so much for diminution of sentimental position and privilege, but for actual abatement of money returns? Many landlords, he believes, would rather dispose entirely of their interests, probably over large areas of their estates some only retaining their demesnes. To further acquisition of land by the actual cultivator, the O'Conor Don would appoint a commission and furnish it with State funds to buy estates offered by existing owners, and empower it to resell to occupiers, who should be required at once to pay down one-fifth of the purchase money, and by annual instalments clear off the remainder in thirty-five years. An alternative scheme is suggested. Dealing with that large class of tenants who have not the desiderated money to pay down one-fifth the value of their holding, and reserving rights of quarries, minerals, turbary, and shooting, many landlords would cheerfully grant perpetuities, and allow rents to be fined down. In the supplementary report which he furnished to the Commissioners of Inquiry into the Landlord and Tenant Act of 1880 the O'Conor Don further suggests that 'these perpetuities should be sold to the public, or the perpetuity grants should be made to the occupiers at an annual payment which would repay four-fifths of the purchase money, interest and principal, in thirty-five years; and this should be paid to the commission simply as interest on rent until such time as the first sale of the tenant's interest took place, when out of the purchase money realised by such sale the original one-fifth should be paid to the commission, and that from that date the repayment of principal should commence (p. 47). Under any of these schemes an increasing number of occupiers would become owners, to their own benefit and that of their country.

The O'Conor Don lives a mile from Castlereagh. Near

P

his old tree-embowered home he has just built in the more open portion of the park a handsome mansion. Commodious stabling and farm buildings evidence sporting and farming tastes. In the park are a number of capital shorthorns and useful Down sheep, which for three years have, however, suffered from liver rot, caused by flukes. The O'Conor Don considers that the Irish climate has of late undergone untoward change ; the summers are wetter, with less sunshine ; the winters more severe. Skating, hitherto unknown in the West, has become a familiar pastime. More shelter and greater stores of dry food he regards as essential for the successful wintering of all descriptions of live stock. In Ireland, as in England, several dry summers are sadly wanted to insure, not only remunerative crops, but the better health and greater profit of the animals of the farm.

The O'Conor Don has 11,500 acres, comprising small mixed farms in Sligo, and larger grazing farms in Roscommon. Of 500 tenants only twenty-three pay over 20*l.* of annual rent ; more than half are charged less than 10*l.* ; on one townland all are under 20*l.* ; on another only three out of twenty-six reach 20*l.* For forty years no accession has been made to the rents, which range from 25 per cent. under to as much over Griffith's valuation. No case has ever been taken into the Land Courts. The tenants have perfect security. Since the great famine there have been no changes among them, and little opportunity for the desirable rolling together of the smaller holdings. Reserving a veto on the solvency and respectability of the new comer, no other restriction is put upon the disposal of the tenant-right, which even in these bad times brings a high figure, often reaching eight or ten years' rental. A holding of three acres reclaimed by the tenant and rented at 21s. a year was recently bought for 60l. Rents are moderate ; 25 per cent. deduction was nevertheless offered to all holders under 20l. ; but payments come in very tardily. Lord Dillon having given 30 per cent., this allowance is expected on all neighbouring properties, whether high or low rented. Several tenants have indulgently been allowed to fall three or four years behind, and some of those who can pay will not. Such old arrears can never be recovered ; but since the passing of The Protection of Life and Property Act and the recent arrests, current rents in the West and South have been rather better paid, and tenants of their own accord drop in and show some legitimate anxiety to get out of debt.

The grass farms of Roscommon range from fifty to 500 acres. During the best of the season they will carry one beast per statute acre ; they are let at 25s. to 40s., and are generally taken annually from May Day. They are independent of tenant-right. A single grazier sometimes rents a dozen farms. There are no buildings, except a herd's miserable cabin, and occasionally the hovel of a squatter. The fields are divided by clay banks or stone walls, are without shelter either from wild winter storms or scorching summer heat, but intelligent graziers are discovering the want of shelter, willingly give more for farms where there are a few trees, and would cheerfully join with the landlord in planting belts and clumps. Rents and prospects of grass farms are not, however, what they have been ; even substantial men have demurred to meet rents. Many who have rendered themselves obnoxious to the Land League have had their gates and fences broken down, their cattle of different sorts driven together, and sometimes sent in the night several miles along the roads, while their herds are terrorised into resigning office. This programme is obviously devised to deter graziers taking those grass farms, and thus to coerce landlords to divide them among small holders. Any considerable breaking up of grass land would, however, be a dubious and temporary benefit either to occupier or owner. With an accumulated store of plant food, those old pastures, without trouble or expense for some years, would produce full crops of oats and roots. But the damp western climate is more suitable for pasture than for tillage. Cultivation of the type generally met with would steadily depreciate the value of the farms. They would produce less weight of food than they now do, and soon retrograde in value, while the reduced rents would be more troublesome to collect. Numerous illustrations of such retrogression are met with. A good one occurs in the townland of Ballinbella, in the parish of Ballindine, where, at their own request and on their own terms, permission was some years ago granted to the tenants to plough up some good pasture. The land has gradually deteriorated. The tenants declare that the old rents cannot be made, and allowances have to be given to the extent of 25 per cent. It is often wise to leave well alone.

Mr. Sandford, of Castlereagh, has an estate of 26,000 acres; nearly half of it is red bog, some of it 30 feet deep, not capable of profitable improvement, but the remainder is useful, the most easterly portions largely in grass, and, like the land generally in Roscommon, desirable and profitable. The occupations are larger than on Lord Dillon's and many other western estates. With the reputation of a good landlord, who adopts the live-and-let-live principle, Mr. Sandford never has a vacant farm. He endeavours to limit the amount given for tenant-right, has the transaction made through the office, and believes that, in their wild, thoughtless competition for land, incoming tenants often promise more than they can afford to give ; an excessive premium for their entry leaves them with nothing to till or stock the land. Within the last few years, 500*l.* has been given for the goodwill of a holding rented at 20*l.* ; 200*l.* has been paid for six acres ; in another instance 250*l.* was the premium for twenty acres, and 150*l.* for twenty-five acres.

West of Castlereagh, round Ballyhaunis, are thousands of acres of poor red bog, 15 feet to 20 feet deep, offering small encouragement for the exertions of the most enterprising improver. To bring such subjects into cultivation requires an outlay of 12*l.* to 15*l.* an acre. Is the landlord or the State justified in transplanting from overcrowded districts their pauperised supernumeraries and placing them on such unpromising lands, nursing them while they bring into cultivation sufficient for their subsistence, and exercising besides further superintendence, in order that the poor thriftless bog, even when reclaimed, shall not revert to its original profitless state? The small, precarious returns of late years obtained from most Irish estates naturally check the ardour even of enthusiastic improvers. Their exertions and outlay do not seem greatly to add to the prosperity and contentment of the tenantry, and certainly bring to the landlord no adequate pecuniary return. Tnose who have devoted time and money to their estates and their people in the present annoying agitation are often as unpopular, and have almost as much difficulty in getting their just rents, as those who are notoriously unpopular, arbitrary, or grasping.

Lord Clanmorris has 12,337 acres in Mayo, with a Government valuation of 6,200*l.*, and 5,295 acres in Galway, with a valuation of 1,899*l.* He has about 665 tenants, upwards of 400 of whom pay less than 5*l.* of annual rent. He and his family have always been good and popular landlords; on the occasion of his recent marriage an address and presentation of plate was made to him; his rents are stated to have remained unchanged for thirty years, and to be 17 per cent. under the Government valuation; tenants have had unlimited privilege of sale. Rents, nevertheless, are not paid; a 20 per cent. reduction is clamoured for. The stand against rents has been general on most estates in this part of Mayo. Mr. Edward Moore O'Ferral, Treemere, offered to take one half-year's rent and give a receipt in full for the three that are due. Armed with this liberal proposal the agent confidently expected to collect 1,000*l.*, but did not obtain one shilling. Poverty, which is generally pleaded, cannot here be the invariable excuse; one of the recalcitrants is a Poor-Law guardian, the other a man with considerable landed property. Mr. J. D. H. Browne, London, on his Mayo property of 3,629 acres in 1879 and 1880, was liberal with money relief, seed potatoes, and labour; his land is good and his rents moderate; but, although offering a reduction of 6*s.* 8*d.* in the pound, payments, often twelve months overdue, are not coming in. Mr. Emanuel Churcher, of Gosport, makes the same complaint; his tenants are two, some three, years in arrears; the well-to-do justify their non-payment by declared dread of Boycotting.

Lord Oranmore's inability to collect rents is somewhat

more easy to understand; he has raised among his people considerable ill-feeling by displacing tenants, by interfering with old rights of common, by charging the villagers high prices for the grazing of their cows, and in one townland by changing their allotments year by year, in order that the holders should not acquire claims for disturbance. Mr. Blake, of Castle Glass, has heavy arrears; out of the last three gales he is understood not to have had more than one paid up, but his tenants are said to be smarting under recently-raised rents and unfulfilled promises of leases and needful improvements. On some estates ill-feeling has been engendered by excessive game preservation, by shooting and poisoning herds' and tenants' dogs, and by fines for disturbing or pursuing game. On many more there has been an absence of all sympathy and interest in the people and no effort to guide or help them.

In satisfactory contrast to absenteeism, to careless and ignorant neglect, or to inconsiderate mismanagement, is the Heath Estate, Ballindine, five miles south of Claremorris. Mr. Thomas Tighe, High Sheriff of the county, has here 1,720 acres, with a rental of about 1,000*l.*, divided among thirty-five tenants. Of these, five are under 4*l.* of rent, all are industrious and prosperous, well looked after, and helped by their landlord. The Heath was bought twenty-five years ago by Mr. Tighe's father, who made his money in business in Ballinrobe; 10,000*l.* has since been laid out in improvements, comprising buildings, roads, draining, reclamation, and planting. The tenants are encouraged and assisted; guano and implements are got for them on the best terms; employment is found in dull times; several families have had assisted passages to America; money is advanced to those who are short of capital. One man paying about 20*l.* of rent, unfortunate in 1879, in 1880 was opportunely helped to buy lambs and cattle ; after selling out in autumn and paying up his rent he had a profit of 58*l.*

Within a mile of Claremorris is a useful farm formerly held by a relative of Captain Boycott, who, becoming unpopular, was compelled to leave it. For a year the gates have been thrown off, the fences are broken down, the landlord unable to find a tenant. Until the Land League authorities, forsooth, are consulted and propitiated, there is small hope of a tenant. Mr. Anthony Ormsby, Ballinamore, Killamore, has two farms of thirty to forty acres lying vacant. The bankrupt tenants, desirous to leave for America, agreed to transfer their possessory interest to the landlord, who sacrificed several years' rent and contributed to the purse made up for the Transatlantic trip. The Land League, however, intervened, got the way-going tenants to make over their interest to one of their creatures ; in spite of the landlord, carried on the farm for a year, and sold off the crops ; one of the houses was meanwhile burnt ; with much trouble and cost, and after an appeal to the Court, the intruding tenant has been got rid of, but hitherto no one else dares to occupy either holding. These are not solitary cases.

Mr. Walter M. Bourke, J.P., Curraghleigh, Claremorris, has 4,192 acres in county Mayo and 1,882 in county Galway. Previous to 1845 the Mayo estate was in rundale ; it has been striped, drained, and roads made at an outlay which, between 1845 and 1861, reached 7,000*l.* There are 175 tenants, of whom 120 pay less than 10*l.* of annual rent. A few leases are outstanding ; new ones for twenty-one years would cheerfully be given, but are seldom applied for. The leasehold and yearly rents are about the same. There is no appreciable difference in the condition or prosperity of the leasehold and yearly tenants on this or, indeed, on other western estates. Sale of tenant-right has reached four or five years' rental. The present rental is 26*l.* less than it was twenty years ago. Rents, although hitherto paid regularly and uncomplainingly, have not been recently met; the arrears extend back for two or even three years; reductions varying from 15 to 25 per cent. have not secured settlement; large remissions of old arrears have been promised from the rents of 1879-80; 1,000*l.* has already been remitted; one man was told if he could pay up last year's rent of 21*l.* his accumulated debt of 57*l.* would be written off, but an organised stand has been made against all rents. Mr. Bourke served several ejectment notices on tenants with long arrears and well able to pay; the cases went into court; no defence was offered; a few payments have since been made, but no evictions have occurred. The Mayo tenantry appear generally instructed to offer Griffith's valuation, irrespective of any improvements or outlay effected by the landlord. On many estates a permanent reduction of 25 to 33 per cent. is demanded from present rents. The evident aim is to pull down rents, in view of an anticipated arrangement under which occupiers hope, at public expense, to be converted into owners on payment of about twenty years' reduced rental.

Although Mr. Bourke's tenants repudiate for the present their liability to pay rent, many of them appear friendly towards their landlord, in affectionate terms inquire for sick and absent members of his family, and with pious zeal ejaculate, 'God help them!' I visited and conversed with a large number of tenants on this estate, most of whom, if let alone, would be contented; no complaints are made of excessive rent or insecure tenure; considering recent bad times, most are fairly well-to-do. Home-grown potatoes, oatmeal, and milk, with an occasional fowl and some eggs, constitute the principal dietary. The sale of the yearlings or two-year-olds, of pigs and poultry, and occasionally of butter, make the rent, rates, and other expenses, which do not exceed those of an English agricultural labourer.

Subjoined is the acreage and rental in 1863 and at the present date of three tenants living immediately outside the demesne, occupied in dairying, keeping four or five milking cows, like their neighbours, rearing the calves and selling them as yearlings or two-year-olds. From this single source the rent is readily made:—

	Acreage	Rent 1863 £ s. d.	Rent 1880 £ s. d.
J. Reilly	58·2	39 0 11	36 0 0
W. Costello	25·3	17 6 6	16 0 0
P. Commons	47·2	32 8 0	28 0 0

John Keen, Curneen, for his sixteen statute acres of useful land pays 12*l*. 15*s*., has three cows, two calves, an ass, and two pigs, all comfortably lodged with his nine healthy-looking children in the end of the house. Peter Healy has lived at Curneen fourteen years, was formerly a cottier, with house and garden costing upwards of 3*l*., and, like many of the class, often found work irregular and difficult to get. To improve his position he took six acres of useful land, has fenced, drained, and cultivated it fairly. His rent is 9*l*. His house is, however, getting considerably out of repair; he has lost two potato crops, small deteriorated seed being evidently the cause. He has no money to buy cattle, but with oat straw, in the end of his house, is foddering five yearlings belonging to a neighbour, who gives him the moderate sum of 15*s.* each for housing and feeding them from December 1 until May Day. Joseph Salmon four years ago took twelve acres inclosed and partially cultivated, and thirty acres of bog, for which, with a comfortable house, he pays 11*l.* a year. The rent was fixed by himself, but with recent indifferent seasons and losses among his stock he declares it is 'more than enough.' He grows about an acre and a half of oats, the same area of potatoes, and a few roods of turnips; he has three useful cows of shorthorn character and three yearlings, which would alone amply meet his annual rent and rates.

The townland of Cultibow extends to 670 acres; the rent is 252*l.* 13*s.* 6*d.*; the soil is poor and shallow, on a limestone conglomerate; a good deal of bog remains unreclaimed; roads and draining have been done at the landlord's expense, usefully finding winter employment and ready money. Michael Royan settled on the common about twenty-two years ago, built his house, took in four acres of land, ditched, drained, and fenced it, pays 3*l.* for rent, keeps a cow, and usually two calves, but sells little or no butter or milk, all being used by his children, of whom there were nine, but only three survive. Indifferently fed, often exposed to inclement weather, seriously overcrowded when indoors, and very ignorantly managed when anything goes amiss, the infant mortality appears in this neighbourhood to be unusually high, and of many large families only one-half reach maturity. Royan, a tall, active man of fifty, after digging his land, planting his crops, and leaving their subsequent treatment to the wife and children, about the end of

May proceeds to a farm near Leeds, where he has been regularly employed for eighteen years, earns 15*s.* a week, often has hoeing by the piece, when he works from 4 A.M. to 9 P.M., returns from Yorkshire about the end of October, and admittedly does not work so hard at home as he does in England.

John Costello, taking advantage of a bright, frosty January day, has untied his two cows and calf, turned them out in the snow, put out the peat fire, converted his house for the nonce into a barn, and, with the help of a neighbour, was thrashing out some oats. The potatoes and bit of dinner are being cooked in the adjacent hovel by the tidy old grandmother. For his premises and nearly twelve acres he pays 3*l.* a year. Like his nine or ten thousand Mayo neighbours, Costello spends the summer in England. He acts regularly as a cattle man in Cheshire, goes to his English work in May, got back this year on Christmas eve, earns while absent 2*s.* 6*d.* or 3*s.* a day, brings home about 10*l.* or nearly half his earnings ; sleeping in a hovel or barn, he has few expenses, except for food. Like many Irishmen who thus reside so far from the scene of their half-year's work, Costello says that it costs much more to rear a family in England than in Ireland, and adds ' that even if he had a bigger house and a better sop he could not live contented all the year out of the ould country.'

Antony Regan holds fifty-one acres, which cost him 26*l.* 10*s.*, or 4*l.* more than it was forty years ago. It is better land and better tilled than that of most of his smaller neighbours. With a stout mule, the soil is turned up more cheaply and effectively than with the spade husbandry of the small cultivators. He has six or eight cows and their produce, which are generally sold at two years old. Three of them fairly well disposed of suffice to make the rent. This constitutes a small proportion of the available receipts. He has erected a useful barn and some sheds, but for extra comfort a favourite sow and her small pigs are in the house with ten rosy children, whose commodious sleeping apartment is, however, partitioned from the kitchen, pig and poultry department. Mr. Bourke's townlands of Lower, Middle, and Upper Mace are better land, are occupied by larger tenants, apparently somewhat more prosperous, but not more willing to pay rent. Above Mr. Bourke's own house, abutting on his demesne, is Murneen South, one of the best bullock farms in the district. Ascending the hill, a fine view is obtained of some fifty miles of undulating, well watered, but treeless country. It would be a great boon in this part of Ireland if extensive and systematic planting of the poorer exposed land were more generally adopted.

CHAPTER XIX.

TENURE AND TENANTS IN NORTH-WEST MAYO.

From Manulla Junction to Foxford, and thence to Swineford, are thousands of acres of poor red bog, much of it flat and difficult to drain, sparsely-scattered villages of mud hovels, numerous small holders on rundale or rudely-striped farms, cultivation done expensively and untidily by the spade, no attempt at autumn clearing or upturning of the soil to the ameliorating influences of frost, thrashing of light indifferently-saved oats effected by the flail, and winnowing in pristine form, conducted outside the barn with the assistance of the western breezes.

Lord Clanmorris and Mrs. Rushley are the chief owners of these poor subjects about Foxford. Mr. Drew, a middleman at Killamore, has twenty-five tenants, whose holdings range from two and a half to four Irish acres; their rents are said to be 30s. an acre; ten evictions are stated to have occurred here in 1880. Miss Gardiner, of Farmhill, has a poor class of tenants, with whom disagreements as to rent and encroachments increased until twenty-four ejectments had been served. Evidently there were faults on both sides. Mr. Macdonald, the Sheriff, being called in during the summer of 1880 to evict, instead of proving an exterminator, with much tact and patience acted as mediator, secured the promises of the defaulters to pay the 140*l.* claimed, allowed them time, and to their credit the money has been faithfully forwarded to Mr. Macdonald. The parish of Killbelfad, in the union of Ballina, near Foxford, belonging to Lord Clanmorris, extends to 475 acres, and is let to thirty-nine tenants. The total land valuation is 70*l.*, the tenement valuation is only 15*l.*, which does not say much for the condition and accommodation of the thirty-nine dwelling-houses. But even here, with scant means of subsistence, the disposition to subdivide occurs, and during 1880 three small holdings had been split into six. On the townland of Cuing Beg, measuring 337 acres, Lord Clanmorris has seventeen tenants; the total valuation of the land is 25*l.* 10*s.*; the tenement valuation is 8*s.* 15*s.*; the rental is about 20 per cent. over the valuation. These tenants have land enough, but it is woefully poor, and, like much else in this neighbourhood, is not made the best of. The Bellass townland, in the Strachean electoral division, is divided among forty-two tenants, whose tenement valuation is only 7*l.* 15*s.*; their land is valued for Poor Law purposes at 112*l.* 5*s.*; many are paying less than 40*s.* of annual rent. It is a most puzzling problem how these poor people on indifferent land can be improved. It is not the rent that pauperises them; it is the want of judiciously-applied systematic industry.

Mr. Edmond H. C. Pery, Coolcronan, Ballina, in a county too notable for absentees for twenty years, has been a popular resident landlord. He has succeeded in making his estate a model one, has built a good house, effected a good deal of reclamation, planted 100 acres, and taken into possession 571 acres for a home farm, giving liberal compensation to the dispossessed tenants, and placing thereon modern buildings, a steam-engine, and other equipments, with a valuable herd of shorthorns, in which both he and Mrs. Pery take an active interest, and which are improving the size, quality, and value of the cattle of the district. The farm wages annually amount to 600*l.* The occasional employment given to tenants in their spare time often enables them to earn much more than their rent. In these and other useful works Mr. Pery, during twenty years, has expended 15,000*l.* About one third of this has been spent in roads, draining, houses, and improvements, directly benefiting the 266 tenants, of whom nearly all, excepting twenty-six, are rated at less than 10*l.* Including the home farm, the estate measures 5,061 acres; the Poor Law valuation, comprising lands in hand, is 2,148*l.* The owner pays the entire rates for eighty-one holdings and county cess amounting to 80*l.* a year. The cottages of the tenants were generally built forty to fifty years ago and many are pleasantly placed round the margin of the lough. Liberal allowances were made, not only in cottage-building, but for other substantial improvements, by the grandfather of the present owner; reclamation, when thoroughly done, has generally been profitable. The lands are now conveniently squared; with many of the cultivated plots a portion of mountain grazing and turf bog is let.

Rents, fixed at their present figures in 1868 and 1869, and varying from 10*s.* to 20*s.* for the best land, are about 25 per cent. over Griffith's valuation, and until recently have not been complained of. An abatement of 15 per cent. was offered from the rent of 1879, much of which is still unpaid. In the winter of 1879–80 Indian meal was distributed at prime cost—namely, 6*l*. 10*s*. per ton ; payment was promised either in money or in labour ; but the debt in great part is still outstanding. Champion potatoes to the extent of fifty tons were also distributed gratuitously to the necessitous, and at cost price to those who were better off. Gratitude for these boons should have stimulated more effort to pay for them ; but here, as elsewhere, both public and private potato funds are still heavily, apparently irrecoverably, in debt. Sale of possessory interest allowed to be made to any solvent party reaches five to seven years' rental, but has recently fallen somewhat owing to agitation and uncertainty as to the land question.

Like all sensible landlords, Mr. Pery has striven hard to increase the independence of his people. He has endeavoured to foster steady industry ; he has provided the work so sadly wanted throughout many districts of Ireland. Upwards of a dozen families are found regular employment on the home farm ; occasional work is furnished, as required, for small tenants. Such supervision and help have produced comfort and prosperity in many homes. The tenants, where they have not run deeply into debt, are rapidly recovering from the bad season of 1879 ; the 10-acre men, quickest pulled down, have received more help in their troubles, and are again recovering more quickly. Like so many thoughtful observers, Mr. Pery states that the ownership of the cultivator conduces to greater economy of production, to greater industry, self-reliance, and thrift, and to a more intelligent interest in the preservation of the law and order which maintain the rights and value of property.

Lord Arran in this part of Mayo has 600 tenants, who multiplied excessively during the lax administration of a former owner; one-half pay under 5*l.* of annual rent; all are yearly holders. Excepting in the case of new comers, rents have not been advanced for twenty-six years. The chief cases of over-renting appear to occur among the tenants of tenants, who number about fifty. But, without holdings into which to deport them, it is probably difficult to remedy the evil. Tenant-right is admitted; the waygoer receives four to six years' rental for his possessory interest. Notwithstanding the teaching of the practical agriculturists whom Lord Arran employed some years ago to give advice and instruction, the agent assures me that since 1870 the tenants have become very independent; they will not be told anything, and their farming generally has fallen off.

Sir Charles Knox Gore, near Ballina, has 17,608 acres, rated for Poor Law purposes at 6,332*l.*, and also some estates in Sligo. The rental averages about 25*s.* an acre, is 25 per cent. to 30 per cent. over the Poor Law valuation. His father and himself have been anxiously alive to the evils of small holdings, and have enlarged them wherever possible to twenty or thirty acres. Of 500 occupiers, more than one-half still, however, have less than ten acres. The Land Act of 1870 renders the consolidating process more troublesome and costly, and recently the crippled resources of the tenantry have diminished competition for the larger holdings. Tenants have enjoyed free sale, which realises six to seven years' rental. Draining and other improvements, to which the landlord has contributed, have improved cultivation. The extended growth of turnips, the better stamp of live stock, the railway facilities, and the growth of Ballina as a market have helped the tenantry of this district. But improved transport and market facilities, four banks instead of one, more and better shops, have enlarged the farmer's expenditure and extended credit, of which Irishmen are too prone to take undue advantage.

An extensive gombeen operator and manure merchant in the west declares that his numerous constituents have so overstretched their resources, have been so idle and careless, and latterly are so indifferent about paying anybody, that he would gladly take, he says, 5,000*l.* for the 15,000*l.* which he has now lying out chiefly in Mayo. Gombeen men have multiplied. A wholesale stationer informs me that he prints the forms and makes up and sells five times the number of bill books that he did ten years ago. With charges and extras, 25 per cent. interest is not unusual on small amounts. Itinerant vendors of groceries and wearing apparel, selling their goods on a costly credit system, have rapidly made handsome competencies. Hard-earned farming profits have not always been wisely spent, and although the farm generally yields more than it did twenty-five years ago, and the produce brings higher prices, the farmer's position has not proportionately improved.

Travelling west of Ballina, the country gets barer and poorer; beyond Bangor is a wilderness of wretched waste reaching to Belmullet, which is forty-four miles from Ballina, on the north-west promontory of Mayo, in a desolate region of sand and bog, the few storm-stunted trees not reaching much over 6 feet. The coast is generally flat, diversified by a few sand-hills, without clay wherewith to improve either the sand or bog. An old ruined castle belonging to the Bynghams stands on the peninsula, exposed to the wild roar of the Atlantic waves. The population generally do not speak English. Their mud hovels are low, small, and often without windows, with poor pretensions to furniture; a bundle of straw in the corner sometimes constitutes the family bed. The small patches of cultivated land are laboriously made out of shifting sand, or deep, deaf bog, or, farther back from the coast, are carved out of the rugged mountain with pick and shovel. The tillage land is held in rundale or imperfectly striped; the mountain is in common. High winds and dripping rain unfit this country for grain-growing. Considering the soil and climate, potatoes, when the seed is changed, do fairly. Young cattle and pigs are the only agricultural produce sold. The sea might yield a better harvest than the land, but there are not sufficient boats, no money to buy them, seldom persevering industry to make the best of them if they were obtained; there are no harbours into which to run them for refuge from the wild Atlantic storms, and no railway nearer than Ballina or Westport for conveyance of either fish or agricultural produce.

Among the small holders from Erris, round Black Sod Bay, on Achill and Clare Islands, and on the opposite mainland shores during the sad winter of 1879–80, there was much destitution, resulting mainly from potato failure, and aggravated by the loss of pigs from contagious typhoid fever. Poor-rates in some unions mounted to 5s. 6d. per pound, but even then were not one-third of the figure they reached in 1847–8. The county cess is generally about 2s. Many of these extreme western people go east to other parts of Ireland and to England for their summer's work. From Erris alone 100 men, I am told, regularly depart for England throughout April, and return in October and November. Their summer earnings pay the rent, which in most cases does not exceed 4*l.*, and provide beside the small stock of winter necessaries. On some estates a miserable redundant population, with the slenderest prospects of subsistence, are culpably allowed to settle. For some of the bare, poor land 10*s.* an acre is given. Tenant-right is not generally recognised. In Shannahee village, I am told of a landlord who is said to advance his rents every second year, and who has one tenant paying 16*l.* 10*s.* for a holding rated at 2*l.* 10*s.*, and raised to its present value by the labours of the occupier.

In Westport, as in many western towns, winter diminishes the irregular, precarious employment, drives in casuals from the country districts, and brings a considerable amount of distress. Notwithstanding high rates and ill-paid accounts, the townspeople during the severe weather in January made handsome subscriptions in aid of the necessitous. The district is in a state of chronic agitation and disaffection. Any reverses to British arms in Afghanistan or at the Cape provoke unmistakable rejoicing. Able-bodied idlers, even when unable to find work and seeking relief, will not now accept the 'Queen's shilling.' Rents and other liabilities are very irregularly discharged. Boycotting of various types is common. Private animosity sometimes thus succeeds in revenging itself. Within three miles of Westport are several grass farms from which tenants have been warned by the League; several strangers, some of them from England, have examined the lands with a view to taking them, but dare not run the risk. Between Westport and Newport, Mrs. Watson has a lease of a grass farm for 170*l.* a year, whence several hundred deer in the great famine were generously given to the soup committees. Although answerable for her own rent, she cannot find a tenant. For such malpractices the apology is, 'The people want the land.'

Ten miles south, towards Louisburg, are several townlands, where overcrowding, poverty, and agitation are widespread and serious. Father Nugent recently visited this miserable district, and vainly endeavoured to persuade families to emigrate. Ten or fifteen years ago his praiseworthy efforts might have been more successful. Now, the priests, the League, and the incendiary newspapers, which are eagerly devoured and implicitly believed, discourage emigration. The Cape Government has lately made a proposal which may, perhaps, remove some of the difficulties. With other inducements, they offer the priest who will accompany his people 20s. per annum for life, or for twenty years, for each family he can bring with him.

The Westport country furnishes not a few cases of small landlords and middlemen reduced to sad straits by continued nonpayment of rent. Establishments have been reduced; the education of families stopped; retrenchments rendered imperative. Mr. Gurvey, Ross Duan, has a large number of small tenants; although he expressed willingness to accept Griffith's valuation, he has not been paid. That his tenants are not very hardly dealt with is evident from the fact that, although he holds under an old lease, his profit rent does not yield him more than 80*l.* a year. Mrs. Carroll owns several townlands in the parish of Killmina, between Westport and Newport, purchased some years ago through the Court. The rents, ranging from 5*l.* to 8*l.*, are rather high; they are said since purchase to have been slightly raised; the arrears have now accumulated to four and some to five years' rent. Impudent cases of pretended inability to pay occasionally come under observation. A well-to-do man on Clare Island had his useful grass farm, with privilege of sea-ware, for 55*l*. a year. The landlord three or four years ago was offered 80*l*. for the holding to divide among several neighbouring farms; but he demurred to disturb the possessor. Six months ago, having dropped considerably behind with his rent, he came complaining and demanding a liberal rebate. Before agreeing, his landlord made a few inquiries, and discovered that his sorely-tried tenant had sub-let the farm for double the rent he was paying, and was endeavouring also to exact 10*l*. extra for the privilege of sea-ware.

Lord Sligo's estates lie around Westport, extend to 114,881 acres, and, including occupiers of houses, make a muster of 1,600 tenants. The large proportion are under 10*l*. of annual value. Although Lord Sligo is a confirmed absentee, the evils of his non-residence are somewhat abated by his brother, Lord John Browne, tolerably constantly living upon the estate. He farms extensively, by precept and example, and by distributing good male animals he has contributed to the advance of the agriculture of his district. Mainly under his auspices, the cottages of the tenants have been improved; people have been cajoled or threatened for converting their houses into cattle or pig pens. But there is still ample room for more tidiness about the premises, for more care of the manure, and for cleaner, more thorough cultivation. Improvements made by tenants are paid for if they remove; but premiums given for entry by incoming tenants are discountenanced. Rents on this estate were freely reduced at the time of the great famine;

several years were considerately allowed to elapse, during which the tenants might recover from their difficulties; on some townlands the rents, however, have since been advanced four times, giving rise to much ill-feeling. The reduced rents of former years are naturally mourned over, but the tenants might reasonably consider whether the present enhanced charges are excessive as compared with the capability of the land and with the valuation of neighbouring estates. Since the reduction of 1847 the townland of Arderry has had four additions to the rent roll, and now stands at 98*l.*, while the Poor Law valuation is 83*l.* 15*s.* The townland of Tonlegee, with a valuation of 82*l.* 11*s.*, and with four accessions of rental angrily complained of, is 94*l.* In neither of these cases, which have been specially declaimed against, is the enhanced rent 20 per cent. over Griffith's valuation, which is admittedly moderate in Mayo, where I have met with instances of tenants paying three times the valuation and making their holdings answer very well.

It is not the rents which are the cause of the misery on this and other western estates. It is rather, as has been repeatedly stated, the want of steady industry, of energy, and of pride in the thorough working of their holdings. On many of these estates healthy emulation and good results might be greatly stimulated by a few pounds spent on prizes for the best-cultivated farms on every townland, with, perhaps, a champion prize for the best in the parish. This system has produced good fruits, especially among small tenants, both in Great Britain and Ireland. Adopted in Mayo, it would, perhaps, bring even absentee landlords and their agents into much-needed personal contact with the tenantry and promote improved profitable farming.

Sir Roger Palmer has 80,000 acres in Mayo, valued for rating at about 15,000*l.*, moderately rented, with liberty of free sale, with a fairly prosperous tenantry, some of them, however, complaining—for there seem to be grievances, real or fancied, almost everywhere—that a mountain which was a good 'stand' for cattle has been taken from one section of the tenants.

Lord Lucan has 60,570 acres in Mayo, part of it around Castlebar, where his substantial old house stands; part of it at Cloona Castle, near Ballinrobe. Griffith's valuation of the estate is 12,940*l.* It presents some contrasts to most of the large neighbouring estates. From several parishes extensive evictions were made from 1846 to 1850; throwing together the smaller holdings, several large grazing and a few considerable tillage farms were made. Lord Lucan, in his terse, incisive style, asserted that 'he would not breed paupers to pay priests.' Some townlands, nevertheless, still remain greatly overcrowded. With a sort of military despotism, he has endeavoured personally to rule his estates. Hurried visits to Mayo have not, however, always furnished him with sound information as to agricultural or social difficulties; his local lieutenants have had small authority; their opinions have often been hastily set aside; little has been done to develop either Castlebar, the villages on the estate, or the agriculture of the country. Although 300*l.* goes to his lordship yearly for tolls and stands at Castlebar Market, and although the need of a market-house for years has been urged, and repeated lots of plans have accumulated in the office, merchants and their customers still do business unsheltered in the open streets. The townspeople, moreover, complain that they cannot get from his lordship sites for better-class houses. The estate appears irregularly rented, more than one good tenant has been lost by want of tact, and a good many farms are unlet. At Castlebar and now at Cloona Castle are farms of upwards of 1,000 acres in hand, apparently not managed very profitably, much of the tillage imperfectly cultivated, and a good deal of the pasture only half-grazed and returning to its pristine rushes and coarse grass.

CHAPTER XX.

ESTATES AND FARMING IN SOUTH MAYO.

BALLINROBE has been one of the strongholds of agitation. Wholesale evictions on neighbouring properties, miserable overcrowding supinely permitted on others, indiscreet interference with old rights of common or turbary, high rents charged on a few small estates, altered arrangements of office and farm management, often good enough in themselves, but introduced without care and conciliation, have furnished grievances which, ingeniously displayed and freely magnified, have roused an ignorant, enthusiastic people to believe themselves generally unjustly and hardly dealt with. The want of knowledge, the thoughtless apathy, and blundering meddling of a few landlords and agents have brought odium, suspicion, and trouble on almost everyone connected with land management. Many landlords, disgusted at the unreasoning and often unreasonable agitation, and with life and property threatened, have left the country. In many districts it has been found difficult to conduct the business of sessions. The landlords and agents who remain mostly walk and drive under care of a couple of armed constables; even over their farms and about their own premises their vigilant guards constantly accompany them; their intended movements are kept very quiet; endeavour is made to go and return from any appointment by different routes. These gentlemen, and, indeed, all classes, suspicious of their neighbours, avoid being out after dusk ; mounted police patrol town and country roads ; most houses in town and country have extra bars and bolts, and, in many, heavy 2-inch deal shutters are every night put up against the windows to arrest the bullet of any murderous marauder.

At Ballinrobe the Church Commission five years ago sold some glebe property in the poorest part of the town, consisting of about fifty cabins, some of them rented at a few shillings a year. Although disposed of at three to ten years' rental, and some of them only realising 5*l.*, not half of the holders were able to raise the needful money, and accordingly many made over their rights of pre-emption to more fortunate friends. Mrs. Egan, a prosperous gombeen, bought several at the time of sale, and has since acquired others on which interest on mortgage was not forthcoming. Several lots which she has more recently bought have cost four times the amount the Commissioners received for them. She has rebuilt some of the tumble-down places ; complains, however, that rents are uncertain and difficult to collect, but will apparently become owner of the bulk of this glebe property. Notwithstanding the popular Irish clamour for abolishing landlords, such a case evidently indicates that labourers in Ballinrobe are not yet sufficiently steady, prudent, and self-sacrificing to grasp even the most favourable opportunity of becoming their own landlords.

Captain Charles Knox, of Ballinrobe, besides a small estate in Donegal, has 24,374 acres in Mayo, valued by Sir Richard Griffith at 8,050*l.* ; the present rental amounts to 9,000*l.* The number of tenants, area, valuation, and rental on different parts of the property are summarised as follows :

	No. of Tenants	Statute Acres	Griffith's Valuation	Rental
Ballinrobe	782	11,090	£6,098	£7,152
Glenhest	184	7,636	811	1,045
Castlelacken*	189	3,481	1,142	1,252
	1,155	22,207	£8,051	£9,449

The Ballinrobe tenants are generally well-to-do; 650 are purely agricultural; their farms are chiefly rented at 10 per cent. over Griffith's valuation; in no case is any one charged 25 per cent. over this valuation; a good many pay under 4*l.* of annual rent. As the town extends and prospers, there is increasing competition for the town parks, which have not however, been raised from the price charged in 1860, the best of them being 4*l.* 10*s.* per Irish acre. No remission was made from rents in 1879, but to meet the difficulties resulting from two bad years 10 to 15 per cent. was offered to all who would settle up their year's rent, due May 15, 1880. Occupiers of town parks, leaseholders, and those paying over 50*l.* a year, were, however, excluded from this deduction. With similar restriction, 15 to 25 per cent. was given throughout Glenhest, and 10 per cent. at Castlelacken. Many of the small people throughout all parts of the estate were excused one-half of the 1879 rents. The highest-rented portion is the mountain property of Glenhest, near Newport. The sea-coast townlands near Killala are low. Tenant-right has never been acknowledged, but liberal payments are made for improvements. Money for goodwill frequently passes between the out-going and in-coming tenants. Very few changes of tenancy, however, occur—a fair indication of the contentment and well-doing of the people, even in this notoriously disturbed district. Although

* On this part of the estate a large house is let for £300 over the valuation.

holding under yearly tenancies, the farms are transmitted in families for generations.

During thirteen years since Captain Knox came into possession, he has lived constantly on his property, and has exerted himself to improve his tenantry and his estate. He has never turned a tenant out; grace has always been generously given in making up rents; arrears are frequently wiped off; employment is largely found when wanted. A few ejectments have been served on idlers drifting three or four years behind; the sheriff has been summoned three times to evict, but even then the tenant has been put back as caretaker; help has been given wisely to assist emigration of families who were doing indifferently at home. To secure employment and furnish the money often needed to buy food, a loan was effected from the Board of Works, and between March 1 and November 1, 1880, 1,663*l*. 10*s*. 10*d*. was usefully expended in deepening a river, in main drains, and in reclamation. This assistance was necessary, even during summer, inasmuch as agricultural depression in England and the general slackness of the building trades, in which Irish labourers are largely employed, greatly diminished the prospects of the Mayo men finding their usual occupation in Great Britain.

Mr. James Simson emigrated from Roxburghshire in 1855, and took from Lord Lucan a twenty-five years' lease of Cloona Castle, two miles north of Ballinrobe, with upwards of 2,000 acres of land, part of it having been indifferently tilled by small occupiers, some of it in rough pasture, bog, and scrub. A large proportion had recently been given up by middlemen; 300 cabins, housing 2,000 souls, had been pulled down in 1848-49. Draining, trenching-out large stones, levelling, and removing tortuous fences had been begun; but under Mr. Simson's energetic and practical auspices more extended and thorough improvements were inaugurated and successfully carried out, large square fields were inclosed by forty miles of stone walls, a capital complete farmstead was erected at a cost of 13,000*l.*, and cottages were built for ploughmen and other servants. Besides this expenditure on the part of the landlord, Mr. Simson has laid out in various additions to buildings upwards of 14,000*l.*, and a similar amount on draining, fencing, and other substantial works. Much labour was also expended in eradicating neglected weeds, and, by liberal manuring, in restoring plant-food to land robbed by continuous cropping and reiterated burning. The Cloona Castle labour bills, like those elsewhere, have steadily advanced. Between 1855 and 1860 they were covered by 900*l.*; from 1861 to 1873 they averaged upwards of 1,000*l.*; from 1875 to 1878 they reached 1,300*l.*; while in 1879 the expenditure was 1,402*l.* This does not include blacksmith, carpenter, or saddler's accounts. Wet seasons greatly increased the costs of hoeing and added fully 100*l.*, to the annual labour bills. Like most enterprising Scotch farmers, Mr. Simson has been a good customer to the cake and manure merchants; his bills for these necessary adjuncts to success, tolerably equally spread over the twenty-five years, are as follow :—

Linseed and cotton cake	£5,617
Oats, beans, and other corn	6,000
Manures	14,852
Total	£26,469

He has introduced capital, hardy, quick-stepping Clydesdales, has a herd of useful shorthorns, and has successfully crossed the Roscommon sheep with well-selected border Leicesters. This cross stands the winter and wet admirably, readily reaches 22lbs. per quarter at 18 months, produces a heavy fleece of superior wool, and the good flock has greatly contributed to the success of the well-managed concern. Griffith's valuation of Mr. Simson's farm is 1,500*l.*; the rent has been 2,200*l.* The lease terminated at Michaelmas, 1880; but Lord Lucan and his enterprising tenant have been unable again to come to terms. Mr. Simson was willing to go on under the old conditions, provided allowance was made for 150 acres erroneously measured in the farm, and for which he had been paying. Lord Lucan at first demanded an advanced rent, and would make no concessions on account of insufficient measurement. Now that Mr. Simson has given up, his lordship cannot find a tenant, and is compelled to include Cloona with the large area he is already farming. Considering the uncertainty of farming and the increased difficulties with labourers, Mr. Simson is glad to leave Cloona Castle and restrict his agricultural operations ; but his claims for improvements and unexhausted tillages have been disallowed, and will have to be settled by the courts. Meanwhile Mr. Simson retains the farm of Killrush, Holly Mount, belonging to Miss Lindsay's trustees, measuring 480 acres, and has also 250 acres of grazing land. Poor-rates on these farms are 1*s.* 2*d.* and the county cess 1*s.* 10*d.*, the owner paying half of both, and also contributing one half towards all repairs.

One of the drawbacks to farming in the West of Ireland is the humid climate. The rainfall ranges from 31 to 57 inches. The Cloona Castle rainfall of 1876 was 44·9 ; of 1877, 47·30 ; of 1878, 37·6 ; that of 1880 was only 31·20— the lightest for ten years. The large number of rainy days etards and adds to the expense of outdoor work and facilitates the troublesome growth of weeds. Although the mean temperature is 2 degrees higher than on the east coast, recent years have wanted sunshine for the healthy maturing of crops. With some French meteorologists, Mr. Simson believes that seasons run in cycles of eleven years, four bad come together, two of them being wet and two cold, and there are three consecutive good seasons; but between each series are two of an intermediate character. It is consolatory to learn that we have got through the worst years of the cycle, are again on the ascending, improving series, and should this year expect a hot summer.

Mr. Simson, at Cloona, required twelve pairs of stout horses to cultivate satisfactorily his usual area of 320 acres of corn and 220 acres of roots. This is more horse-power than is requisite on similarly light loam in Scotland or the North of England. Manual labour, as already stated, is not only more expensive than it was twenty years ago, but wages have advanced from 7$s.$ to 10$s.$ and even 12$s.$ per week. Labourers, moreover, are increasingly difficult to manage; strikes at busy times have lately been common; Scotch and English farmers have been regarded with considerable suspicion, and liberal employers have often been put to inconvenience and loss by cabals among the men. It is difficult to introduce piece-work, so mutually advantageous alike to employers and employed. Holidays and wakes often prove annoying hindrances. Recent organisations have occasionally turned the labourers out on strike and terrorised those who were disposed quietly to continue at work by firing under cover of darkness into their windows. The increased cost of labour discourages arable culture and keeps an undue area unprofitably in grass, not always of the best quality.

Another disadvantage to western farming has been distance and inaccessibility of markets. Mr. Simson estimates that his marketing, alike of dead and live stock, has cost 10s. an acre. Extended railway and steamship communication is somewhat reducing this serious disadvantage, but even now it costs 14s. per ton, under recent enhanced rates, to bring cake or manure 134 miles from Dublin to his nearest station of Claremorris. Expenses of transport also discourage dairying, for which much of the Mayo land is suitable. The cattle stock on the larger farms are mostly brought as calves and yearlings from Kilkenny, Mullingar, Limerick, and Roscommon, are kept one or two years and passed on, generally fit for the butcher, leaving usually 5*l.* of profit for each year's keep.

With ripe experience of land management on both sides of the Channel, Mr. Simson is an ardent reformer. He inveighs against the laws of entail and primogeniture; would relieve the landowner of his trammels, would gradually secure the registration of all landed property, and have branch registers in every county town; would grant owners power to borrow on debenture bonds to the extent of three-fourths of their valued rental, in sums of 100*l.* upwards bearing interest at current rates, transferable and capable of redemption on six months' notice. Such bonds might be paid to a wife's trustees under marriage settlement or to children as their portion. Tenants and others would willingly take such securities, and landlords would thus cheaply obtain money for estate improvements.

James Gibson lives a mile south of Ballinrobe, is owner of a cabin and half an acre of land, which his forefathers acquired as squatters, and for which he assures me he could now obtain 25*l.* or 30*l.* Rough stone walls built with mud, 6 feet high, inclose an interior area of about 16 feet by 12 feet; the roof is rudely thatched; the door and small window furnish a modicum of light and ventilation. In this single room have been reared three generations of Gibsons. The father and grandfather were coopers and noggin makers; Gibson's chief resource is making spade and broom handles. The ash poles for this purpose are generally gratuitously furnished by considerate friends. From this source about 5*l.* a year is earned, and about the same by stone-breaking. The garden grows potatoes and a little wheat. The present family numbers nine; two are dead. The younger branches are at school, educated gratuitously. The eldest daughter, aged seventeen, is married and gone to California. From this neighbourhood numbers of young girls now go as domestic servants to America. They are more steady and saving than the lads; they prove zealous emigration agents; they write glowing accounts of the attractions of the Western Continent, and remit money to help out sisters and brothers. One after another the eleven children of a Ballinrobe limeburner crossed the Atlantic, and eventually the old couple have been persuaded to follow. Emigration is thus going on steadily and widely. I find on inquiry among the national schoolmasters in rural districts that few of the boys who pass through their hands now settle at home; the best go either to England or America. Mr. Cross, the master at Dough, has turned out about fifteen boys annually for fifteen years, and not one-tenth of them, I am told, are in the neighbourhood either as tenants or labourers.

Father John O'Malley has identified himself with the Irish popular movement; has been fourteen years at the

Neils; is a great favourite with his people; and, like many of his class, declares that Ireland's troubles and distress depend upon careless absentee landlords, ignorant, upstart agents, and a bad system of land tenure. The landowners, he complains, are never seen among their people; they have no sympathy with them; they subscribe miserably to charities. He found great difficulty in raising funds when some years ago his church required rebuilding. Owners of property spend, he says, liberally in embellishing their own demesnes or in carrying out their own whims, but little in improving the hovels of the poor or in helping them to reclaim land or to farm properly. The tenants, he urges, have no encouragement for their outlay, no security for their improvements, no protection against arbitrarily advanced rents. But while such sweeping complaints are readily enough made, the cases on which they are founded are neither so numerous nor so serious as his reverence represents. General conclusions ought not to be founded on exceptional cases.

Between Ballinrobe and Cong, at Dough, lives Mr. Thomas Gildea, who has a fee farm grant of 100 Irish acres and a neat house, well placed in the midst of garden, trees, and park. Here in 1798 the rebels met and concocted their plans. Mr. Blake, the then owner of Dough, was an active promoter of the rebellion, and his national zeal brought him to the gallows. Mr. Gildea has incurred the displeasure of the Land League. Artificers and labourers engaged in building a lodge and other improvements were ordered to stop work. The strike, however, must have been worse for the employed than the employer, and, as rents have not come in, he remarks that expenditure has been very opportunely reduced. With extended experience of Mayo, Mr. Gildea concludes that subdivision of holdings has been one of the chief pauperising influences. Without safeguards against sub-letting, small owners and occupiers determinedly plant around them their relatives and friends, and the poor land becomes overpopulated beyond the power of affording decent subsistence. He has an interest in 530 acres of improvable land near Foxford, within a mile of the railway, valued by Griffith at 140*l.*, and rented at 175*l.* per annum. Some years ago it was held by five, now it is in the hands of thirty-two leaseholders, who have numbers of sub-tenants. The occupiers ignorantly cling to the antiquated, inconvenient rundale, and indignantly object to the striping which has been offered to be done for them without expense. Irish tenants are eminently conservative as regards land management, and dislike to be put out of their old ways.

Mr. George Vesey, Ballyhankins, has 8,289 acres in Mayo and Galway, with a rental of about 3,000*l.* At the time of the great famine the best land was thrown into somewhat larger farms. Most of the tenants keep cows and rear a few calves, which thrive well on the palatable herbage of the thin limestone rock. Of 292 tenants, 51 pay less than 5*l.* of annual rental. Dr. Veitch has a considerable estate between Ballinrobe and Cong, where a number of small tenants have been carefully looked after, timeously helped, and are fairly well-to-do. Mr. Blake, Knock, has here 50 Irish acres in his own hands, and about 70 divided among 25 tenants; four hold among them 16 acres, five have one acre each, four have only one rood each. The limestone rock produces a fine, sweet herbage. Like thousands of others in the west, the people have no regular or even frequent employment. Many assure me that 50 days' work a year is all they can usually count upon at home; their own small farming occupies only a few occasional days; it could generally be done, like the English labourer's allotment, in spare time.

The Rev. W. Jamieson several years ago bought on favourable terms Kildun More, which measures 1,831 acres, and is valued at 1,774*l.* His rents have not been raised. They are understood to be within Griffith's valuation, but he has, nevertheless, had to make the 25 per cent. abatement so generally demanded in this district. Not far distant is Mr. J. G. Dawson's estate of 1,120 acres, affording an example of very different treatment. A large portion some years ago was cleared and converted into sheep-walks. It was valued by Griffith at 500*l.* The rental is stated to be nearly double that amount, but for some years considerable abatements have been made both to the larger pastoral and to the smaller tenants.

Sir Benjamin Lee Guinness purchased the Ashford property at Cong, picturesquely situated on the banks of Lough Mask, in South Mayo, in 1852. Estates, some of them of absentees, much neglected and mismanaged, have since been added, and now Lord Ardilaun owns 33,298 acres in Mayo and Galway, producing a rental of 12,000*l.*, divided among 670 tenants, of whom about 316 are rented at less than 5*l.* per annum. During the past twelve years, since Lord Ardilaun came into possession, almost the whole of the rental has been expended on estate works, such as building a magnificent mansion, inclosing and planting a park of 200 Irish acres, making roads, draining extensively, altering the pier for the accommodation of the steamer which plies from Galway to Cong, and building numerous cottages. Four hundred to five hundred artisans and labourers have frequently been engaged, but during the last six months, since rents have been persistently refused, the works have been contracted, and only 100 people are in regular occupation. Wages fifteen years ago were 6s., now they range from 8s. to 10s. per week. In winter the hours are from 8 A.M. until dark; in summer from 6 A.M. to 6 P.M., with an hour for breakfast and another for dinner. With extensive improvements still going on, there does not seem to be sufficient cottage accommodation, and many of the labourers trudge three or four miles morning and night, to and fro. With plenty of remunerative work, fewer of the people here—not one in fifty—proceed to England for summer service. Of the mountain tenants a larger proportion migrate; about 20 per cent. of the flower of the youth go to England in March, and are employed in building work and in the forges; many seem to be taken up at Shields and Jarrow.

Although slow to take in bog or waste, and not always making the best of their farms, the labourers and small holders are fairly well off. Many of the labourers keep a cow, some have a donkey or horse and cart, for which they obtain frequent employment at the rate of 4s. per day. Lord Ardilaun has encountered the same difficulties as other landlords who have endeavoured to increase the size of their smaller holdings and provide better dwellings for their people. Those bought out of small farms, miserably inadequate to provide a livelihood, talk as if they had been dispossessed of a magnificent inheritance without requital. Although liberal terms were given for disturbance, although payments were made for tenants' improvements, and good houses and farms were provided elsewhere, the clearing away of small holders to make Ashford-park has caused considerable heartburning. Clearances from overcrowded spots or from land desired to be taken in hand were mainly effected by the purchase of grazing farms, whence it was no hardship to remove the non-resident yearly tenants, and where, at the landlord's expense, fifteen to twenty-five acres were set out and houses provided. Such changes, judiciously effected, are notably of great permanent benefit ; but the Land Act of 1870 renders them more difficult and costly to carry out.

Notwithstanding extended farms and better dwellings, some of the tenantry are by no means satisfied with their altered position. There is manifest disposition to magnify the value of what has been given up and to underestimate what has been acquired. A poetic sentiment throws its glamour over the past and makes it compare too favourably with the present. The new, substantial stone and slated houses, often of two storeys, to which some are removed, are complained of as too big. At Garracloon the people say that they have too much light and cannot keep the great places warm. Ignoring architectural effect and modern appliances, it is probably economy and wisdom for the present to allow Irish tenants to build their own houses in great part after their own ideas. On various portions of this estate houses have thus been built, the landlord sometimes advancing the money and charging for it 4 per cent. In one mountain district each tenant holds his house and garden separately, but has his grazing for cattle and sheep in common with his neighbours. Very little reclamation is being done by tenants; they usually have gratuitously what turf they require for their own use. Around the park and plantations, which are greatly improving the amenity of the estate, game is becoming plentiful, and is said to do considerable damage.

Rents vary from 5s. to 40s. per Irish acre; the latter figure is given for the best grazing lands, let annually from May-day. Hay is allowed to be cut for the tenants' use or for sale to his successor, but not for removal; the herd's cottage, the only building on these grass holdings, is maintained in repair by the landlord. Grazing farms in Galway are generally let higher than those in Mayo. Yearly tenancies are the rule all over the estate; leases are never asked for, and, under the Act of 1870, are less needful. Since 1868 Lord Ardilaun has issued ten ejectments, several of them for non-payment of rent. Other changes of tenancy were effected voluntarily, considerable money payments and other advantages being given to the waygoer. Besides much continuous employment being found, 3,000*l.* was spent during the winter of 1879-80 in meal and seed potatoes. From the 1879 rents under 20*l.* 30 per cent. was allowed, and half that from the 1880 rents. Farms valued at 20*l.* to 50*l.* received 20 per cent. deduction from the 1879 rent, and 10 per cent. from that of 1880. On this, as on so many other liberally-managed Irish estates, the home farm has greatly helped to teach improved agricultural practices, to bring into notice useful implements, and to place within reach of the smaller tenants valuable improved male animals.

Mr. William Burke, J.P., who acts as agent, not only for Lord Ardilaun, but also for Lord Kilmaine, Lord Clanmorris, and others, tells me that, in spite of all that has been done for the tenantry, rents for more than twelve months have been badly paid throughout Mayo and Galway. Agitation and persistent refusal to pay their just debts have been fomented, not only by meetings and orations, but very largely by a certain portion of the Irish and American Press, which is eagerly read by the people, which expatiates on some real and on many imaginary wrongs, which ministers to cupidity and idleness, and suggests impossible remedies. Mr. Burke rendered himself unpopular, and necessitated his being included among the 157 persons placed under police protection, by serving processes on several of Lord Clanmorris's long-defaulting tenants near Ballinrobe. Holders of long leases and fee-farm grants frequently come under Mr. Burke's observation. They are not, as might be expected, greatly more prosperous than their neighbours under reasonable covenants occupying from year to year. They sell and change quite as frequently as the yearly tenants. An Americanised Irishman with a fee-farm grant of 200 Irish acres, on which the rent is 30*l.*, is at present offering his estate for sale. Another fee-farm owner of sixty Irish acres, with a good house built by himself, offers his property to Lord Ardilaun, desiring to become a yearly tenant and willing to pay as rent 5 per cent. on the purchase money. Ownership, unfortunately, is no guarantee against dissipation and waste. On Lord Kilmaine's estate, the holder of a lease of sixty acres for three lives has just drunk himself to death. He had sub-let the holding under a sort of conacre for two years, received his rents in advance, but owed his landlord one and a half year's arrears. This is an unsatisfactory entry for the new leaseholder.

Political and religious differences cause here, as in other

parts of Ireland, loss of time and of temper, and interfere considerably with education and progress. Lord Ardilaun has built a capital school at Ashford, and took pains to have a first-rate master, but he happens to be a Protestant, and although, of course, no religious teaching is given in a national school, and no suspicion of proselytism is hinted at, Roman Catholic farmers and labourers are dissuaded from sending their children, and many of the little people have the disadvantage of tramping three miles to the approved school at Cong. Although so much money has recently been circulated in this district, business does not flourish in Cong. Of the three flour-mills which were wont to be driven by the abundant water-power, only one is now in operation, and is not always running; there are no other manufactories.

Mr. William Joyce, of Blakehill, Clonbur, has 100 Irish acres on lease from Lord Ardilaun; by rebuilding his old-fashioned, ivy-clad house he could prolong his lease, but he does not think that the present prospects of farming justify such outlay. He has six sub-tenants, each holding five acres, paying 10*l.* of rental, thinking as much of their cottage and cabbage-garden as Lord Ardilaun does of his castle, and, although zealous members of the Land League, meeting their rents regularly. On the edge of this farm is the spot where Lord Mountmorres was murdered. Mr. Joyce has also 560 acres of land at Headford. Paying 36*s.* to 40*s.* an acre of rent, 3*s.* 9*d.* of poor-rates, and 2*s.* of county cess, and taking into account the increased cost of production and the inconvenient remote markets, he believes his farming to be unremunerative, and has accordingly given up a considerable part of his land.

CHAPTER XXI.

LAND TENURE: GENERAL CONCLUSIONS.

THE land question in Ireland presents varying aspects in various parts of the island, on different estates, and on farms of different descriptions. Almost side by side are well and ill-managed estates; great tracts of land liberally and profitably treated, and equally large areas neglected and starved, and which under better treatment might readily produce double their present returns. Irish tenants enjoy more privileges, freedom of action, and security of tenure, than any in Europe; but exceptional cases are met with of tenants ruthlessly rackrented and smarting under grievances which the present laws fail to prevent. Fair profits have been secured from the larger better cultivated farms in most localities, and especially from grazing and dairying. Complaints of distress and difficulty have, however, occurred very generally among small holders on poor, wet, and foul land. In many parts of Ireland few and indifferent roads, and distance from markets, tell seriously upon prices of agricultural produce and reduce rents. Mainly from these causes the value of land differs considerably in the four provinces. Official statistics indicate that the acreable agricultural rent throughout Leinster is 18*s.* 11*d.*, in Ulster 15*s.* 8*d.*, in Munster 11*s.* 2*d.*, in Connaught 6*s.* 9*d.* With better roads and transit facilities rents in the Southern and Western provinces might more nearly approach those in the east and north.

The preceding letters on land tenure and estate management, although describing only scattered properties in Leinster, in Waterford, Cork, and Kerry, throughout Ulster, and in Mayo, afford ample illustration of many phases in the relation of landlord and tenant. They justify the statements made in our introductory observations, that a large proportion of the 7,000 landlords of Ireland, owners of 500 acres and upwards, are strenuously, sometimes of late rather thanklessly, doing their duty and improving their estates and their people. On many large estates described, as on those of the Duke of Leinster, Lord Fitzwilliam, the Duke of Devonshire, Lord Ardilaun, and Messrs. Musgrave, as well as on the properties of most of the public companies, large sums are annually expended in improvements which furnish profitable labour during their execution, and further permanently benefit the tenant. Deducting such expenditure, with allowances and arrears, which have been heavy of late years, Irish landlords generally secure poor and precarious returns for their land investments. Outside their own estates, and for the development of the material and social condition of the people, many have zealously promoted the making of roads and railways, and exerted themselves to provide piers and harbours, to secure steam communication for the transport of agricultural produce and to foster local industries. In many districts there is still ample scope for the prosecution of such good work. In all parts of Ireland landlords generally have come forward with personal exertion and purse to tide over those frequently recurring periods of distress and famine depending mainly on the smallness of the holdings, the indolence and improvidence of the people and their undue dependence on the precarious potato crop. In almost every district are liberally managed estates belonging to English as well as to Irish families, where example, precept and judicious help have promoted the tenants' well doing. The estates of the Marquis of Waterford, Sir Henry Gore-Booth, Mr. E. Pery, and Mr. Tighe, afford illustrations of thoughtful regard for the interests of the tenantry. Ireland can ill afford to alienate or remove such landlords or minimise the good which they are doing.

Unfortunately there are landlords of less favourable type, devoid of public spirit, and with an indifferent sense of their duties and responsibilities, sometimes so impoverished and hampered with debt that they are impelled to rackrenting and any other devices for the raising of money. Of the holders of estates exceeding fifty acres about one-third, or 2,973, are absentees, who every year abstract from their impoverished country upwards of 2,500,000*l.* One of these gentlemen, visiting his estates after many years of absence, showed the too common indifference of his class by declaring that 'he cared not if he never saw them again.' On several estates I visited the people have never seen their landlord; frequently the agent is also non-resident; rarely goes over the estate; is only met by the tenants once or twice a year when rents are collected. Under such auspices, especially with small and ignorant holders, not much progress can be expected. Such a state of matters, although to be deplored, is difficult to amend by Act of Parliament. The Western counties are the stronghold of absenteeism.

In Mayo, for example, nine owners hold upwards of 20,000 acres each, amongst them draw annually 100,000*l.* from this poor Western county, and spend not one-tenth of their income on their estates. Many properties, great and small, are heavily encumbered ; the nominal owner has nothing to lay out in much-needed improvements ; rents, even when punctually paid, were all required to meet interest on mortgages, settlements, and charges. Under such circumstances there can be no timeous help initiating and encouraging improvements. Needy landlords are apt to produce needy tenants. Dire necessity demands the uttermost shilling of rent that can be screwed out of the property ; pauperising subletting is apt to flourish, for it is expensive as well as troublesome to remove and provide for the multiplying families that helplessly sprawl over impoverished Irish properties. For the advantage alike of such encumbered owners and their miserable tenants it has been reasonably urged that when an estate is burthened to the extent of three-fourths of its value—an unpleasant fact which is not always however made public—the nominal owner should be compelled to sell. With extended facilities and provision for the security of the remainder man, many encumbered Irish properties would now be willingly disposed of, and would obviously furnish a ready means of multiplying small owners.

Irish landlords generally have not only been reasonable in the matter of rent, but, even before the Land Act of 1870, they have seldom exerted their rights of eviction and distraint. The annual evictions have fallen to 460, or one-half the number they averaged previous to 1870. Landlords have respected the old tribal traditional usages ; and not only in Ulster, but throughout most parts of Ireland, there has grown a tacit admission, unknown in Great Britain, that the tenant has a possessory interest in his holding. The strong affection for the place of birth or early location, the infrequent changes of occupancy—held often undisturbed for many generations—the building, reclamation, and other permanent work done by the tenant instead of, as in Great Britain, by the landlord, have concurred to root the occupier to the soil, and despite his usual yearly and parole agreement to give him an equitable claim to security of tenure. The concurrent interest of landlord and tenant in the Irish holding has been amusingly illustrated by Lord Dufferin by comparing them to two fellows occupying one bed. Much fear is, however, expressed that the strongest and least scrupulous may kick the other out. The tenant having acquired a statutory right to continuous possession, cuckoo-like, may be disposed to claim more than his share, and if possible edge his landlord out. Despite this risk, in all parts of the country, well-informed landlords of various shades of politics recognise this possessory interest in their dealings with their tenantry, and believe that with certain safeguards its general concession will not injuriously affect their interest.

The Royal Commissioners, in their report on the working of the Landlord and Tenant (Ireland) Act of 1870, state that 'the occupiers have as a general rule acquired rights to continuous occupancy which in the interest of the community it is desirable to recognise.' This interest constitutes the chief feature of the Ulster custom. As pointed out in many of the letters, the value of tenant right in the North often exceeds the fee simple; while the landlord would receive perhaps 25*l.* per acre, or twenty-five years' purchase, for his share in the property, the tenant frequently commands even double that, or sometimes as much as fifty years' rental.

The Irish occupier's tenure is hence more permanent than that of his British fellow worker. To formulise and impress the uncertain tenant right custom with the authority of law, was the chief object of the Land Act of 1870. While granting the tenant this important recognition, the Act does not however give him any direct means of protecting his right. The occupier of an ordinary arable or mixed farm, on the voluntary surrender of his holding, claims from his landlord compensation for all improvements made by himself and his predecessors in title. In the absence of proof to the contrary, all improvements are presumed to be made by the tenant. If with the landlord's consent the tenant or his predecessor has paid any premium for good will on entry, if not allowed to sell his interest, and not receiving any payment for compensation, he is entitled to remuneration for such premium. The tenant cannot be evicted for non-payment of rent until one year's rent is in arrear, and by paying up the claim and expenses within six months of the eviction may demand reinstatement. The tenant is not liable for tithes; if his valuation is under 4*l*. the landlord must pay poor-rates; if over 4*l*. the landlord pays half the poor-rates, and on many estates the custom is also to share the county cess. The Irish tenant valued at less than 50*l*. cannot contract himself out of the benefits conferred by the Act. If the tenant is served with a notice to quit, or is otherwise disturbed in his holding, he must be paid by his landlord not only full compensation for any improvements effected by himself or his predecessors in title, but a solatium varying from one to seven years' rent. Even if evicted for non-payment of rent, he must be paid by his landlord for all improvements; and when his rent does not exceed 15*l.*, and if the court determines that the rent has been exorbitant, he is entitled moreover to a sum of money varying from one to seven years' rent. Irish tenants moreover have facilities for the purchase of their lands when sold through the Landed Estates Court.

These valuable privileges belonging to the Irish tenant are liable however to be materially restricted or even nullified. The intentions of the Land Act are sometimes misinterpreted, and its provisions are occasionally evaded. Exorbitant rents are sometimes charged; senseless restrictions are imposed; security is only attained by payment of a repeatedly raised rent which leaves the tenants small margin for subsistence. Rents are sometimes arbitrarily and unadvisedly raised by periodical valuation, at the termination of leases, or on changes of tenancy. The advance is not always justified by the improved state of the holding. It is usually dependent upon unwise competition among small farmers who desire a home, and if they make a bad bargain have nothing to lose. Any real accession to the value of the holding has generally been the result of the outlay and labour of the tenant. A few such cases of taxing and confiscation naturally produce uncertainty and ill-feeling throughout a wide district. Even in Ulster, where tenant right has greatly improved the occupiers' position, there are loud complaints of reiterated raising of rent especially on changes on tenancy, with the obvious effect of proportionately reducing the value of the tenant right.

Every 1s. added to the rent is estimated to take 20s. from the value of the tenant right.

Rearrangement as to rent, redistribution of land amongst adjacent tenants, the change from a lease to yearly tenancy, have been interpreted to break the continuity of tenancy, and thus prove a bar to the tenant's claims for improvements and compensation. Such limitations and exceptions might be reduced or abandoned. The leaseholder with an equitable claim is sometimes as much entitled to compensation as the yearly tenant. The occupier of a holding over 50*l.* of annual value usually deserves as much consideration as the smaller occupier. The conjoined interests of landlord and tenant are not inimical; fairly defined they should prove mutually beneficial; their permanence should ensure the best being made of the land; there should be every inducement to prevent the deterioration and waste which occur in tenancies at will or towards the termination of leases.

To mete out justice between landlord and tenant, to prevent arbitrary treatment of the weaker party, to settle disputes before they become serious grievances, a land court of arbitration and appeal is greatly wanted. To such a tribunal would be referred all disputes as to rent, tenure, or sale. Difficulties might thus be settled amicably without the two parties as now being brought into antagonism, without the disagreeable intervention of an ejectment, and without the risk of the tenant losing his holding in fighting for his compensation.

Tenants' interests, it was at one time believed, might be secured, as they have been to some extent in Great Britain, by leases. But these have disadvantages. They demand more independence and intelligence on the part of both contracting parties than are generally found in Ireland. The present popular remedy for Irish Land troubles are the three F's—Fixity of Tenure, Free Sale, and Fair Rents. With certain limitations, these new conditions of tenure are already widely recognised. Adopted on some of the best managed estates, they might with advantage to the agriculture and peace of Ireland be generally insisted on.

No just landlord objects to give his tenants Security, or even with certain limitations Fixity of Tenure. He does not seek to disturb a good tenant. He desires to reserve minerals, quarries and turbary, power to make watercourses, drains, roads and other public improvements, liberty on payment of compensation, as granted under the Land Act of 1870, to take sites for cottages for other building purposes or for gardens. He stipulates for ingress, egress and regress, for concurrent sporting rights, for protection against subdividing, subletting, dilapidation, and waste. He covenants for regular payment of rent, and for prompt and easy redress in case these reasonable conditions are unfulfilled or contravened. Landlords would have power to remove a tenant only by decree of the Land Court compelling him to sell in the event of his being convicted of any serious criminal offence, falling one or more years in arrears with his rent, subdividing, or subletting, or interfering with the landlords' rights enumerated, after being ordered in writing to desist, or being guilty of dilapidation or waste.

Free Sale under certain limitations proves a benefit both to landlord and tenant. It secures a reserve fund from which the owner is always sure of his rent, as is well illustrated in Ulster, where losses from arrears are trifling. With an admitted interest in his holding the tenant ought to be at liberty to make the best of it, and sell it either privately or publicly. The knowledge that he can do so must stimulate his exertions, and induce him to make the best of his occupation—a benefit alike to himself and his landlord. In case of difficulties the sale enables him to settle with his landlord and other creditors, and probably besides secures funds with which to make a fresh start. In legalising Free Sale on estates where hitherto it has not been recognised, care must obviously be taken that the tenant does not dispose of anything which does not belong to him. Landlord's improvements, the privilege of an admittedly low rent, the landlord's possession of the tenant right must be jealously guarded from appropriation. As has been frequently suggested, and as is urged by the Royal Commissioners, the present value of a landlord's improvements might be capitalised and made a first charge on the tenant's interest. Or again in the case of rent being regarded by the landlord as too low, and hence increasing unduly the value of the possessory interest, at the expense of the value of the fee simple it would not be difficult to fix and record a fair rent which any subsequent tenant would have to pay. The landlord, moreover, would retain a *veto* in regard to the respectability, solvency and practical ability of the proposed tenant, might insist on his being resident, and would have the privilege of pre-emption at the highest *bonâ fide* price offered for the holding.

The Fair Rent is the most troublesome to adjust of the three proposed new conditions of tenure. It is more difficult to determine in Ireland than in England. It is not necessarily the absolute commercial value. Old customs have sanctioned, and the Land Act of 1870 has legalised, the tenant's right to any improvements made by himself or his predecessors which have added to the letting value, and in the case of small tenancies, any money which has been paid down on entry. The real or fancied excess of rent has been the chief cause of the land grievance. The question of fair rents is complicated by old relations under which they have sometimes remained unaltered for half a century. Recent rack renting, on the other hand, affords the tenant scant margin for subsistence. The fair rent may practically be regarded as that to which both contracting parties willingly agree, or which within the last twenty years and for a period of ten years has been paid without objection, or which has been or shall be settled in the usual way by arbitration. To facilitate such arrangements standing committees of local arbitrators have been proposed. The fair rent may sometimes happen to conform with Griffith's valuation; occasionally it will be under; more often it will be considerably above it. Opportunity and facility should be given to tenants, with of course the consent of the owner, to fine down the rent. On some estates the present low rents would be raised to a fair standard, or some arrangement made by which the fair rent should be recognised and recorded in order, as already stated, that the tenant, exercising his right of sale, should not dispose of what did not belong to him. The purchaser would enter at the advanced standard rent, or, if the landlord chose to allow a continuance of tenure at the lower rent, he might receive from the produce of the first sale the capitalised value of his annual remission. No court would interfere with existing rents unless when disputes occur. Thoughtful landlords consider that no change should be made in rents once determined, except by mutual consent, or at intervals of twenty-one, twenty-five, or, as some advise, thirty-one years. Even at these prolonged periods the general concurrence of opinion declares that no increase of rent should be exigible unless by mutual agreement, excepting under three conditions, namely: (*a*) the advanced price of agricultural produce as fixed by the *Gazette* returns of the district for a period of not less than five years; (*b*) outlay on the part of the landlord on or outside the farm, adding to its letting value; (*c*) an unearned increment such as the making of a railway, the rising of a town, or the improvement of markets.

Her Majesty's Commissioners recommend that one-half of this unearned increment should be credited to the landlord, one-half to the tenant. The former, however, will be mainly instrumental in such exoteric advances; in most parts of the county his money interest in the holding considerably exceeds that of the tenant, and hence in justice he should enjoy a larger proportion, probably three-fourths of this unearned increment. All accession of value not coming under these three heads would accrue to the tenant.

The fixing of a fair rent, it has been urged, might be facilitated by an immediate general revaluation. A period of agitation is, however, unsuitable for such an undertaking. Its execution would, moreover, occupy at least two years. Such a postponement of the rent difficulty is inadmissible. Besides, no valuation, however good, would be likely to prove, any more than Sir Richard Griffith's laborious and careful valuation has done, an infallible criterion of value. A Court of Arbitration and Appeal such as is now proposed would still be requisite. It is more hopeless in Ireland than in England to attempt, as has been suggested, a valuation which shall serve both for rent and for rating.

The harmonious relations of landlord and tenant, and

the successful working of an Irish Land Act, must greatly depend on the formation of a good land court. Under the Act of 1870 the County Court judge who tries land cases does not always possess practical knowledge of the questions brought before him. Two thoroughly competent agriculturists with a legal assessor would probably make a fitting tribunal. It would go on circuit to county and other principal towns, probably every three months or as required. Such a court would possess the confidence both of landlord and tenant. To it would be referred all disputes in regard to land. The party losing his case or making unreasonable or unjust demands would be charged with costs. In many instances, being early appealed to, it would redress grievances before they became serious, and secure harmony between landlord and tenant ; instead of arranging as the Act of 1870 mainly does for their separation, it should provide for their amicable working. It should be constituted to prevent fully as much as to cure disputes. Without the court's decree no ejectment would be granted. Whilst usurping part of the authority hitherto belonging to the landlord, a properly constituted land court would relieve him of some of his most difficult and painful duties. As already indicated, it would often anticipate and prevent troubles. It would be a dead letter on most well managed estates, but prove a barrier to the capricious arbitrary treatment of tenants. Whilst protecting the occupier against any unreasonable advance of rent, or injurious interference in his management or in the sale of his possessory interest, it would relieve the landlord of much odium, as for example in preventing subdivision or waste, in objecting to an unsuitable purchaser of the tenant right, in insisting on the removal of an occupier who had dropped into arrears, and in securing from the proceeds of the sale settlement for rent and other reasonable claims.

For the agricultural and social regeneration of Ireland, further land measures are anxiously canvassed. Even with the beneficial operation of the Encumbered Estates Act, the Bright Clauses of the Land Act of 1870, and the Church Act of 1869, it is very generally admitted that there is in Ireland a disproportion in the number of owners and occupiers. The estates exceeding fifty acres are held by less than 20,000 persons. Half the area of Ireland is divided amongst 750 owners. The total occupiers exceed 600,000; one-half of these hold only fifteen acres and under; about one-fifth of the farms are under 4*l*. of annual rent. Between the great owners of lordly domains and the small, often wretched, occupiers there is a wide chasm. The yeoman class, which own ten acres to 500 acres, and possess one-third of the land of England, hold only one-eighth of the soil of Ireland. The well-to-do men renting 100 acres and upwards, and numerous in England and Scotland, are usually liberal employers of labour, advance greatly the productive capabilities of the soil, and constitute an important section of the middle class, but are rare in Ireland. The multiplication of these few and far scattered yeomen and substantial tenant farmers would in many ways benefit Ireland. Legislation may encourage their creation. Delays and expenses of the transfer of land may still be greatly reduced. Greater facilities may be granted for the acquisition of small portions of land by the occupier.

Small owners throughout Ireland have not hitherto been particularly conspicuous for their success. Their farming has not invariably been better than that of their neighbouring tenants-at-will. When established they have not been very permanent. The Cromwellian grants of 100 acres, freely given throughout Ireland, have almost all disappeared. Most neighbourhoods present unhappy records of perpetuity owners and long leaseholders gradually wasting their substance and having to dispose of their farms. The dignity of ownership has sometimes foolishly prevented steady work, and dangerously provided credit which has been woefully abused. The general atmosphere of *dolce far niente* has often been two strong for the smaller owner. The moist mild climate of the west, and the absolute dearth of work at many seasons, have contributed to enervating idleness. The 6,000 small owners recently created under the Church Act are doing better; most have made substantial improvements; their arrears, owing to the commissioners, do not amount to 10 per cent., and are regarded as all recoverable. They have been orderly, and even where compelled by bad times or domestic calamity to give up their newly acquired estates, they have done so quietly and without coercion. These are hopeful evidences of a better state of things. School teaching, the education of example, steadier habits, and the opportunities of better markets, are inculcating more industry and thrift. Amongst the agricultural population generally there are greater incentives to exertion, and more helps to prudence and saving. Recovering rapidly from the effects of the bad season of 1879, the more careful of the agricultural classes are again in a position to find ready money towards the purchase of their holdings. In all parts of the country tenants express anxiety to have a more permanent interest in the soil they till, and thoughtful landlords, even when doubtful as to the means by which such a scheme can be carried out, are anxious that the experiment should have a fair trial.

There is no difficulty in obtaining estates on which occupiers can be converted into yeomen and peasant proprietors. In many districts, especially in the west, are estates, portions of estates, and outlying townlands, which would be willingly sold at little over twenty years' rental. Chief amongst the offerers of such lands will be many absentees, numerous encumbered owners, some of the public companies, not a few landlords who believe that their rights have been tampered with, others who have been disappointed in carrying out their ideas of social or material improvements, still more who have found their estates provokingly unremunerative and their rents difficult and uncertain to collect.

The satisfactory working of the Church Act of 1869, in disposing of the Irish glebe lands, encourages the further creation of small owners. The Irish Church Commissioners, at the period of the disestablishment, were the largest landowners in Ireland, and had estates worth about 229,000*l.* a year, held by 10,563 tenants, of whom nearly one-fifth were perpetuity tenants or leaseholders; 8,432 were yearly tenants. Of these, 6,057 have bought the fee-simple of their holdings, representing an annual value of 73,759*l.*, paying on an average twenty-two and two-thirds years' purchase. 2,326 other tenants were unable to take advantage of their power of pre-emption, on account of their inability to find the ready money, consisting in the case of holdings not exceeding 50*l.* of the whole of the purchase money, in the case of larger holdings of one-fourth. The three-fourths generally left unpaid was secured either on simple mortgage, bearing interest at 4 per cent. per annum, or on an instalment mortgage providing for payment of both principal and interest in half-yearly instalments, spread over thirty-two or any lesser number of years. As already stated, the obligations of these numerous tenants have been punctually met, and even during the recent period of general indisposition to pay rents the arrears do not exceed 10 per cent.

The successful working of the Church Act affords a good basis for any new land scheme. The Commission gave every tenant pre-emption of the lands in his occupation, and provided simple information and instructions as to his proceedings. The expenses of purchase were very much less than those under the Bright clauses of the Land Act. There was no restriction as to the purchaser borrowing as best he could on the security of a second mortgage. For manipulating estates and disposing of them to the occupying tenantry, a commission would be appointed. As recommended by the Royal Commission and other competent authorities, lands purchased would be paid for, not in cash, but in bonds or stock similar to 3 per cents. or India Stock, transferable in the same manner, bearing half-yearly dividends at the rate of $3\frac{1}{2}$ per cent., redeemable in a defined number of years by a sinking fund. Tenants under these Acts, having to obtain at least one-fourth of their purchase money, were on this account sometimes debarred from exercising their power of pre-emption; others to procure this advance frequently had to borrow, paying 10 per cent. and in some instances much more. This obligation contrasted unfavourably with the $5\frac{1}{2}$ per cent. charged by the Commission for the unpaid purchase money, and which cleared off principal and interest in thirty-two years.

If estates are judiciously bought on the terms now offered and the Commission is economically worked, even if squaring roads and main drainage operations require to be overtaken, it will usually be possible to sell the farms at twenty-five years' purchase. The few tenants who could at once settle in full would be encouraged to do so; any part payment would be accepted; and the residue arranged as a charge, to be cleared off at the furthest within fifty years. It seems undesirable to deny pre-emption to any resident occupier who has lived several years on his farm or has purchased his tenant right, even although he can make no preliminary payment. The repayment of the whole principal with interest discharged in half-yearly instalments might be extended over a period not exceeding fifty years. It would make small difference if the amount thus fixed slightly exceeded, as it occasionally might do, the present rent. Surely the prospect of ultimate ownership should reconcile the cultivator to any small extra payment. The administrative body would run small risk of loss. As frequently occurred on the first passing of the Land Act of 1870, pride in the more firmly secured holding would prove a stimulus to improvement and better cultivation, which could not fail to appreciate the value of the farm. Every payment would reduce risk of loss to the Commission. In the event of the death of the new owner or of his falling into difficulty or arrears, the farm would be readily sold. Amongst the recently created owners of the Church lands no losses have occurred, and no difficulties even during the last two years had been found in quietly transferring the holdings of the few defaulters to responsible solvent persons. The tenant right, worth at a low estimate five times the yearly rent, constitutes from the date of purchase a security on which the Commission would have the first claim. The embryo owner or his representative at any time should have power to sell *in globo*. Until indebtedness to the Commission was entirely liquidated no tenant without permission should be permitted to subdivide or sublet. In manipulating these estates conveyances might be simplified and cheapened, and the farms handed over to the tenant free of legal expenses, as is done for purchasers of quit and Crown rents under the Department of Woods and Forests. Mr. Walter L. Bernard, chief clerk to the Commissioners of Church Temporalities in Ireland, has suggested in the case of transactions under 5*l*. that instead of a conveyance mortgage there should be substituted a simple charging order which should be free of stamp duty. A duplicate copy would remain with the tenant, and when reconveyance was made or the mortgage claims liquidated, the transaction should be registered for a fee of 2*s*. 6*d*. on the charging order.

When these yeoman and peasant proprietors have got their holdings, will they keep them? Small owners in Ireland have not been so permanent as could be desired. Many have drifted into difficulties. No statutory safeguard can be devised to prevent this. Bad seasons, want of energy, family troubles, will sometimes necessitate resale. Men who have made a little money in the towns or abroad will doubtless seize such opportunities and lay several of these farms into small estates; the owner of a few short years will revert to his position as a tenant-at-will; but on the ruins, as it were, of these peasant proprietors will gradually arise a most valuable substantial yeoman class.

Besides other important considerations, the question occurs, What should be the minimum size of holdings? The benefits anticipated from peasant proprietorship will be jeopardised if the farms permanently set out are insufficient to furnish subsistence for an industrious occupier and his family. Between 1841 and 1861 the number of holdings under fifteen acres declined 55 per cent. Although this salutary rolling together of small occupations goes steadily on, the farms throughout Ireland are still much too small. In most parts of the country twenty statute acres of fairly cultivated or cultivatable land should certainly be the minimum. On superior soils near towns, one-half or even one-fourth of this area properly cultivated should secure a decent maintenance. Where the land is chiefly bog or mountain, and little of it fit for cultivation, forty or fifty acres would generally be required to furnish a modest livelihood. Sir Richard Griffith and other good authorities have declared that Irish farms should range from twenty-five acres to forty acres. In many poorer overcrowded districts, in order that each small tenant should possess this area, considerable numbers would have to be displaced. On some estates room would be found for these supernumeraries by subdividing and breaking up second-rate grass farms. The conversion of really good grassland into tillage, as frequently recommended, would be a retrograde step and only of temporary benefit. The climate of Ireland and the relative price of grain and live stock alike indicate the desirability of promoting a system of agriculture which will most profitably keep the largest number of cattle and sheep. On many neglected Western estates, where the land is poor, and where no other means of subsistence is attainable, clearances must be gradually and judiciously made by migrating or emigrating the surplus population in families. A commission, with estates in different parts of the country, would have special facilities at no very serious cost for thus relieving hopeless overcrowding.

The four and a half million acres (4,630,059 acres) of uncultivated land, which the statistics set forth as still remaining in Ireland, are often spoken of as promising happy homes for thousands of industrious peasant proprietors. An examination of some of these waste lands demonstrates the futility of this view. More than three-fourths of the area at present scheduled as 'uncultivated' is bog and barren mountain, some of it at such an altitude that it can never do more than afford a brief summer subsistence for a few sheep or goats. The mountains of Donegal, Sligo, and Mayo, the bare limestone rocks of Galway, the mountain tracts of Cork and Kerry, with a few cheap surface drains, in the expressive phrase of the country, may furnish better summer 'standing' for rough stock, but will chiefly continue as now to be held by considerable graziers rather than by resident tenantry or peasant proprietors. Many of the great bogs gradually stripped of turf will eventually be converted into tillage and grazing land, but the process of reclamation will be slow, often expensive, and the result not always remunerative. The Bog of Allen in Counties Carlow and Dublin, extending to 350,000 acres, is twenty to forty feet deep. Lying low, before it could be tilled great draining operations would require to be adopted. To bring either bog or mountain into profitable cultivation necessitates, as has been repeatedly shown in these letters, an outlay of 12*l.* to 20*l.* an acre. Unless soil, climate, and situation are tolerably favourable, this outlay is seldom very remunerative. In many parts of the country are considerable areas, especially of mountain land, which have been reclaimed and allowed to revert to their natural state of furze and poor grass. The labours of Lord Lifford at Meen Glas in Donegal, and of the Trappist monks, of Mount Mellaray in County Waterford, illustrate the meagre results which are frequently obtained even from the continued judicious treatment of these intractable wastes. It is mainly in isolated favourable spots, by slow degrees, and by the occasional spare labour of small occupiers of adjacent cultivated and better land, that any considerable reclamation can be economically made. Greatly more hopeful results are obtained by encouraging the better cultivation of land already reclaimed. In many districts are thousands of acres inadequately drained, a great deal of tillage land imperfectly cultivated, and pastures often poor and thriftless from everything being taken from them and nothing put back. As in many parts of England, along the banks of streams and rivers, are considerable areas of good land, poached and scoured by constant flooding, which might be doubled in value by the better management or removal of weirs, dams, and other obstructions to the outflow of water. The improvement and more profitable use of these lands, hitherto only partially cultivated, promise for many years ample scope for advancing the agricultural resources of Ireland; for securing more constant work for the numerous irregularly employed labourers; for planting from overcrowded localities tenants secured in the enjoyment of better managed holdings; and for finding space besides for an extended creation of peasant and yeoman proprietors.

INDEX.

ABE

ABERCORN, Duke of, 138; outlay for improvements, 140
Absentee landlords, 8, 100, 187, 254
Alexander, Mr. T., Londonderry, 138
Allowances, serious sacrifice to owners, 41, 112, 249
Allowances to tenants, 25, 41, 59, 191, 217, 226
Antrim, estates in, 98
Ardilaun, Lord, 246; extensive improvements, 247

BACHELORS, prosperous, 150
Ballina and neighbourhood, 227
Ballinrobe, disturbed district, 235
Ballyconnell, wretched coast villages, 196
Bandon, Lord, 73
Bank deposits diminished, 107
Barber, Frank, Lissadell, 195
Barron, Sir Henry P. T., 57
Begging expeditions less common, 162
Belfast, estates near, 103
Belmullet, a poor district, 227
Bessborough, Lord, 31
Bishops' leases, 109
Blarney estates, Sir G. Colthurst's, 67
Blessington village, county Wicklow, 13
Borrows, Major, 19
Bourke, Walter M., Curraghleigh, 216
Boycotting, 167, 185, 229, 241
Bremner, James, Valentia, 95
Brooke, Thomas, Lough Eske, 168
Browne, Lord John, Westport, 231

DEA

Buncrana fair, 134
Burke, William, Ashford park, 249
Bustard, Ebenezer, Mayo estate, 174

CABIN-HOLDERS, county Kerry, 91
Cahirciveen, Dingle Bay, 84
Capital needed in farming, 44, 70
Caskay, James, Drenagh, 124
Cattle feeding, 122
Church (Irish) Act of 1869, 9, 266
Church lands, 88, 109, 170, 185, 236
Clanmorris, Lord, county Mayo, 114, 222
Cloncurry, Lord, county Kildare, 25
College of Physicians, Waterford estates, 50
Colthurst, Sir George, 67
Commission for handling estates, 268
Conolly estates, Donegal and Sligo, 172
Conyngham, Marquis, 164
Cork, estates in, 65
Courts of Arbitration and Appeal, 263, 264
Credit unduly stretched, 52, 164
Crindle Myroe, county Derry, 123
Cromwellian grants, 104, 146, 266
Cropping clauses uncommon, 37
Currey, E. S., Lismore, 55

DAIRYING, county Mayo, 196
Dairying, Waterford, 49
Daunt, Mr. Derry Grey, county Cork, 75
Deazeley, Charles, M.D., Pembroke, 173

DEV

Devonshire, Duke of, Lismore, 54; railway enterprises, 54; rental, 55
Dillon, Lord, county Mayo, 200; help in bad times, 203; tenantry migrate to England, 204
Dingle Bay, 84, 89
Dixon, Thomas, Sligo, 174
Dobbs, Mr., of Castle Dobbs, 110
Donegal, Lord, Carrickfergus estates, 105, 109
Donegal mountain estates, 158
Dowries for daughters, 46, 146, 205
Draining, 58, 70, 87, 183, 195
Drumraighland, county Derry, 156

EMIGRATION, 243
Encumbered Estates Court, 4, 174, 176, 255
Ennishowen Peninsula, 133
Estates of various acreages, 2
Evictions declining, 255

FAIR rents, how determined, 261
Fences, turf and clay, 194
Fishing profits reduced, 199, 228
Fishmongers' Company, county Derry, 119; tenants' leases, 120; liberal arrangements, 120
Fitzgerald, Sir Maurice, Knight of Kerry, 95
Fitzwilliam, Earl of, 32; charities, 32; emigration aided, 34; improvements, 34; leases and agreements, 37; rental, 41
Free sale, 45, 97, 260
Fixity of tenure, 10, 145, 256, 260
Forrest, James, Drumraighland, 155
Foster, Arthur H., 168; rabbit farming, 170
Foxford, a poor district, 222

GAGE, C. W., Ballykelly, 119
Game Acts, 27
Gardiner, Miss, Farmhill, Mayo, 222
Gildea, Thomas, Dough, Ballinrobe, 244
Glebe lands, 88, 109, 170, 185, 236
Gombeen men, 227, 236
Gore-Booth, Sir Henry, Lissadell,

KER

190; judicious management, 191; resources of tenantry, 194
Gore, Sir Charles Knox, Ballina, 226
Government loans extended, 71
Grand Jury cess, 26
Grass farms, 211, 249; depreciated by breaking up, 212
Griffith's valuation, 15, 56
Guinness, Sir Benjamin Lee, 246

HALLARAN, Rev. Thomas, Cahirciveen, 88
Hamilton, Major, Broomhall, 182
Hanna, W. T., Carrigans, 136
Harvey, Sir Robert Bateson, 136
Hegarty, J., Mill street, 68; spirited reclamation, 69
Herbert, A. H., Muckross, 80
Hertford, Marquis of, 100
Heygate, Sir Frederick, 122
Hill-Trevor, Lord Arthur, Glencoe, 105
Hogg, Sir James M'Garel, 110
Holdings, acreage of, 31, 271
Home farms, 34, 51, 163, 223, 249
Horse-breeding, county Waterford, 60
Humphries, Major, Strabane, 140
Hussey and Townsend, estate agents, 65

IMPROVEMENTS by landlords, 26, 36, 69, 76, 159, 175, 183, 191
Improvements by tenants, 38, 69, 195, 240
Industries should be encouraged, 178
Irish Society, 128; long leases, 128; liberal expenditure, 129
Ironmongers' Company, 117
Irrigation in county Waterford, 61

JAMIESON, Rev. W., Kildunmore, 246
Johnson, T., Kinlough, 183
Joyce, William, Blake Hill, Clonbur, 261

KENMARE, Lord, 76
Kerry, cattle, 89; estates in, 83

KER

Kerry, Knight of, 93
Killarney improvements, 76
King, Michael, Dungiven, 132
Knox, Captain Charles, Ballinrobe, 236

LABOURERS, badly off, 63; wages, 204, 220, 228; work in England, 118, 188
Land Act, 1870, 45, 104, 139, 145, 267
Land Commission needed, 259
Land League, 71, 211, 216, 244
Land, map of, 1
Landlords, divers types, 7
Lansdowne, Marquis of, 83
La Touche, John, Kildare, 19
Leases and agreements, 26, 37, 141, 250, 259
Leinster, Duke of, Kildare and Meath, 20
Lifford, Lord, Meen Glas, 158; small returns from outlay, 164
Limavady estates, 124
Lissadell estate, 190
London companies, 110, 111, 113
Londonderry, Marquis of, 106
Lucan, Lord, Castlebar, 233

M'AULIFFE, George, Belfast, 106
M'Caul, Hugh, Lisburne, 105
M'Causland, D. T., Drenagh, 125; restricted tenant-right, 126
M'Clintock, Captain, Buncrana, 135
M'Neil, Captain Duncan, Coollattin, 40
Magan, Miss, Kildare and Meath, 17
Magee Island, county Down, 110
Malamore estates, Sligo, 184
Markets difficult of access, 242
Martin, Sir Samuel, county Derry, 132; cultivation of wilderness, 133
Maynooth, 21
Mayo estates, 208
Mercers' Company, county Derry, 114
Middlemen, 9, 85, 181
Monks of Mellaray, 61
Mugrave, John and James, Carrick, 174; enterprising improvers, 176

SIM

NAAS Union, 14
Nolan's, Major, Seed Act, 14

O'CONNELL, Daniel, birthplace, 84
O'Connell, Sir Maurice J., 93
O'Conor Don, The, 208
O'Malley, Father John, the Neils, 243
O'Neill, the Right Hon. Earl, Shanes Castle, 111
Oranmore, Lord, Claremorris, 214
Ormsby, Antony, Ballinamore, 216
Owen, William, Blessington, 17
Owners, encumbered, 255; occupying own land, 145, 148, 151; small, 105, 123, 148, 156, 182, 265

PALMER, Sir Roger, county Mayo, 233
Peasant proprietors, 156, 269
Perry, Edmond H. C., Belleck Castle, 223
Plunkett, Hon. A.C.C., Derry, 129
Poor-rates, 16, 257
Possessory interest, 46, 186, 256, 261
Power, Joseph, O'Neil, county Waterford, 52

RAINFALL, 240
Reclamation, 62, 69, 74, 83, 84, 137, 159, 189, 215, 272
Redhill estates, county Down, 108
Remedies for Irish troubles, 196, 209, 263
Rents, not increased so rapidly as in Great Britain, 11; perpetuity, 146, 147; reduced by fines, 146, 262; excessive, 174, 229; badly paid, 217, 230
Roe Valley of, county Derry, 122; reclamations, 122
Rundale superseded, 127, 157, 175, 192, 222

SANDFORD, J., Castlereagh, 212
Schools, National, 14, 33, 86, 243, 251
Simson, James, Cloona Castle, 238; liberal management, 239

SKI

Skinners' Company's estates, 116
Sligo estates, 171
Sligo, Lord, 231
Squaring and striping, 157, 193, 202
Squireens, 104
Strickland, Charles, 202
Subdivision, 146–148, 156, 183, 245

TABLE of owners, 2
    Lord Abercorn's improvements, 140
    Lord Fitzwilliam's rental, etc., 32
    Lord Waterford's tenantry, 49
    Resources of Lissadell tenantry, 194
    Sales of tenant-right in Ulster, 130, 131, 142
Teeven, Mr. S., purchaser of Conolly estates, 174
Tenant-right, 39, 52, 121; limited, 126; sales of, 79, 108, 121, 130, 139, 166, 188, 193, 261
Tenants, bankrupt, 3, 92; compensation for disturbance, 258; compensation for improvements, 258; small, 10, 52, 91, 101, 144, 196
Thomson, George, a prosperous yeoman, 151
Thornton, Colonel Todd, Ennishowen, 136
Tighe, Thomas, High Sheriff of Mayo, 215

YEO

Tillie and Henderson, shirt factories, Derry, 124
Townsend, Robert, estate agent, Cork, 66
Transport facilities needed, 178
Trinity College estates, county Kerry, 82; Sligo, 178; leases, 179
Tyrone, estates in, 132

ULSTER custom, 10, 98, 107, 124; restricted, 126

VALENTIA Island, 93
    Valuation, is a new one necessary? 263
Veitch, Dr., county Mayo, 245
Ventry, Lord, county Kerry, 83
Vesey, George, Ballyhankins, 245

WAGES, county Antrim, 112; Derry, 137; Donegal, 168; Galway, 247; Mayo, 141; Valentia island, 95; Waterford, 50, 63
Wallace, Sir Richard, county Down, 100
Westport, relief funds, 229
Work interfered with, 241
Wynne, Owen, Sligo estates, 189

YEOMEN, 149, 151, 265, 270

FEBRUARY 1881.

GENERAL LISTS OF NEW WORKS

PUBLISHED BY

Messrs. LONGMANS, GREEN & CO.

PATERNOSTER ROW, LONDON.

HISTORY, POLITICS, HISTORICAL MEMOIRS &c.

Armitage's Childhood of the English Nation. Fcp. 8vo. 2s. 6d.
Arnold's Lectures on Modern History. 8vo. 7s. 6d.
Bagehot's Literary Studies, edited by Hutton. 2 vols. 8vo. 28s.
Browning's Modern France, 1814-1879. Fcp. 8vo. 1s.
Buckle's History of Civilisation. 3 vols. crown 8vo. 24s.
Chesney's Waterloo Lectures. 8vo. 10s. 6d.

Epochs of Ancient History:—
    Beesly's Gracchi, Marius, and Sulla. 2s. 6d.
    Capes's Age of the Antonines, 2s. 6d.
    — Early Roman Empire, 2s. 6d.
    Cox's Athenian Empire, 2s. 6d.
    — Greeks and Persians, 2s. 6d.
    Curteis's Rise of the Macedonian Empire, 2s. 6d.
    Ihne's Rome to its Capture by the Gauls, 2s. 6d.
    Merivale's Roman Triumvirates, 2s. 6d.
    Sankey's Spartan and Theban Supremacies, 2s. 6d.
    Smith's Rome and Carthage, the Punic Wars, 2s. 6d.

Epochs of English History, complete in One Volume. Fcp. 8vo. 5s.
    Creighton's Shilling History of England (Introductory Volume). Fcp. 8vo. 1s.
    Browning's Modern England, 1820-1875, 9d.
    Cordery's Struggle against Absolute Monarchy, 1603-1688, 9d.
    Creighton's (Mrs.) England a Continental Power, 1066-1216, 9d.
    Creighton's (Rev. M.) Tudors and the Reformation, 1485-1603, 9d.
    Rowley's Rise of the People, 1215-1485, 9d.
    Rowley's Settlement of the Constitution, 1688-1778, 9d.
    Tancock's England during the American & European Wars, 1778-1820, 9d.
    York-Powell's Early England to the Conquest, 1s.

Epochs of Modern History:—
    Church's Beginning of the Middle Ages, 2s. 6d.
    Cox's Crusades, 2s. 6d.
    Creighton's Age of Elizabeth, 2s. 6d.
    Gairdner's Houses of Lancaster and York, 2s. 6d.
    Gardiner's Puritan Revolution, 2s. 6d.
    — Thirty Years' War, 2s. 6d.

London, LONGMANS & CO.

Epochs of Modern History—*continued*.
    Hale's Fall of the Stuarts, 2s. 6d.
    Johnson's Normans in Europe, 2s. 6d.
    Longman's Frederick the Great and the Seven Years' War, 2s. 6d.
    Ludlow's War of American Independence, 2s. 6d.
    Morris's Age of Queen Anne, 2s. 6d.
    Seebohm's Protestant Revolution, 2s. 6d.
    Stubbs's Early Plantagenets, 2s. 6d.
    Warburton's Edward III., 2s. 6d.

Froude's English in Ireland in the 18th Century. 3 vols. crown 8vo. 18s.
  — History of England. 12 vols. 8vo. £8. 18s. 12 vols. crown 8vo. 72s.
  — Julius Cæsar, a Sketch. 8vo. 16s.
Gardiner's England under Buckingham and Charles I., 1624-1628. 2 vols. 8vo. 24s.
  — Personal Government of Charles I., 1628-1637. 2 vols. 8vo. 24s.
Greville's Journal of the Reigns of George IV. & William IV. 3 vols. 8vo. 36s.
Hayward's Selected Essays. 2 vols. crown 8vo. 12s.
Ihne's History of Rome. 3 vols. 8vo. 45s.
Lecky's History of England. Vols. I. & II. 1700-1760. 8vo. 36s.
  — — — European Morals. 2 vols. crown 8vo. 16s.
  — — — Rationalism in Europe. 2 vols. crown 8vo. 16s.
Lewes's History of Philosophy. 2 vols. 8vo. 32s.
Longman's Lectures on the History of England. 8vo. 15s.
  — Life and Times of Edward III. 2 vols. 8vo. 28s.
Macaulay's Complete Works. Library Edition. 8 vols. 8vo. £5. 5s.
  — — — Cabinet Edition. 16 vols. crown 8vo. £4. 16s.
  — History of England :—
    Student's Edition. 2 vols. cr. 8vo. 12s. | Cabinet Edition. 8 vols. post 8vo. 48s.
    People's Edition. 4 vols. cr. 8vo. 16s. | Library Edition. 5 vols. 8vo. £4.
Macaulay's Critical and Historical Essays. Cheap Edition. Crown 8vo. 3s. 6d.
    Student's Edition. 1 vol. cr. 8vo. 6s. | Cabinet Edition. 4 vols. post 8vo. 24s.
    People's Edition. 2 vols. cr. 8vo. 8s. | Library Edition. 3 vols. 8vo. 36s.
May's Constitutional History of England, 1760-1870. 3 vols. crown 8vo. 18s.
  — Democracy in Europe. 2 vols. 8vo. 32s.
Merivale's Fall of the Roman Republic. 12mo. 7s. 6d.
  — General History of Rome, B.C. 753—A.D. 476. Crown 8vo. 7s. 6d.
  — History of the Romans under the Empire. 8 vols. post 8vo. 48s.
Minto (Lord) in India from 1807 to 1814. Post 8vo. 12s.
Rawlinson's Seventh Great Oriental Monarchy—The Sassanians. 8vo. 28s.
Russia Before and After the War, translated by E. F. Taylor. 8vo. 14s.
Russia and England from 1876 to 1880. By O. K. 8vo. 14s.
Seebohm's Oxford Reformers—Colet, Erasmus, & More. 8vo. 14s.
Sewell's Popular History of France to the Death of Louis XIV. Crown 8vo. 7s. 6d.
Short's History of the Church of England. Crown 8vo. 7s. 6d.
Smith's Carthage and the Carthaginians. Crown 8vo. 10s. 6d.
Taylor's Manual of the History of India. Crown 8vo. 7s. 6d.
Todd's Parliamentary Government in England. 2 vols. 8vo. 37s.
  — — — — the British Colonies. 8vo. 21s.
Trench's Realities of Irish Life. Crown 8vo. 2s. 6d.
Trevelyan's Early History of Charles James Fox. 8vo. 18s.
Walpole's History of England, 1815-1841. Vols. I. & II. 8vo. 36s. Vol. III. 18s.
Webb's Civil War in Herefordshire. 2 vols. 8vo. Illustrations, 42s.

London, LONGMANS & CO.

BIOGRAPHICAL WORKS.

Bagehot's Biographical Studies. 1 vol. 8vo. 12s.
Burke's Vicissitudes of Families. 2 vols. crown 8vo. 21s.
Cates's Dictionary of General Biography. Medium 8vo. 28s.
Gleig's Life of the Duke of Wellington. Crown 8vo. 6s.
Jerrold's Life of Napoleon III. Vols. I. to III. 8vo. price 18s. each.
Lecky's Leaders of Public Opinion in Ireland. Crown 8vo. 7s. 6d.
Life (The) and Letters of Lord Macaulay. By his Nephew, G. Otto Trevelyan, M.P. Cabinet Edition, 2 vols. post 8vo. 12s. Library Edition, 2 vols. 8vo. 36s.
Marshman's Memoirs of Havelock. Crown 8vo. 3s. 6d.
Memoirs of Anna Jameson, by Gerardine Macpherson. 8vo. 12s. 6d.
Mendelssohn's Letters. Translated by Lady Wallace. 2 vols. cr. 8vo. 5s. each.
Mill's (John Stuart) Autobiography. 8vo. 7s. 6d.
Missionary Secretariat of Henry Venn, B.D. 8vo. Portrait. 18s.
Newman's Apologia pro Vitâ Suâ. Crown 8vo. 6s.
Nohl's Life of Mozart. Translated by Lady Wallace. 2 vols. crown 8vo. 21s.
Overton's Life &c. of William Law. 8vo. 15s.
Spedding's Letters and Life of Francis Bacon. 7 vols. 8vo. £4. 4s.
Stephen's Essays in Ecclesiastical Biography. Crown 8vo. 7s. 6d.

MENTAL AND POLITICAL PHILOSOPHY.

Amos's View of the Science of Jurisprudence. 8vo. 18s.
— Fifty Years of the English Constitution, 1830-1880. Crown 8vo. 10s. 6d.
— Primer of the English Constitution. Crown 8vo. 6s.
Bacon's Essays, with Annotations by Whately. 8vo. 10s. 6d.
— Works, edited by Spedding. 7 vols. 8vo. 73s. 6d.
Bagehot's Economic Studies, edited by Hutton. 8vo. 10s. 6d.
Bain's Logic, Deductive and Inductive. Crown 8vo. 10s. 6d.
          PART I. Deduction, 4s. | PART II. Induction, 6s. 6d.
Bolland & Lang's Aristotle's Politics. Crown 8vo. 7s. 6d.
Brassey's Foreign Work and English Wages. 8vo. 10s. 6d.
Comte's System of Positive Polity, or Treatise upon Sociology. 4 vols. 8vo. £4.
Congreve's Politics of Aristotle; Greek Text, English Notes. 8vo. 18s.
Grant's Ethics of Aristotle; Greek Text, English Notes. 2 vols. 8vo. 32s.
Griffith's A B C of Philosophy. Crown 8vo. 5s.
Hillebrand's Lectures on German Thought. Crown 8vo. 7s. 6d.
Hodgson's Philosophy of Reflection. 2 vols. 8vo. 21s.
Kalisch's Path and Goal. 8vo. 12s. 6d.
Lewis on Authority in Matters of Opinion. 8vo. 14s.
Leslie's Essays in Political and Moral Philosophy. 8vo. 10s. 6d.
Macaulay's Speeches corrected by Himself. Crown 8vo. 3s. 6d.
Macleod's Economical Philosophy. Vol. I. 8vo. 15s. Vol. II. Part I. 12s.
Mill on Representative Government. Crown 8vo. 2s.
— — Liberty. Post 8vo. 7s. 6d. Crown 8vo. 1s. 4d.
Mill's Analysis of the Phenomena of the Human Mind. 2 vols. 8vo. 28s.
— Dissertations and Discussions. 4 vols. 8vo. 47s.
— Essays on Unsettled Questions of Political Economy. 8vo. 6s. 6d.
— Examination of Hamilton's Philosophy. 8vo. 16s.

London, LONGMANS & CO.

Mill's Logic, Ratiocinative and Inductive. 2 vols. 8vo. 25s.
— Principles of Political Economy. 2 vols. 8vo. 30s. 1 vol. crown 8vo. 5s.
— Subjection of Women. Crown 8vo. 6s.
— Utilitarianism. 8vo. 5s.
Müller's (Max) Chips from a German Workshop. 4 vols. 8vo. 36s.
— — Hibbert Lectures on Origin and Growth of Religion. 8vo. 10s. 6d.
— — Selected Essays on Language, Mythology, and Religion. 2 vols. crown 8vo. 16s.
Sandars's Institutes of Justinian, with English Notes. 8vo. 18s.
Swinbourne's Picture Logic. Post 8vo. 5s.
Thomson's Outline of Necessary Laws of Thought. Crown 8vo. 6s.
Tocqueville's Democracy in America, translated by Reeve. 2 vols. crown 8vo. 16s.
Twiss's Law of Nations, 8vo. in Time of Peace, 12s. in Time of War, 21s.
Whately's Elements of Logic. 8vo. 10s. 6d. Crown 8vo. 4s. 6d.
— — — Rhetoric. 8vo. 10s. 6d. Crown 8vo. 4s. 6d.
— English Synonymes. Fcp. 8vo. 3s.
Williams's Nicomachean Ethics of Aristotle translated. Crown 8vo. 7s. 6d.
Zeller's Socrates and the Socratic Schools. Crown 8vo. 10s. 6d.
— Stoics, Epicureans, and Sceptics. Crown 8vo. 15s.
— Plato and the Older Academy. Crown 8vo. 18s.
— Pre-Socratic Schools. 2 vols. crown 8vo. 30s.

MISCELLANEOUS AND CRITICAL WORKS.

Arnold's (Dr. Thomas) Miscellaneous Works. 8vo. 7s. 6d.
— (T.) Manual of English Literature. Crown 8vo. 7s. 6d.
— English Authors, Poetry and Prose Specimens.
Bain's Emotions and the Will. 8vo. 15s.
— Mental and Moral Science. Crown 8vo. 10s. 6d.
— Senses and the Intellect. 8vo. 15s.
Becker's *Charicles* and *Gallus*, by Metcalfe. Post 8vo. 7s. 6d. each.
Blackley's German and English Dictionary. Post 8vo. 7s. 6d.
Conington's Miscellaneous Writings. 2 vols. 8vo. 28s.
Contanseau's Practical French & English Dictionary. Post 8vo. 7s. 6d.
— Pocket French and English Dictionary. Square 18mo. 3s. 6d.
Davison's Thousand Thoughts from Various Authors. Crown 8vo. 7s. 6d.
Farrar's Language and Languages. Crown 8vo. 6s.
Froude's Short Studies on Great Subjects. 3 vols. crown 8vo. 18s.
German Home Life, reprinted from *Fraser's Magazine*. Crown 8vo. 6s.
Gibson's Cavalier's Note-Book. Small 4to. 14s.
Greville's (Lady Violet) Faiths and Fashions. Crown 8vo. 7s. 6d.
Hume's Essays, edited by Green & Grose. 2 vols. 8vo. 28s.
— Treatise on Human Nature, edited by Green & Grose. 2 vols. 8vo. 28s.
Latham's Handbook of the English Language. Crown 8vo. 6s.
— English Dictionary. 1 vol. medium 8vo. 14s. 4 vols. 4to. £7.
Liddell & Scott's Greek-English Lexicon. Crown 4to. 36s.
— — — Abridged Greek-English Lexicon. Square 12mo. 7s. 6d.
Longman's Pocket German and English Dictionary. 18mo. 5s.
Macaulay's Miscellaneous Writings. 2 vols. 8vo. 21s. 1 vol. crown 8vo. 4s.

London, LONGMANS & CO.

General Lists of New Works.

Macaulay's Miscellaneous Writings and Speeches. Crown 8vo. 6s.
Macaulay's Miscellaneous Writings, Speeches, Lays of Ancient Rome, &c. Cabinet Edition. 4 vols. crown 8vo. 24s.
Mahaffy's Classical Greek Literature. Crown 8vo. Vol. I. the Poets, 7s. 6d. Vol. II. the Prose Writers, 7s. 6d.
Müller's (Max) Lectures on the Science of Language. 2 vols. crown 8vo. 16s.
Rich's Dictionary of Roman and Greek Antiquities. Crown 8vo. 7s. 6d.
Rogers's Eclipse of Faith. Fcp. 8vo. 5s.
— Defence of the Eclipse of Faith Fcp. 8vo. 3s. 6d.
Roget's Thesaurus of English Words and Phrases. Crown 8vo. 10s. 6d.
Savile's Apparitions, a Narrative of Facts. Crown 8vo. 5s.
Selections from the Writings of Lord Macaulay. Crown 8vo. 6s.
The Essays and Contributions of A. K. H. B. Crown 8vo.
- Autumn Holidays of a Country Parson. 3s. 6d.
- Changed Aspects of Unchanged Truths. 3s. 6d.
- Common-place Philosopher in Town and Country. 3s. 6d.
- Counsel and Comfort spoken from a City Pulpit. 3s. 6d.
- Critical Essays of a Country Parson. 3s. 6d.
- Graver Thoughts of a Country Parson. Three Series, 3s. 6d. each.
- Landscapes, Churches, and Moralities. 3s. 6d.
- Leisure Hours in Town. 3s. 6d. Lessons of Middle Age. 3s. 6d.
- Present-day Thoughts. 3s. 6d.
- Recreations of a Country Parson. Three Series, 3s. 6d. each.
- Seaside Musings on Sundays and Week-Days. 3s. 6d.
- Sunday Afternoons in the Parish Church of a University City. 3s. 6d.

White & Riddle's Large Latin-English Dictionary. 4to. 21s.
White's College Latin-English Dictionary. Royal 8vo. 12s.
— Junior Student's Lat.-Eng. and Eng.-Lat. Dictionary. Square 12mo. 12s.
Separately { The English-Latin Dictionary, 5s. 6d.
{ The Latin-English Dictionary, 7s. 6d.
Wit and Wisdom of the Rev. Sydney Smith. 16mo. 3s. 6d.
Yonge's English-Greek Lexicon. Square 12mo. 8s. 6d. 4to. 21s.

ASTRONOMY, METEOROLOGY, GEOGRAPHY &c.

Freeman's Historical Geography of Europe. 8vo. 31s. 6d.
Herschel's Outlines of Astronomy. Square crown 8vo. 12s.
Keith Johnston's Dictionary of Geography, or General Gazetteer. 8vo. 42s.
Neison's Work on the Moon. Medium 8vo. 31s. 6d.
Proctor's Essays on Astronomy. 8vo. 12s. Proctor's Moon. Crown 8vo. 10s. 6d.
— Larger Star Atlas. Folio, 15s. or Maps only, 12s. 6d.
— New Star Atlas. Crown 8vo. 5s. Orbs Around Us. Crown 8vo. 7s. 6d.
— Other Worlds than Ours. Crown 8vo. 10s. 6d.
— Saturn and its System. 8vo. 14s. Proctor's Sun. Crown 8vo. 14s.
— Universe of Stars. 8vo. 10s. 6d.
Smith's Air and Rain. 8vo. 24s.
The Public Schools Atlas of Ancient Geography. Imperial 8vo. 7s. 6d.
— — — Atlas of Modern Geography. Imperial 8vo. 5s.

NATURAL HISTORY & POPULAR SCIENCE.

Arnott's Elements of Physics or Natural Philosophy. Crown 8vo. 12s. 6d.
Brande's Dictionary of Science, Literature, and Art. 3 vols. medium 8vo. 63s.

London, LONGMANS & CO.

Buckton's Town and Window Gardening. Crown 8vo. 2s.
Decaisne and Le Maout's General System of Botany. Imperial 8vo. 31s. 6d.
Dixon's Rural Bird Life. Crown 8vo. Illustrations, 7s. 6d.
Ganot's Elementary Treatise on Physics, by Atkinson. Large crown 8vo. 15s.
— Natural Philosophy, by Atkinson. Crown 8vo. 7s. 6d.
Goodeve's Elements of Mechanism. Crown 8vo. 6s.
Grove's Correlation of Physical Forces. 8vo. 15s.
Hartwig's Aerial World. 8vo. 10s. 6d. Polar World. 8vo. 10s. 6d.
— Sea and Its Living Wonders. 8vo. 10s. 6d.
— Subterranean World. 8vo. 10s. 6d. Tropical World. 8vo. 10s. 6d.
Haughton's Six Lectures on Physical Geography. 8vo. 15s.
Heer's Primæval World of Switzerland. 2 vols. 8vo. 16s.
Helmholtz's Lectures on Scientific Subjects. 2 vols. cr. 8vo. 7s. 6d. each.
Helmholtz on the Sensations of Tone, by Ellis. 8vo. 36s.
Hullah's Lectures on the History of Modern Music. 8vo. 8s. 6d.
— Transition Period of Musical History. 8vo. 10s. 6d.
Keller's Lake Dwellings of Switzerland, by Lee. 2 vols. royal 8vo. 42s.
Lloyd's Treatise on Magnetism. 8vo. 10s. 6d.
— — on the Wave-Theory of Light. 8vo. 10s. 6d.
Loudon's Encyclopædia of Plants. 8vo. 42s.
Lubbock on the Origin of Civilisation & Primitive Condition of Man. 8vo. 18s.
Macalister's Zoology and Morphology of Vertebrate Animals. 8vo. 10s. 6d.
Nicols' Puzzle of Life. Crown 8vo. 3s. 6d.
Owen's Comparative Anatomy and Physiology of the Vertebrate Animals. 3 vols. 8vo. 73s. 6d.
Proctor's Light Science for Leisure Hours. 2 vols. crown 8vo. 7s. 6d. each.
Rivers's Orchard House. Sixteenth Edition. Crown 8vo. 5s.
— Rose Amateur's Guide. Fcp. 8vo. 4s. 6d.
Stanley's Familiar History of British Birds. Crown 8vo. 6s.
Text-Books of Science, Mechanical and Physical.
    Abney's Photography, 3s. 6d.
    Anderson's (Sir John) Strength of Materials, 3s. 6d.
    Armstrong's Organic Chemistry, 3s. 6d.
    Ball's Astronomy, 6s.
    Barry's Railway Appliances, 3s. 6d. Bloxam's Metals, 3s. 6d.
    Goodeve's Principles of Mechanics, 3s. 6d.
    Gore's Electro-Metallurgy, 6s.
    Griffin's Algebra and Trigonometry, 3s. 6d.
    Jenkin's Electricity and Magnetism, 3s. 6d.
    Maxwell's Theory of Heat, 3s. 6d.
    Merrifield's Technical Arithmetic and Mensuration, 3s. 6d.
    Miller's Inorganic Chemistry, 3s. 6d.
    Preece & Sivewright's Telegraphy, 3s. 6d.
    Rutley's Study of Rocks, 4s. 6d.
    Shelley's Workshop Appliances, 3s. 6d.
    Thomé's Structural and Physiological Botany, 6s.
    Thorpe's Quantitative Chemical Analysis, 4s. 6d.
    Thorpe & Muir's Qualitative Analysis, 3s. 6d.
    Tilden's Chemical Philosophy, 3s. 6d.
    Unwin's Machine Design, 3s. 6d.
    Watson's Plane and Solid Geometry, 3s. 6d.
Tyndall on Sound. New Edition in the press.

London, LONGMANS & CO.

Tyndall's Contributions to Molecular Physics. 8vo. 16s.
— Fragments of Science. 2 vols. post 8vo. 16s.
— Heat a Mode of Motion. Crown 8vo. 12s.
— Notes on Electrical Phenomena. Crown 8vo. 1s. sewed, 1s. 6d. cloth.
— Notes of Lectures on Light. Crown 8vo. 1s. sewed, 1s. 6d. cloth.
— Lectures on Light delivered in America. Crown 8vo. 7s. 6d.
— Lessons in Electricity. Crown 8vo. 2s. 6d.

Von Cotta on Rocks, by Lawrence. Post 8vo. 14s.
Woodward's Geology of England and Wales. Crown 8vo. 14s.
Wood's Bible Animals. With 112 Vignettes. 8vo. 14s.
— Homes Without Hands. 8vo. 14s. Insects Abroad. 8vo. 14s.
— Insects at Home. With 700 Illustrations. 8vo. 14s.
— Out of Doors. Crown 8vo. 7s. 6d. Strange Dwellings. Crown 8vo. 7s. 6d.

CHEMISTRY & PHYSIOLOGY.

Buckton's Health in the House, Lectures on Elementary Physiology. Cr. 8vo. 2s.
Crookes's Select Methods in Chemical Analysis. Crown 8vo. 12s. 6d.
Kingzett's Animal Chemistry. 8vo. 18s.
— History, Products and Processes of the Alkali Trade. 8vo. 12s.
Miller's Elements of Chemistry, Theoretical and Practical. 3 vols. 8vo. Part I. Chemical Physics, 16s. Part II. Inorganic Chemistry, 24s. Part III. Organic Chemistry, Section I. price 31s. 6d.
Reynolds's Experimental Chemistry, Part I. Fcp. 8vo. 1s. 6d.
Thudichum's Annals of Chemical Medicine. Vol. I. 8vo. 14s.
Tilden's Practical Chemistry. Fcp. 8vo. 1s. 6d.
Watts's Dictionary of Chemistry. 7 vols. medium 8vo. £10. 16s. 6d.
— Third Supplementary Volume, in Two Parts. PART I. 36s.

THE FINE ARTS & ILLUSTRATED EDITIONS.

Doyle's Fairyland; Pictures from the Elf-World. Folio, 15s.
Dresser's Arts and Art Industries of Japan. [In preparation.
Jameson's Sacred and Legendary Art. 6 vols. square crown 8vo.
Legends of the Madonna. 1 vol. 21s.
— — — Monastic Orders. 1 vol. 21s.
— — — Saints and Martyrs. 2 vols. 31s. 6d.
— — — Saviour. Completed by Lady Eastlake. 2 vols. 42s.
Longman's Three Cathedrals Dedicated to St. Paul. Square crown 8vo. 21s.
Macaulay's Lays of Ancient Rome. Illustrated by Scharf. Fcp. 4to. 21s. imp. 16mo. 10s. 6d.
— — — Illustrated by Weguelin. Crown 8vo. 6s.
Macfarren's Lectures on Harmony. 8vo. 12s.
Moore's Irish Melodies. With 161 Plates by D. Maclise, R.A. Super-royal 8vo. 21s.
— Lalla Rookh, illustrated by Tenniel. Square crown 8vo. 10s. 6d.
Perry on Greek and Roman Sculpture. 8vo. [In preparation.

THE USEFUL ARTS, MANUFACTURES &c.

Bourne's Catechism of the Steam Engine. Fcp. 8vo. 6s.
— Examples of Steam, Air, and Gas Engines. 4to. 70s.

London, LONGMANS & CO.

Bourne's Handbook of the Steam Engine. Fcp. 8vo. 9s.
— Recent Improvements in the Steam Engine. Fcp. 8vo. 6s.
— Treatise on the Steam Engine. 4to. 42s.
Brassey's Shipbuilding for War. 2 vols. 8vo.
Cresy's Encyclopædia of Civil Engineering. 8vo. 25s.
Culley's Handbook of Practical Telegraphy. 8vo. 16s.
Eastlake's Household Taste in Furniture, &c. Square crown 8vo. 14s.
Fairbairn's Useful Information for Engineers. 3 vols. crown 8vo. 31s. 6d.
— Applications of Cast and Wrought Iron. 8vo. 16s.
— Mills and Millwork. 1 vol. 8vo. 25s.
Gwilt's Encyclopædia of Architecture. 8vo. 52s. 6d.
Hobson's Amateur Mechanic's Practical Handbook. Crown 8vo. 2s. 6d.
Hoskold's Engineer's Valuing Assistant. 8vo. 31s. 6d.
Kerl's Metallurgy, adapted by Crookes and Röhrig. 3 vols. 8vo. £4. 19s.
Loudon's Encyclopædia of Agriculture. 8vo. 21s.
— — — Gardening. 8vo. 21s.
Mitchell's Manual of Practical Assaying. 8vo. 31s. 6d.
Northcott's Lathes and Turning. 8vo. 18s.
Payen's Industrial Chemistry Edited by B. H. Paul, Ph.D. 8vo. 42s.
Piesse's Art of Perfumery. Fourth Edition. Square crown 8vo. 21s.
Stoney's Theory of Strains in Girders. Royal 8vo. 36s.
Ure's Dictionary of Arts, Manufactures, & Mines. 4 vols. medium 8vo. £7. 7s.
Ville on Artificial Manures. By Crookes. 8vo. 21s.

RELIGIOUS & MORAL WORKS.

Abbey & Overton's English Church in the Eighteenth Century. 2 vols. 8vo. 36s.
Arnold's (Rev. Dr. Thomas) Sermons. 6 vols. crown 8vo. 5s. each.
Bishop Jeremy Taylor's Entire Works. With Life by Bishop Heber. Edited by the Rev. C. P. Eden. 10 vols. 8vo. £5. 5s.
Boultbee's Commentary on the 39 Articles. Crown 8vo. 6s.
— History of the Church of England, Pre-Reformation Period. 8vo. 15s.
Browne's (Bishop) Exposition of the 39 Articles. 8vo. 16s.
Bunsen's Angel-Messiah of Buddhists, &c. 8vo. 10s 6d.
Colenso's Lectures on the Pentateuch and the Moabite Stone. 8vo. 12s.
Colenso on the Pentateuch and Book of Joshua. Crown 8vo. 6s.
— — PART VII. completion of the larger Work. 8vo. 24s.
Conder's Handbook of the Bible. Post 8vo. 7s. 6d.
Conybeare & Howson's Life and Letters of St. Paul :—
  Library Edition, with all the Original Illustrations, Maps, Landscapes on Steel, Woodcuts, &c. 2 vols. 4to. 42s.
  Intermediate Edition, with a Selection of Maps, Plates, and Woodcuts. 2 vols. square crown 8vo. 21s.
  Student's Edition, revised and condensed, with 46 Illustrations and Maps. 1 vol. crown 8vo. 7s. 6d.
Ellicott's (Bishop) Commentary on St. Paul's Epistles. 8vo. Galatians, 8s. 6d. Ephesians, 8s. 6d. Pastoral Epistles, 10s. 6d. Philippians, Colossians, and Philemon, 10s. 6d. Thessalonians, 7s. 6d.
Ellicott's Lectures on the Life of our Lord. 8vo. 12s.
Ewald's History of Israel, translated by Carpenter. 5 vols. 8vo. 63s.

London, LONGMANS & CO.

General Lists of New Works.

Ewald's Antiquities of Israel, translated by Solly. 8vo. 12s. 6d.
Gospel (The) for the Nineteenth Century. 4th Edition. 8vo. 10s. 6d.
Hopkins's Christ the Consoler. Fcp. 8vo. 2s. 6d.
Jukes's Types of Genesis. Crown 8vo. 7s. 6d.
— Second Death and the Restitution of all Things. Crown 8vo. 3s. 6d.
Kalisch's Bible Studies. PART I. the Prophecies of Balaam. 8vo. 10s. 6d.
— — — PART II. the Book of Jonah. 8vo. 10s. 6d.
— Historical and Critical Commentary on the Old Testament; with a New Translation. Vol. I. *Genesis*, 8vo. 18s. or adapted for the General Reader, 12s. Vol. II. *Exodus*, 15s. or adapted for the General Reader, 12s. Vol. III. *Leviticus*, Part I. 15s. or adapted for the General Reader, 8s. Vol. IV. *Leviticus*, Part II. 15s. or adapted for the General Reader, 8s.
Lyra Germanica: Hymns translated by Miss Winkworth. Fcp. 8vo. 5s.
Martineau's Endeavours after the Christian Life. Crown 8vo. 7s. 6d.
— Hymns of Praise and Prayer. Crown 8vo. 4s. 6d. 32mo. 1s. 6d.
— Sermons, Hours of Thought on Sacred Things. 2 vols. 7s. 6d. each.
Mill's Three Essays on Religion. 8vo. 10s. 6d.
Missionary Secretariat of Henry Venn, B.D. 8vo. Portrait. 18s.
Monsell's Spiritual Songs for Sundays and Holidays. Fcp. 8vo. 5s. 18mo. 2s.
Müller's (Max) Lectures on the Science of Religion. Crown 8vo. 10s. 6d.
Newman's Apologia pro Vitâ Suâ. Crown 8vo. 6s.
Passing Thoughts on Religion. By Miss Sewell. Fcp. 8vo. 3s. 6d.
Sewell's (Miss) Preparation for the Holy Communion. 32mo. 3s.
— — Private Devotions for Young Persons.
Smith's Voyage and Shipwreck of St. Paul. Crown 8vo. 7s. 6d.
Supernatural Religion. Complete Edition. 3 vols. 8vo. 36s.
Thoughts for the Age. By Miss Sewell. Fcp. 8vo. 3s. 6d.
Whately's Lessons on the Christian Evidences. 18mo. 6d.
White's Four Gospels in Greek, with Greek-English Lexicon. 32mo. 5s.

TRAVELS, VOYAGES, &c.

Baker's Rifle and Hound in Ceylon. Crown 8vo. 7s. 6d.
— Eight Years in Ceylon. Crown 8vo. 7s. 6d.
Ball's Alpine Guide. 3 vols. post 8vo. with Maps and Illustrations :—I. Western Alps, 6s. 6d. II. Central Alps, 7s. 6d. III. Eastern Alps, 10s. 6d.
Ball on Alpine Travelling, and on the Geology of the Alps, 1s.
Brassey's Sunshine and Storm in the East. 8vo. 21s.
— Voyage in the Yacht 'Sunbeam.' Cr. 8vo. 7s. 6d. School Edition, 2s.
Edwards's (A. B.) Thousand Miles up the Nile. Imperial 8vo. 42s.
Hassall's San Remo and the Western Riviera. Crown 8vo. 10s. 6d.
Macnamara's Medical Geography of India. 8vo. 21s.
Miller's Wintering in the Riviera. Post 8vo. Illustrations, 7s. 6d.
Packe's Guide to the Pyrenees, for Mountaineers. Crown 8vo. 7s. 6d.
Rigby's Letters from France, &c. in 1789. Crown 8vo. 10s. 6d.
Shore's Flight of the 'Lapwing', Sketches in China and Japan. 8vo. 15s.
The Alpine Club Map of Switzerland. In Four Sheets. 42s.
Tozer's Turkish Armenia and Eastern Asia Minor. 8vo. 16s.
Weld's Sacred Palmlands. Crown 8vo. 10s. 6d.

London, LONGMANS & CO.

WORKS OF FICTION.

Blues and Buffs. By Arthur Mills. Crown 8vo. 6s.
Buried Alive, Ten Years of Penal Servitude in Siberia. Crown 8vo. 10s. 6d.
Crookit Meg (The). By Shirley. Crown 8vo. 6s.
Endymion. By the Right Hon. the Earl of Beaconsfield, K.G. 3 vols. post 8vo. 31s. 6d.
Hawthorne's (J.) Yellow-Cap and other Fairy Stories. Crown 8vo. 6s.

Cabinet Edition of Stories and Tales by Miss Sewell:—

    Amy Herbert, 2s. 6d.
    Cleve Hall, 2s. 6d.
    The Earl's Daughter, 2s. 6d.
    Experience of Life, 2s. 6d.
    Gertrude, 2s. 6d.
    Ivors, 2s. 6d.
    Katharine Ashton, 2s. 6d.
    Laneton Parsonage, 2s. 6d.
    Margaret Percival, 3s. 6d.
    Ursula, 3s. 6d.

Novels and Tales by the Right Hon. the Earl of Beaconsfield, K.G. Cabinet Edition, Ten Volumes, crown 8vo. price £3.

    Lothair, 6s.
    Coningsby, 6s.
    Sybil, 6s.
    Tancred, 6s.
    Venetia, 6s.
    Henrietta Temple, 6s.
    Contarini Fleming. 6s.
    Alroy, Ixion, &c. 6s.
    The Young Duke, &c. 6s.
    Vivian Grey, 6s.

The Modern Novelist's Library. Each Work in crown 8vo. A Single Volume, complete in itself, price 2s. boards, or 2s. 6d. cloth:—

By the Earl of Beaconsfield, K.G.
    Lothair.
    Coningsby.
    Sybil.
    Tancred.
    Venetia.
    Henrietta Temple.
    Contarini Fleming.
    Alroy, Ixion, &c.
    The Young Duke, &c.
    Vivian Grey.

By Anthony Trollope.
    Barchester Towers.
    The Warden.

By the Author of 'the Rose Garden.'
    Unawares.

By Major Whyte-Melville.
    Digby Grand.
    General Bounce.
    Kate Coventry.
    The Gladiators.
    Good for Nothing.
    Holmby House.
    The Interpreter.
    The Queen's Maries.

By the Author of 'the Atelier du Lys.'
    Mademoiselle Mori.
    The Atelier du Lys.

By Various Writers.
    Atherstone Priory.
    The Burgomaster's Family.
    Elsa and her Vulture.
    The Six Sisters of the Valleys.

Lord Beaconsfield's Novels and Tales. 10 vols. cloth extra, gilt edges, 30s.

Whispers from Fairy Land. By the Right Hon. Lord Brabourne. With Nine Illustrations. Crown 8vo. 3s. 6d.

Higgledy-Piggledy; or, Stories for Everybody and Everybody's Children. By the Right Hon. Lord Brabourne. With Nine Illustrations from Designs by R. Doyle. Crown 8vo. 3s. 6d.

POETRY & THE DRAMA.

Bailey's Festus, a Poem. Crown 8vo. 12s. 6d.
Bowdler's Family Shakspeare. Medium 8vo. 14s. 6 vols. fcp. 8vo. 21s.
Cayley's Iliad of Homer, Homometrically translated. 8vo. 12s. 6d.
Conington's Æneid of Virgil, translated into English Verse. Crown 8vo. 9s.

London, LONGMANS & CO.

General Lists of New Works. 11

Goethe's Faust, translated by Birds. Large crown 8vo. 12s. 6d.
— — translated by Webb. 8vo. 12s. 6d.
— — edited by Selss. Crown 8vo. 5s.
Ingelow's Poems. New Edition. 2 vols. fcp. 8vo. 12s.
Macaulay's Lays of Ancient Rome, with Ivry and the Armada. 16mo. 3s. 6d.
Ormsby's Poem of the Cid. Translated. Post 8vo. 5s.
Southey's Poetical Works. Medium 8vo. 14s.

RURAL SPORTS, HORSE & CATTLE MANAGEMENT &c.

Blaine's Encyclopædia of Rural Sports. 8vo. 21s.
Francis's Treatise on Fishing in all its Branches. Post 8vo. 15s.
Horses and Roads. By Free-Lance. Crown 8vo. 6s.
Miles's Horse's Foot, and How to Keep it Sound. Imperial 8vo. 12s. 6d.
— Plain Treatise on Horse-Shoeing. Post 8vo. 2s. 6d.
— Stables and Stable-Fittings. Imperial 8vo. 15s.
— Remarks on Horses' Teeth. Post 8vo. 1s. 6d.
Nevile's Horses and Riding. Crown 8vo. 6s.
Ronalds's Fly-Fisher's Entomology. 8vo. 14s.
Steel's Diseases of the Ox, being a Manual of Bovine Pathology. 8vo. 15s.
Stonehenge's Dog in Health and Disease. Square crown 8vo. 7s. 6d.
— Greyhound. Square crown 8vo. 15s.
Youatt's Work on the Dog. 8vo. 6s.
— — — Horse. 8vo. 7s. 6d.
Wilcocks's Sea-Fisherman. Post 8vo. 12s. 6d.

WORKS OF UTILITY & GENERAL INFORMATION.

Acton's Modern Cookery for Private Families. Fcp. 8vo. 6s.
Black's Practical Treatise on Brewing. 8vo. 10s. 6d.
Buckton's Food and Home Cookery. Crown 8vo. 2s.
Bull on the Maternal Management of Children. Fcp. 8vo. 2s. 6d.
Bull's Hints to Mothers on the Management of their Health during the Period of Pregnancy and in the Lying-in Room. Fcp. 8vo. 2s. 6d.
Campbell-Walker's Correct Card, or How to Play at Whist. Fcp. 8vo. 2s. 6d.
Edwards on the Ventilation of Dwelling-Houses. Royal 8vo. 10s. 6d.
Johnson's (W. & J. H.) Patentee's Manual. Fourth Edition. 8vo. 10s. 6d.
Longman's Chess Openings. Fcp. 8vo. 2s. 6d.
Macleod's Economics for Beginners. Small crown 8vo. 2s. 6d.
— Elements of Economics. Small crown 8vo. [*In the press.*
— Theory and Practice of Banking. 2 vols. 8vo. 26s.
— Elements of Banking. Fourth Edition. Crown 8vo. 5s.
M'Culloch's Dictionary of Commerce and Commercial Navigation. 8vo. 63s.

London, LONGMANS & CO.

Maunder's Biographical Treasury. Fcp. 8vo. 6s.
— Historical Treasury. Fcp. 8vo. 6s.
— Scientific and Literary Treasury. Fcp. 8vo. 6s.
— Treasury of Bible Knowledge, edited by Ayre. Fcp. 8vo. 6s.
— Treasury of Botany, edited by Lindley & Moore. Two Parts, 12s.
— Treasury of Geography. Fcp. 8vo. 6s.
— Treasury of Knowledge and Library of Reference. Fcp. 8vo. 6s.
— Treasury of Natural History. Fcp. 8vo. 6s.
Pereira's Materia Medica, by Bentley and Redwood. 8vo. 25s.
Pewtner's Comprehensive Specifier; Building-Artificers' Work. Crown 8vo. 6s.
Pole's Theory of the Modern Scientific Game of Whist. Fcp. 8vo. 2s. 6d.
Scott's Farm Valuer. Crown 8vo. 5s.
— Rents and Purchases. Crown 8vo. 6s.
Smith's Handbook for Midwives. Crown 8vo. 5s.
The Cabinet Lawyer, a Popular Digest of the Laws of England. Fcp. 8vo. 9s.
West on the Diseases of Infancy and Childhood. 8vo. 18s.
Wilson on Banking Reform. 8vo. 7s. 6d.
— on the Resources of Modern Countries 2 vols. 8vo. 24s.

MUSICAL WORKS BY JOHN HULLAH, LL.D.

Hullah's Method of Teaching Singing. Crown 8vo. 2s. 6d.
Exercises and Figures in the same. Crown 8vo. 1s. or 2 Parts. 6d. each.
Large Sheets, containing the 'Exercises and Figures in Hullah's Method,' in Parcels of Eight, price 6s. each.
Chromatic Scale, with the Inflected Syllables, on Large Sheet. 1s. 6d.
Card of Chromatic Scale. 1d.
Exercises for the Cultivation of the Voice. For Soprano or Tenor, 2s. 6d.
Grammar of Musical Harmony. Royal 8vo. 2 Parts, each 1s. 6d.
Exercises to Grammar of Musical Harmony. 1s.
Grammar of Counterpoint. Part I. super-royal 8vo. 2s. 6d.
Wilhem's Manual of Singing. Parts I. & II. 2s. 6d.; or together, 5s.
Exercises and Figures contained in Parts I. and II. of Wilhem's Manual. Books I. & II. each 8d.
Large Sheets, Nos. 1 to 8, containing the Figures in Part I. of Wilhem's Manual, in a Parcel, 6s.
Large Sheets, Nos. 9 to 40, containing the Exercises in Part I. of Wilhem's Manual, in Four Parcels of Eight Nos. each, per Parcel, 6s.
Large Sheets, Nos. 41 to 52, containing the Figures in Part II. in a Parcel, 9s.
Hymns for the Young, set to Music. Royal 8vo. 8d.
Infant School Songs. 6d.
Notation, the Musical Alphabet. Crown 8vo. 6d.
Old English Songs for Schools, Harmonised. 6d.
Rudiments of Musical Grammar. Royal 8vo. 3s.
School Songs for 2 and 3 Voices. 2 Books, 8vo. each 6d.

London, LONGMANS & CO.

Spottiswoode & Co. Printers, New-street Square, London.

www.ingramcontent.com/pod-product-compliance
Lightning Source LLC
Chambersburg PA
CBHW032049230426
43672CB00009B/1539